T0322381

SYNDROME K

SYNDROME K

HOW ITALY RESISTED THE FINAL SOLUTION

CHRISTIAN JENNINGS

For Sylvia, who always strives to seek out the humanity and the good, both in history and in life. With thanks that reach to the stars.

Back cover quote: Caitlin Hu, 'An Italian doctor explains "Syndrome K," the fake disease he invented to save Jews from the Nazis', *Quartz Magazine*, 8 July 2016. qz.com/724169/an-italian-doctor-explains-syndrome-k-the-fake-disease-he-invented-to-save-jews-from-the-nazis/.

First published 2022

The History Press
97 St George's Place, Cheltenham,
Gloucestershire, GL50 3QB
www.thehistorypress.co.uk

British Library Cataloguing in Publication Data.
A catalogue record for this book is available from the British Library.

ISBN 978-0-7509-9655-6

Typesetting and origination by The History Press
Printed and bound in Great Britain by TJ Books Limited, Padstow, Cornwall.

Trees for LYfe

CONTENTS

ACKNOWLEDGEMENTS

Thanks must go, as always, to my outstanding literary agent, Andrew Lownie. I'm very grateful as well to Mark Beynon at The History Press, who saw the idea and story behind the book, and published it with verve, style and commitment. Along the way, friends and family have stood watch: Giulia Avataneo, Kat Sacco, my brothers Anthony and James, and sister Flora. I'm grateful, too, to David Kenyon, for his expert advice and help on things cryptanalytical.

Complex war crimes investigations, especially when dealing with a subject as monumental and epochal as the Holocaust, are always far from easy. In seventeen years on the road as a foreign correspondent, across countries such as Rwanda, Burundi, Democratic Congo, Kosovo and Bosnia, I was lucky to have good friends and colleagues. I learned rather a lot from them about writing and investigating such stories: Nerma Jelacic, Corinne Dufka, Beth Kampschror, Adam Boys, Peter Bouckaert, Elida Ramadani, Lejla Hadzimesic and Jonah Hull.

THE POSTCARD FROM THE TRAIN

Verona, December 1943

Nobody survived to tell the story of how Wanda Abenaim wrote the last message to her family. There would have been witnesses, that winter day at Verona Station, as the convoy of cattle cars clattered and rumbled through the city. But probably none of them remained alive for very long, because the train's final destination was the camp complex at Auschwitz-Birkenau, and because Wanda was an Italian Jew who'd been betrayed. From the writing on the old postcard she wrote, it seems as though she had somehow managed to conceal a fountain pen somewhere on her person as the *Schutzstaffel* (SS) and Italian Fascist police arrested her. If she'd been writing the card in the cattle car, there would have hardly been space to move her arm or write, as there would have been so many people jammed into the carriage alongside her. But, from the look of the smeared ink, she may have licked her finger and smudged out the writing of the former address on the card. Writing diagonally on one side of it and straight on the other, she scribbled her message. She might have done this in the German lorry on the way to Verona Station or before she got on the train, and then dropped the postcard onto the railway tracks. Or maybe she had written it on the train itself and then, when it was done, reached up to the small window on the side of the railway wagon and pushed the slip of cardboard out, so it fluttered down and fell onto the tracks. As Wanda said on her postcard, she had no idea of her destination.

Other prisoners deported on German Holocaust transport trains from Italy had dropped last postcards, desperate messages written on pieces of paper or envelopes. On 18 October 1943, for instance, a railway worker at Padua Station had found a railway ticket, thrown from a train, which must have had an address and message on it, as the man forwarded it on to an unknown recipient. The train in question, passing through Padua on that day, was the first convoy of Italian Jews to leave Rome after the German roundup on 16 October. So, in December, as Wanda Abenaim's train pulled out of Verona, one of the soldiers guarding the station, or a railway worker, must have found her postcard on the platform or the tracks. And somehow they forwarded it on or gave it to somebody, as it survives today. Written in ink are the following words:

> My dear Signora,
>   With a heavy heart I leave my native land. I leave for distant lands alone, but I will be brave. Kiss my dear mother and brother and tell them to pray for me and that I will never forget them. I will do everything to send my news. I'm well. Tell Carlo to remember that those two are not with me, and that he should protect them and help them as if they were his. I hope we see each other again soon. I kiss and hug you. Ciao, your most affectionate Wanda.[1]

Over a week previously, the SS and Italian Fascist police had burst into the convent in Florence where she and other Italian Jews had been hidden by Franciscan nuns. They'd been betrayed.[2] Wanda had had no news from her husband in Genoa, nor from his family, for three weeks. As the SS men shouldered their way into the convent, it's uncertain whether they would have bothered giving Abenaim and the other Jews the customary slip of paper that was handed to other Jewish deportees in Italy as their flats, houses, offices and workplaces were raided by the

Gestapo, SS and Italian Fascists. It was the official list of what Jews were allowed to take with them:

> Together with your family, and any other Jews in your home, you are being relocated.
> You must bring the following with you: food for at least eight days; ration cards, identity card, glasses, suitcases with personal effects, underwear and blankets.
> Bring money and jewels.
> Close and lock your flat, any sick people, however ill, cannot be left behind. There is an infirmary in the camp.
> You have twenty minutes to be ready for departure.[3]

Only Wanda and one other family member would be taken away from the Franciscans in Florence. Nobody else was there. Her husband Riccardo was in Genoa, where he was the Chief Rabbi, and that was where her two brothers, Carlo and Ettore, and her mother were as well. Half an hour later, she and a group of other Jewish families were outside on the pavement, their suitcases at their sides. The group were herded onto lorries that took them first to a prison in Florence, and then on to Verona, 150 miles to the north. That December, with the Allied and American armies bogged down around Monte Cassino, south of Rome, both Florence and Verona were way behind the front lines of the German armies who had occupied Italy in that summer of 1943, after the Italians had surrendered.

On 6 December, Wanda was forced at rifle point onto the convoy of cattle cars waiting at Verona Station. Some of the cars would have been already full, for the train had formed up on Milan's Platform 21, from which Holocaust deportations from that city took place. Prisoners arrested in other cities such as Turin and Genoa would have been transported to Milan. Deportation Convoy No. 5 would now pass from Milan to Verona, Padua and Treviso, on the west side of the Venetian lagoon, before heading east towards Tarvisio, the Austrian border at Arnoldstein, and thence Vienna. Thankfully, the 37-year-old Wanda didn't have her two children with her. Raffaele, who was 5, and Emanuele, 13, were both in hiding in another convent on the hills above Florence.

At the same time, a 34-year-old Roman Catholic priest called Don Francisco Repetto was working with an organisation called *Delegazione Assistenza Emigranti Ebrei* (Delegation for the Assistance of Jewish Emigrants, DELASEM) in Genoa. Wanda's children were just two of the hundreds of Jews whom Repetto had helped to hide – in Florence, in the towns and villages along the Ligurian coast, in the hills and valleys of the province of Cuneo that lay to the north of it, along the border that divides France from north-western Italy. Jewish families hid in family homes, churches, convents, seminaries, disused army barracks and farm buildings, until it was time to move them across the border into Switzerland or France, or stayed hidden in Italy itself. An Italian lawyer in Switzerland, Lelio Valobra, channelled money to DELASEM in Italy, which was working hand-in-hand with the Genoa curia.

The money came in from the United States via bank transfers to Geneva, from donations managed by the American Jewish Joint Distribution Committee. This paid for such vital things as false identity cards, food, transport, medical supplies, clothes, bribes to Italian Fascist and German officials – everything needed by the thousands of Jews on the run inside Italy. Up until the beginning of November 1943, the main liaison and point of contact for DELASEM and Repetto inside the Jewish community of Genoa had been their Chief Rabbi, Riccardo Pacifici, the husband of Wanda Abenaim.

But Fascist informers betrayed him for money to the *Sicherheitsdienst* (SD), the SS's intelligence service. One SS Lieutenant who operated for them in Genoa and Milan was in charge of arranging the deportations of Jews from Genoa and Liguria, and also of appropriating their property on behalf of the SS's economic department at the Reich Security Main Office in Berlin.

So when the Fascist informers told the SS that Rabbi Pacifici was focally involved in hiding Jews, this SS officer acted. Pacifici was arrested on 3 November, questioned in Genoa and then transferred to Milan, where he was put onto a deportation convoy heading for Auschwitz.

He left Milan on Convoy No. 5 on 6 December, travelling through Italy, to Austria, and then a final destination at Auschwitz-Birkenau.

Meanwhile, British cryptanalysts at Bletchley Park in England had cracked some of the codes used on the Enigma machine by the *Reichsbahn*. This was the Third Reich's railway system whose responsibilities included running the network of Holocaust transport trains: every time a convoy of cattle cars loaded with deportees left Turin, Vienna, Lublin or Munich for one of the camps in the *Konzentrationslager* (KL) network, messages announcing departure times, arrival times, destinations and number of prisoners were sent to the Reich Security Main Office in Berlin. The messages were first encoded on an Enigma machine, and the subsequent message encoded again, for security. This was a process known as 'superencipherment' but, although it guaranteed increased cryptographical security, it didn't make the message uncrackable if somebody – in this case the British at Bletchley – knew what the coded Enigma settings were. And the men and women at 'The Park', as the British Government Code and Cypher School was nicknamed, had cracked three of the crucial code settings used by the *Reichsbahn*. Bletchley had named them Blunderbuss, Culverin and Rocket.

So, between this network of people so closely involved in the Holocaust in Italy, some details about some SS deportation trains were known. However, what neither the SS officer in Genoa, the OSS, Bletchley Park, DELASEM nor perhaps even Riccardo Pacifici knew was this. That, on 6 December at Verona, another party of Jews was forced aboard the cattle cars of Convoy No. 5, the same convoy as Rabbi Pacifici. Among them was his wife, Wanda Abenaim. Nobody knows if the couple were aware of each other's presence on the train, or if they travelled up the line to death separated from each other.

Seventy-five years on from that frozen morning at Verona Station, little physical reminder remains of the fate of Riccardo Pacifici, Wanda Abenaim, or their uncle from Genoa, who was another rabbi. Riccardo arrived at Auschwitz on the night of 11 and 12 December 1943 and was immediately selected for the gas chamber.

Nowadays, a small brass plaque set in the pavement outside Galleria Mazzini commemorates the point where he was arrested in Genoa. '*Qui e stato arrestato,*' it says, '*3.11.1943, Reuven Riccardo Pacifici, Rabbino Capo di Genova. Nato 1904, Assassinato 11.12.1943, Auschwitz.*'[4] It's a *pietra d'inciampo* in Italian, a *stolperstein* in German, just one of tens of thousands of such memorial stones set into pavements across Europe, outside houses, businesses and apartment buildings where Jews were arrested during the Holocaust.

Pacifici's niece, Elena, was on the same deportation convoy as him in December 1943, and three years ago, DNA was used to help identify her remains, disinterred from a graveyard in the small Catholic cemetery in the village of Swierklany Dolne. It sits 30 miles west of the town of Oswiecim, where the camps of the Auschwitz complex stood.

Wanda Abenaim, Riccardo Pacifici, Monsignor Francisco Repetto and the SD lieutenant in Genoa – who was called Guido Zimmer – were just four people, four parts among thousands in the Holocaust in Italy, which lasted from August 1943 to April 1945. Yet they mattered so much, not just because of who they were, or what happened to them – especially those murdered in the concentration camp system – but because of what they did. They were all middle-level, mid-ranking officials, members of the religious curia, SD officers, etc. – but it was people like them who were the organisational cogs in the German implementation of the Final Solution in Italy, and the Allied and Italian resistance to it. These were people who did things.

Of the approximately 45,000 Jews who were physically present on Italian territory when the Germans occupied the country in August and September 1943, the majority were Italian. Some were refugees from other countries in Europe, such as Holland, Austria and Poland, where the Holocaust had swung into action from 1940 onwards. Adolf Eichmann and the SS had estimated that there were 58,000 Jews in Italy and Sardinia in January 1942, a number that would have dropped by the time the Germans occupied Italy in August 1943, as some Jews took refuge abroad. But Yad Vashem, the Holocaust Memorial Centre in

Jerusalem, puts the total at 44,500 Jews present in Italy. By April 1945, just under two years later, about 8,400 had been arrested and deported, some 750–800 had survived the Holocaust and an estimated 7,680–8,000 had died.[5] A further 36,820 had survived, whether by escaping, emigrating or hiding. Horrific as these figures are, they still represent the second highest survival rate of any national Jewish community in Europe – the highest was Denmark. At over 80 per cent, this rate was enormous, given the Germans' huge efforts to implement the Final Solution in European countries. Faced with these figures, a mathematical statistical analyst could argue convincingly that the German implementation of the Final Solution had failed to achieve its objectives in Italy.

The spirits of 8,000 murdered Jewish people, along with partisans, communists, Roma, homosexuals and political detainees, would stand to temper the use of this word 'failure'. But when compared to the percentage of Jews arrested in a country like the Netherlands, where 105,000 out of 150,000 Dutch Jews were deported and murdered in the KL network, Italy's survival rate is astonishing. This book looks at the principal reasons why, through the eyes of some of the people of all ranks, levels of importance and nationalities who found themselves involved with the Holocaust in Italy.

Resistance to the Final Solution in the country can roughly be divided into the two areas of what the Italians and the Allies did to prevent it, slow it down or resist it, and a third area of the operational failings of the Germans – what they did that short-circuited or blocked their own plans.

The Italians' greatest triumph was hiding their fellow countrymen everywhere they could, from churches and convents to farms and city apartments. Their next triumph lay in their partisan operations, which denied the Germans logistical stability in their areas of occupation in Italy to carry out the necessary round-up, arrest and deportation operations.

In other countries, such as France, Poland and Austria, the Holocaust was carried out once the Germans had invaded and pacified the country. The opposite was the case in Italy – the Allied armies were fighting their way up the country from July 1943 onwards, bombing railways, roads and logistical links, while behind the lines, thousands of partisans kept the Germans tied down. These resistance groups also absorbed Jews into their ranks, effectively hiding them. The Vatican was fundamentally involved in concealing Jews and supporting the resistance against Hitler, at the price of not speaking out vociferously and directly against the deportation of Rome's Jews.

The Germans' main failing was that their Gestapo and SS officials were often incompetent, while some were operating as intelligence agents for the Allies, and other Wehrmacht officers and diplomats were actively supporting operations to hide Jews. A huge Allied advantage was that they could read the codes both of their enemies and of neutral countries like Switzerland and, occasionally, the Vatican.

Predominantly, though, the Final Solution didn't work in Italy because the Italian population decided to fight it, to resist it in any way they could. They had decided that enough was enough: that the Germans' genocidal policies were not going to succeed in Italy, simply because Italians had decided that they wouldn't allow it and were prepared to do whatever was required, however dangerous, however much bravery, intelligence or determination was needed to stop the Holocaust in its tracks.

Over seventy-five years later, signals that detail the operations of the Germans in Rome that summer and autumn of 1943, as they commenced the implementation of the Final Solution in Italy, are now spread across several countries, like four electronic winds. The original translations from the German, made long ago in huts at Bletchley Park, are all in archives now. So are the covert memos, the analyses, the explanations of how the Allies deciphered the codes of the German concentration camp system, enabling them to know how many inmates of each camp were dying, or being murdered, each day. The original signal translation 'flimsies' are stapled to pages of A4, as a form of frame. Many have disappeared, but many survive. They're in Bletchley Park's libraries; they're in the American National Archives at College Park in Maryland; and they're in the British National Archives at Kew. They're also in Rome, and at the German Foreign Ministry in Berlin. Some are in Jerusalem, Istanbul and Prague. The Finns have some, too.

In two 'record groups' alone there are 6,300 messages. HW 19/237, now in the British National Archives, is just one subseries of messages intercepted by Bletchley, concerning the activities of the SD in Italy after the occupation of the country. In it, there are 1,500 decoded signals alone. In HW 238–240 there are an estimated 4,800 more. The signals, their transmissions and their contents were like a constant humming, electronic soundtrack to the daily operations of the Germans as they undertook the Holocaust, both in Italy and elsewhere.

And understanding how the Allies intercepted these signals, decrypted and translated them, and how they then acted on this intelligence, shines a (sometimes) clear light onto the tactical and strategic decisions made by the Allies regarding the Holocaust in Italy – what they knew, and what they did or didn't, could or couldn't, do to stop, resist or sabotage it. The British, for instance, knew a lot of what the Germans were doing in Italy when it came to the execution of the Final Solution, which is why they forwarded a selection of carefully screened pertinent information to their ambassador at the Vatican. This was censored and discreetly camouflaged so that it did not reveal the secret of Bletchley Park's successes with the Enigma decrypts, which they code-named 'Ultra'.

Even though both the Italians and Germans could read some British diplomatic traffic, neither side deduced that their enemies and other neutral protagonists knew what they, in turn, were doing when it came to code-breaking. The Germans, in particular, did not work out from the contents of the British diplomatic messages they intercepted that their enemies had been able to decrypt their own messages encoded on Enigma.

For example, the British were able to read Gestapo chief Herbert Kappler's encrypted radio message from Rome to Berlin on 24 September 1943. This said that the Vatican had been 'selling' Portuguese, Spanish, Argentine and Mexican visas to Jews who wanted to smuggle themselves out on a train that was carrying Spanish diplomats from Rome back to Spain. As mentioned above, the British Government Codes & Cypher School, as Bletchley was formally known, had also managed by this point to decrypt some parts of the Enigma settings that were used by the German Reich Transport Ministry. This gave British code-breakers an additional advantage in gaining intelligence into the wider, logistical movements of Germany's war-machine in action across Europe.[6] When it came to the coded messages coming out of Rome by 17 October 1943, they left nobody in any doubt as to what was taking place:

> The SD is now pillaging Rome … Himmler has sent SS men who have had experience of this work in Russia to Rome …

This was one Enigma-encrypted signal read by Bletchley Park on 17 October, sent back to the foreign ministry in Berne by the Swiss Ambassador to the Holy See.

While the Vatican knew the Germans' intentions for Italy at the beginning of October, the Germans, for their part, still didn't know whether the Pope would formally and strongly object to a round-up of Italy's Jews. The pontiff was lobbying the United States to receive Jewish refugees and the Germans feared Italy's Jews would escape, while Italy's Fascist Republic had said it would assist the Germans in the execution of the Final Solution.

All of this had given the Vatican vital advance warning, in turn allowing most of Italy's 38,000 remaining Jews to escape, hide, take cover or fight back. The Pope, meanwhile, was also circulating coded instructions and secret letters via his staff and his Cardinal Secretary of State, Luigi Maglione. These were sent and hand-delivered, not just to Vatican *nuncios* in European capitals, but to selected Catholic convents, churches and seminaries in Rome to put into operation plans to conceal thousands of the capital's Jews. Adolf Eichmann later wrote in his diary that 'the objections given and the excessive delay in the steps necessary to complete the implementation of the operation resulted in a great part of Italian Jews being able to hide and escape capture'.

The amount of solid operational, decipherable information in existence in October 1943 was small, but crucial: the intentions of the SS; German military deployments across Italy; what the Pope had said;

when the German arrest operations would commence. But where effective cryptanalysis and subsequent intelligence deciphering came into its own was by allowing each protagonist a head start in predicting each other's operational intentions and knowing what they were doing.

The British, for instance, knew the Germans were committed to the execution of the Final Solution in Italy and had undertaken its operational implementation. Short of invading the country – which they'd already done in September 1943 – and bombing railway lines ahead of Holocaust transport trains, which they'd also done, one of their most effective options was to persuade the Pope to protest to the Germans as vociferously as possible. This would slow down the German operation, as the Vatican's protests would have to be transmitted via diplomats and generals to Berlin and back; it would hopefully buy the Vatican time to warn Jews and advise Catholic seminaries and convents to prepare to hide them. In the event, this plan worked out differently than expected.

Other Allied initiatives to help Italy's Jews in some cases bore more fruit. These involved parachuting Jewish SOE agents into Italy to lead partisan resistance groups, who in turn would try to disrupt Holocaust transports from Florence, Rome, Milan, Turin and Trieste. The American OSS went one step further and put into action a plan to 'turn' as many as possible of the key SS and Gestapo officials operating inside Italy, in charge of implementing the Final Solution, into double agents.

There were nine such men in Rome, Turin, Milan, Berlin, Verona and Florence. By the war's end, it became apparent that four, if not five, of them had actively been working on behalf of American intelligence or were about to do so. These are just some of the reasons why, in the final reckoning, only 8,000 of Italy's 45,000 Jews were arrested and suffered the horrors of deportation and concentration camps. These were 8,000 stories of loss, death and disappearance, but around 37,000 stories of escape, flight, hiding, escaping, surviving and living to see the liberation of Italy – 37,000 stories of life.

Looking at the story of the resistance by Italian civilians and partisans, the cracking of Holocaust codes, the duplicitous accounts of the SS and Gestapo in Italy, the Allied military and intelligence operations, and the stories of some of Italy's Jews, *Syndome K* investigates what really happened, how it happened and why it happened.

THE PIPERNO FAMILY
AND THE JEWS OF ROME

'We're Italian first, Jewish second, monarchist third, and Fascist last.' That was how Clotilde Piperno described herself and her family when people asked. A large middle-class clan of wholesale textile merchants, the Pipernos had always lived in Rome. They had a house near Piazza Giudea, within a few hundred yards of the Jewish ghetto. Since the 1500s, this had stood next to the River Tiber and the ruins of the old open-air Theatre of Marcellus, designed and built by the nephew of the Emperor Augustus and by Julius Caesar, just before the latter was murdered. Rome, ancient and modern, had surrounded each generation of the Pipernos at every step. There had been Jews in Italy since 200 BC, during the period of the Roman Republic. They were concentrated among communities of Sephardic and Ashkenazi Jews, who had originated in Spain and the lands of the former Holy Roman Empire, as well as Persian, Libyan and Italian Jews.

The Jews of Rome had always been forced to live in the cramped, crowded, walled ghetto, until Napoleon's generals invaded Rome in 1798. In that year, the Roman Republic was formed and took over the Papal States: this made a huge and direct difference to the life of Clotilde's great-grandparents, since one of the sweeping changes instituted under the new republic was to abolish the requirement for the city's Jews to live in the ghetto.

This reprieve did not last long. In 1799, the Vatican states were introduced, and the Jews had to return to within their walled enclave. It was to be nearly 100 years before King Re Umberto finally tore down the ghetto in 1888. Clotilde's father said that this king had brought them freedom from centuries of repression. He himself was to be decorated in 1866 for his part in the Third Italian War of Independence, fighting to push the Austrians out of north-eastern Italy.

On his return to Rome after the war, he married, and Clotilde was the first child. She grew up to see King Vittorio Emanuele III crowned in 1900, and by the time she married the son of another Jewish family from Rome, Italy was heading for another war with Austria. Her husband Giacomo became an officer – Jewish men formed the highest single percentage of commissioned ranks in the Italian Army, due to their educational advantages.

Lieutenant Giacomo was sent to fight against the Austro-Hungarians in the successive battles at the Isonzo River, north-east of Venice. For two years, the pride of the Italian Army hammered against the Austro-Hungarians in twelve confrontations, losing 300,000 men, and sometimes advancing less than a mile across the valleys and snow-covered mountain slopes before becoming bogged down in stalemate.

The twelfth and final battle of the Isonzo took place in October 1917 near the town of Caporetto. Austro-Hungarian units had been reinforced by German stormtroopers, including a company led by a young Lieutenant Erwin Rommel. Under cover of a massive phosgene gas attack, the Austro-Hungarians and Germans finally broke through the Italian lines. It was a staggering defeat for Italy. Half of Italy's total casualties in the First World War fell at the Isonzo, and at Caporetto, 265,000 of the country's soldiers were taken prisoner. But out of this chaos of defeat and imprisonment, Clotilde Piperno's husband, Giacomo, returned safely to Rome.

One of the many casualties of the battles at the Isonzo was a young former journalist turned army sergeant called Benito Mussolini. He was born in 1883 in Forli, in the central Italian region of Romagna. His father was a blacksmith, his mother a schoolteacher. The former was an ardent socialist, and the young Mussolini grew up to the sound of his father's opinions about nationalism, anarchism and socialism – he was named after the liberal Mexican president, Benito Juarez. Reportedly grumpy, shy and prone to hubris and violence, he became a schoolteacher in 1901.[1] Radical socialist politics followed, before he volunteered for the army at the outbreak of the First World War. In February 1917, during a training exercise near the Isonzo, a mortar bomb exploded prematurely, leaving him invalided out of the army with forty-four pieces of shrapnel inside him. Despite his wounds, and Italy's appalling defeats against the Austro-Hungarians, he was a staunch supporter of the war, and afterwards founded an ultra-nationalist, anti-socialist political movement along with a group of disaffected veterans. They called themselves the *Fasci di Combattimento*, after the Roman '*fasces*', a bundle of rods and a single axe which had originally represented the power and discipline of Etruscan magistrates.

In October 1922, with a mass demonstration known as the March on Rome, Mussolini's Fascist Party launched an insurrection in the capital, which called the bluff of the Liberal prime minister. He stood down immediately, and King Vittorio Emanuele III appointed Benito Mussolini the country's youngest-ever prime minister.

Over the succeeding five years, helped by his security militia, known as the *Camicie Nere*, or Blackshirts, he created a one-party dictatorship and a Fascist state. He outlawed labour strikes and trade unions and strengthened the role of capitalist enterprises. He began to expand Fascism's overseas empire, starting colonial wars to take over both Libya and Ethiopia and establish what he called Italian East Africa, merging Somalia, Eritrea and Ethiopia.

The Organization for Vigilance and Repression of Anti-Fascism (OVRA) was Mussolini's secret police force, founded in 1927 following an assassination attempt against him. Its 50,000 agents were infiltrated into every level of public, political and domestic life. Their role was simple – to prevent any 'actions directed to violently subvert the social, economic or national order or undermine national security'. They spied on everybody – from the Vatican and the police to factory workers and industrialists.

Mussolini rose to power on a new-found tide of economic and nationalist optimism that blamed the defeats of the First World War on socialists and the monarchist ruling classes. For families like the Pipernos, economic prosperity followed. Italy became self-supporting in terms of agriculture, and more cash was available for the commodities in which the Pipernos traded – textiles, cotton and wool. Wholesale manufacturing expanded, assisted by state subsidies, which had also helped Italy stave off the worst of the Great Depression. People had jobs, Italian industry was showcased abroad, and at home, enormous naval rearmament programmes created work.

Clotilde and Giacomo's two sons, born in 1897 and 1902, were called Adolfo and Giacomo '*Due*' (or Giacomo No. 2). They married two sisters from the same family, called Vanda and Nella Sed, and each of them in turn had two children. Giacomo's first son, born in 1922, was called Piero.

Two photographs from the early 1930s show the family in Rome. In one, *Nonna* or Grandma Clotilde holds court in a rattan chair, sitting at a table in the garden of a large house. Around her are her boys and their wives. The atmosphere is elegant, relaxed, affluent, at ease. Everybody is smiling.

There were some 50,000 Jews in Italy at that time, who were descendants of one of the four main, long-established communities: Spanish and Portuguese Sephardi Jews, originally expelled from the Iberian Peninsula in 1492; French Jews, similarly forced out of their own country; Italian Jews, who had lived in the country since Roman times; and the Ashkenazi Jews of northern Italy. The Jewish communities had been assimilated into Italian society, at different levels, for hundreds of years. Within the Italian Fascist Party, there were leading Fascist theorists, such as the occultist, Fascist intellectual philosopher and antisemitic conspiracy theorist, Julius Evola, who thought that harsher laws needed to be introduced, as in Nazi Germany, to restrict the Jews' activities.

Mussolini disagreed. He largely rejected Hitler's views on race. In 1934, after a speech in Rome, he laid out his views on racial politics:

> Thirty centuries of history allows us to look with supreme pity on certain doctrines which are preached beyond the Alps by the descendants of those who were illiterate when Rome had Caesar, Virgil and Augustus.[2]

Key figures within the Fascist regime were Italian Jews. These included Aldo Finzi, a politician and second-in-command of the air force; Giorgio Morpurgo, who led Italy's mission in the Spanish Civil War; Renzo Ravenna, who became Mayor of Trieste; and the highly influential and wealthy banker from Turin, Ettore Ovazza, who ensured that all key positions in the Jewish community in Turin were held by Fascist supporters.

Ovazza had marched with Mussolini on Rome in 1922. He met him in 1929 when he was part of a delegation of Jewish war veterans visiting Rome. After meeting the dictator, he said:

> On hearing my affirmation of the unshakeable loyalty of Italian Jews to the Fatherland, His Excellency Mussolini looks me straight in the eye and says with a voice that penetrates straight to my heart: 'I have never doubted it'. When Il Duce bids us farewell with a Roman salute, I feel an urge to embrace him, as a fascist, as an Italian, but I can't; and approaching him at his desk I say: 'Excellency, I would like to shake your hand'. It is not a fascist gesture, but it is a cry from the heart ... Such is the man that Providence has given to Italy.[3]

One of Mussolini's close friends, as well as his propaganda adviser, mistress and biographer, was called Margherita Sarfatti. A Jewish art critic, she wrote a highly popular book about the dictator called *Dux*.

The Italian Fascist regime went further in its allegiance with Jews. It helped establish what would, one day, become the Israeli Navy. In 1943, an officers' training camp was established at Civitavecchia, on the coast outside Rome, where naval personnel from Mandated Palestine, then under British control, came for training by the Italians. Mussolini thought that by doing this, he would be able to adversely affect the naval balance of power in the Mediterranean in his favour, against that of the British Royal Navy.

In this environment, the Piperno family felt safe, even when Clotilde's second son Adolfo died in 1936, leaving his children to be brought up by his elder brother, Giacomo. Piero Piperno went to elementary school close to the family home, and then to one of the capital's most well-known high schools, the *Liceo Classico Ennio Visconti*, 500 yards away from the house.

One day in November 1938, the cheerful, happy child found himself on his way to class. He was 16. Without warning, he and his 13-year-old sister Giovanna, along with forty-eight of his school friends and colleagues, were told to gather in the lecture hall of the building, a large, long room with Renaissance frescoes decorating the walls. The pupils waited. The headmaster entered. The children gathered there, he said, could no longer attend the school, take their exams or even appear on the official school roster. A law had been passed by the government, he explained to the shocked and horrified pupils. He was deeply saddened to have to tell them that, from now on, they were officially to be termed as 'non-people'.

Piero and his sister ran home in tears. What was happening? they asked their mother and grandmother. Clotilde gathered the members of the family and told them that a law had been made by the Fascist government: as Jews, their lives were about to change. Their civil rights were now restricted, their books were to be banned and they couldn't go to school. Papa Giacomo could not consider sending them to university. But why? the children asked. Why? Simply, said their grandmother, because we're Jews. Their father's business activities were to be closely monitored, and they were not going to be able to travel. Mussolini's Racial Decree of 17 November 1938 had come into effect.

The children were not to know it, and their grandmother hadn't mentioned it because she didn't believe it but, for half of that year, there had been numerous articles in the newspapers and broadcasts on the radio that heralded the introduction of the Race Law. Earlier that year, several leading Fascists who styled themselves as 'race scientists' had published what they called a 'Manifesto of Race', which asserted that Europeans were to be considered superior to other races. These latter included Jews. This manifesto recommended the restriction of the civil rights of Jews, banned their books, both educational and cultural, and effectively excluded Jews from any form of public office and higher education. Additional laws stripped Jews of their assets, restricted their travel and finally provided for their confinement in internal exile, as had been done for political prisoners.

The Grand Council of Fascism had held a meeting on 6 and 7 October in Rome, where supporters of Nazi Germany had strongly supported the new law. Jews were no longer allowed even to marry Italians. In July, Pope Pius XI had made a speech against the decree, saying that 'anti-Semitism is a movement with which Christians can have nothing to do … it is impossible for a Christian to take part in anti-Semitism, it is inadmissible … spiritually we are all Semites'. Cardinal Schuster, who was the Archbishop of Milan, went further, describing the law as racism, and therefore heresy, and an international danger – as much as Bolshevism.

Born in 1880, Alfredo Ludovico Schuster was a Benedictine, who served in Milan from 1929 until he died in 1954. He led the Milanese archdiocese during the entire war and, at the beginning of Mussolini's regime, he was a supporter of Fascism. But after the annexation of Austria and the introduction of the Racial Laws in 1938 he became a supremely vocal critic of Il Duce. He made the comment about racism on 13 November 1938, four days before the law was formally announced, and one of Grandmother Clotilde's relatives had heard about it and contacted the family in Rome. It was then that *Nonna* started to think about preparing an escape plan. As 1938 turned into spring 1939, and everybody could see the thunderous clouds of war thickening on the horizon, it was becoming increasingly difficult for the Piperno family to carry on making a living, legally at least.

Giacomo Piperno could no longer trade under his family business name. The imports of cotton, flax and wool he relied upon from Egypt, the Middle East and Spain had to pass through customs at the ports of Taranto and Naples – his family name barred him from access to them.

He managed, in late 1938, to circumvent this by borrowing the name of a business colleague who was not Jewish.

However, his mother saw which way the wind of racial change was blowing and knew that it was time to find somewhere else to live, outside of Rome. Clotilde thought it was a good idea to try and buy a house in the countryside to which she, her children and her grandchildren could flee if they needed to. Several Jewish friends had done the same thing.

One of Clotilde's brothers had a house on the outskirts of Siena, in Tuscany. It was big enough to accommodate the extended family and was in a small town from which the family could move easily without attracting attention. The local property agent was a business colleague of her brother's and the purchase of a large farmhouse in the town of Monaciano could be handled in his name. The incriminating word 'Piperno' would not appear on any documentation.

For the time being, they were safe. The children, including Piero and his sister Giovanna, were receiving school lessons at home by now: they had no high school to attend, no university to look forward to. And then, one day, at the beginning of September 1939, their father Giacomo came into the family living room in their house in Rome, holding a newspaper. The headline announced in broad black type that Britain and France had declared war on Germany.

For the Jewish supporters of Benito Mussolini, the declaration of war was proof made manifest of everything they most feared. Il Duce would side with Hitler, in their mutually assuring 'Pact of Steel' – or Pact of Friendship and Alliance between Italy and Germany, as it was formally named. Italy would find itself dragged into a war for which it was hopelessly underprepared, against the rest of Europe.

In Turin, one of Mussolini's most loyal and powerful supporters was the banker, Ettore Ovazza, who had sworn such unyielding loyalty to the Italian dictator and marched with him back in the 1920s. He and the Jewish community in Turin, a significant number of whom were members of the Fascist Party, met to decide what to do. It was inconceivable to them that they should not continue to support Mussolini, to continue their lives as before, despite the restrictions that the new racial law placed on them. After all, thought Ovazza, he was still financially supporting the Fascist Party of Turin, even though the perversities of the law made it illegal for the party to accept his contributions. He felt he had much in common with the country's leader, and much in common with the business leaders in the country's Jewish community. He had never met the Piperno family, but had he known them, he would have seen the same lines of history, upbringing and experience that made him who he was.

Born in 1892, he was one of three brothers in the Ovazza family, an immensely wealthy Jewish family who lived in Turin, the capital of the Piemonte region of north-western Italy. Along with Milan, the city was the centre of Italy's economic heartland and the Ovazza banking dynasty functioned right in the middle of it. The Jewish community in Turin was some 5,600 strong at the turn of the century, and despite their strong religious differences from Roman Catholicism, they were completely integrated into the society of the city.

Ovazza and his brothers, along with his father, volunteered to fight as officers in the First World War, and Ettore fought on the same Isonzo River front and suffered the same humiliating defeat at Caporetto as Giacomo Piperno. He was a committed Fascist and saw the social turmoil and general strikes of the early 1920s as disastrous for Italy. The industrial socialism that Mussolini so despised affected the Ovazza family business. Ettore published a selection of letters about his experiences at Caporetto, which Mussolini read and praised.

In the 1930s, the gradual introduction of anti-Jewish legislation initially seemed to push the Ovazza family further towards Fascism. Ettore and some banking colleagues even founded a patriotic newspaper called *La Nostra Bandiera* (*Our Flag*), in which they combined stories of the Jewish military sacrifice in the Great War with encouragement to support Mussolini's regime.

At this point, all of the key positions in the Turin banking industry were held by Fascists, whether they were Jews or not. Ettore even volunteered to serve in Abyssinia, and the government in Rome rewarded him and his family with preferential contracts and even invited him to be part of the Royal Honour Guard which took on the duty of overseeing the tombs of Italy's monarchs in the huge church of the Superga, which sits on a hill overlooking Turin.

Then came 1938, and the passing of the Racial Decree. Although the clauses of the law that forbade Jews from marrying Aryans did not affect the family, the ones concerning education did. Ettore and his brothers could no longer send their children to the same schools as Italians and, crucially, could not employ more than 100 people in their banking institutions, nor could they still continue to be the owners of the numerous buildings that belonged to their bank.

By 1939 things had passed a line in the sand, when Jews were no longer allowed in shops or cafés, and – the Ovazza family included – couldn't even undertake any form of skilled job. To his horror and disbelief, Ettore was expelled from the Fascist Party and his brother was removed from the army. Both of his brothers left the country, urging him to do the same, but he was reluctant to, as he couldn't believe that all of the hard work on which he had focused his life in Italy, his military service, his commitment to Fascism and his devotion to the Jewish faith, would all come to nothing. So, he wrote a letter to Mussolini, in which he begged the dictator to reconsider his views and to change his mind:

> Was it all a dream we nurtured?
>
> I can't believe it. I cannot consider changing religion, because this would be a betrayal – and we are Fascists. And so? I turn to You – DUCE – so that in this period, so important for our revolution, you do not exclude that healthy Italian part from the destiny of our Nation.[4]

Ettore Ovazza and his family were by no means the only affluent, middle-class Jewish families to feel a raw sense of smarting betrayal and humiliation at the passing of the Racial Laws. One other family who saw their life implode were the Montalcinis, and they had a daughter.

From the day she was born, everyone who met her remembered her smile.

Virginia Montalcini was born in 1920 in the centre of Turin, just behind Largo Vittorio Emanuele II. Situated at the junction of four main roads, this open square dominated its surroundings with a 120ft-high statue of the first king of a united Italy, Vittorio Emanuele II. Unveiled in 1899 and erected at the behest of his son, King Umberto I, it rises on four Doric columns, and at the bottom of it are four monuments to the 'Great Virtues' of unity, brotherhood, work and freedom.

Every day, on the way to school, Virginia would walk past it. Her father, Eugenio, was a businessman, and her mother, Adriana, looked after the three of them. Virginia went to elementary school in nearby Corso Matteotti, a wide boulevard spread under chestnut trees, lined with large *palazze*, apartment buildings built in the mid-nineteenth century.

When she was 10, the society photographer from Turin's newspaper, *La Stampa*, had come to the family house and taken a portrait photograph of her. Shortly afterwards, her parents accompanied her to the former Royal Palace of the Duchy of Savoy, in the city's central Piazza Castello. Along with a group of other young girls, Virginia was presented to an aged, wealthy, old woman, a descendant of the House of Savoy, and 'came out' in Torinese society. That same year she celebrated her Bat Mitzvah, with the traditional photograph showing her, pensive and shyly beautiful, in a white dress and half-veil.

In 1933, when she was 13, she moved to the secondary school, and then to high school at the far eastern end of the boulevard. The *Liceo Classico Massimo d'Azeglio* was named after a nineteenth-century statesman and novelist from the Piemonte region, who also became Prime Minister of Sicily. The school was well known not just for its specialisation in Classics, but for the anti-Fascist stance of several of its leading professors. Everywhere Virginia walked, the history of her country, past and present, seemed to tower around her.

There were other children in the school from Jewish families, and one of them was a very bright, shy and nervous teenage boy, who excelled at chemistry and physics. The school bullies picked on him, not because he was Jewish, but because he was physically clumsy and very clever.

His family lived in an apartment building on Corso Re Umberto, not far from Virginia's home. He was a year older than her, and his name was Primo Levi. Both families were born into Turin's professional and academic middle class, and both were easily and seamlessly integrated into society.

The Racial Laws changed that overnight. At the end of the summer of 1938, when Virginia came to enrol in her third year at the Massimo d'Azeglio high school, the school's supervisors told her and her parents that she couldn't, nor could Primo Levi, nor could the four other Jewish teenagers in her class, and the five in his. Forty-six schoolchildren deemed to be 'of Jewish race' could no longer attend the high school. They had become non-citizens. She could continue, however, to live in Turin.

2

MUSSOLINI IS LISTENING TO YOU

Clotilde Piperno, like everybody else, called them '*delatori*' – informers. In Mussolini's Italy, they were everywhere. They could be the concierge in the apartment building, the person sitting on the next seat on the train, the barman, the newspaper seller, the postman. There were people keeping their eyes and ears open for any anti-Fascist comments, anything critical of Italy's economic prowess, its colonial wars, or the government; there were people ready to inform on neighbours, employers, colleagues and complete strangers. They were ready to sell or trade the most banal information about anyone who transgressed the myriad rules and regulations and regulations of OVRA – the secret police. OVRA was the *Organizzazione per la Vigilanza e la Repressione dell'Antifascismo*, or Organization for Vigilance and Repression of Anti-Fascism; its intelligence wing was known in an abbreviated form by some people as the 'PolPol' due to them being from the *Polizia Politicale* (Department of Political Police).

His official title as Leader of the Fascist Party, or *Duce del Fascismo*, might have appealed to his extraordinary vanity, but to huge numbers of citizens living in Fascist Italy, Il Duce was simply a brutal, intolerant dictator who ran a surveillance state. '*Taci, Mussolini t'ascolta*' was a phrase used by everybody – 'Shut up. Mussolini is listening to you.' And if there was one section of the country's population that he was listening to more than anybody else, it was the Jews – and those suspected of employing Jews, befriending Jews, hiding Jews, knowing Jews or sympathising with Jews. Next on the list were Communists, anti-Fascists and anybody critical of the glorious prowess of Italy and its empire, the *Imperia Italiana*.

Mussolini had only been prime minister for less than a year when in January 1923 he had famously sent a message to his undersecretary of state at the Interior Ministry, a former wartime pilot turned politician called Aldo Finzi. He came from a wealthy and long-established Italian Jewish family and was one of nine Jewish members of the National Assembly. Like the Pipernos and the Ovazza family in Turin, he was a loyal Fascist and remained one of Mussolini's trusted confidants and supporters until the introduction of the Racial Laws in 1938.

Mussolini had ordered him to make sure that all of the transcripts of every single conversation intercepted in Italy through phone-tapping be sent to him, and to him alone. By the mid-1920s, some 400 stenographers worked for the Ministry of the Interior, transcribing what the citizens of the country said on their telephones. Il Duce wanted to know what his people were doing, and he wanted to be the first to know and to retain control over this information.

There were thousands of incidents involving *delatori*, the dreaded informers who would swap or barter or give information to OVRA, the PolPol, the Blackshirt militias or the *Polizia di Stato*, the state police. Everyone had a story; everyone knew someone who had had their fingers burnt when saying the wrong thing in the wrong place at the wrong time near the wrong person.

There was the poor carpenter, Luciano Livi, who was taking a train to Rome in the early summer of 1936. He got talking to the people sitting next to him, and before long was complaining about how badly he was paid and how there was a lot of hunger and unemployment in Mussolini's Italy. The person to whom he was talking was a Fascist official. He arrested Livi once the train arrived in Rome and took him to a police station to file a complaint against him. To the horror of the carpenter, the three other people who had been sitting in the train compartment with them came too, and also added their signatures to the form detailing Livi's alleged offence. The slip of the tongue saw him taken to a detention centre in the Apennine Mountains. There was the case of Nicola Conte, who was a 25-year-old agricultural consultant from the southern region of Basilicata. He also taught mathematics, and one day he told his students an anti-fascist joke: they denounced him the same day. In July 1939, the Provincial Commission of Naples gave him five years in a detention centre.

The case of Maria Tulli, an 18-year-old high-school student from Milan, was even more extreme, but in the lengthy list of alleged offences committed by every kind of Italian against the Fascist authorities across twenty years, it became almost commonplace. Tulli's high-school class were writing essays about politics and Italian literature. Their teacher told them that the title of their essay should be 'Il Duce, the Modern Prince', drawing similarities between Mussolini and the central character in the sixteenth-century political treatise by Niccolò Machiavelli.

Maria Tulli knew that one of the themes of the discourse was how princes could justify the use of immoral behaviour to hold on to glory and power. She therefore argued that there was no link between the behaviour of Italy's Fascist leader and Machiavelli's sixteenth-century fictitious character. In theory, this should have been seen as praising Mussolini, but the school's teacher misunderstood it. How could the young student have the audacity to suggest that Il Duce bore no resemblance to a prince? Maria Tulli was sentenced to five years in an internment centre.

With incidents such as these regarded as commonplace by 1940, Clotilde Piperno had drummed into her children and her grandchildren the absolute necessity to keep their mouths shut, except when they were with trusted friends or members of their extended family. The Piperno clan were still living in the old family house near the ruins of the Theatre of Marcellus. There was grandmother, Clotilde, and her husband, Giacomo, her son, Giacomo *Due*, and his wife, Nella, their son, Piero – now 18 – and daughter, Giovanna. In addition, there was her second daughter-in-law, Vanda, and the two children of her second son, Adolfo, who had died of tuberculosis in 1936.

It was as though the family inhabited a netherworld. Around them, the movements and activities of an entire state were being monitored; Europe was at war; Mussolini was making a ham-fisted attempt to recreate his vision of the Roman Empire across six countries; and the Jews were waiting, hiding or running. Clotilde's husband, Giacomo, was still selling off the old stock of textiles that he had stored in a warehouse, and once a month trying to do a deal under a borrowed name. He had just enough money to support the family, the children did some maths and history and Italian at home, and more and more regularly there was a dusty emptiness on the sideboard, shelves or dining room table where candles or silverware had stood. The family had been stripped of their livelihood and civil rights, and consigned to the status of third-class citizens, and Clotilde, Vanda, Nella couldn't go into most shops in Rome, apart from the ones, in and around the ghetto owned by fellow Jews. But, unlike a lot of communists, political agitators, anti-Fascists, members of the Roma community and those who made the mistake of getting caught by the *delatori*, the Pipernos hadn't actually been interned.

The Fascist authorities started building fifteen detention centres, or concentration camps, or re-settlement centres across Italy: the name varied, but they were disused army barracks, summer schools or factories under the guard of police officers, with basic living conditions, enough to eat but nothing to do, and although the regime was strict, it was predominantly not violent. The aim was to have them ready by the summer of 1940, when Mussolini planned to intern as many of Italy's Jews as he could.

Every day for the people of Italy brought a blizzard of Fascist propaganda: on posters emblazoned across the cities; on the radio; or in the pages of the Fascist newspaper, *Il Popolo d'Italia*, 'The People of Italy'. The airwaves and the newsprint sang to the tunes of Imperial Italian triumphalism.

Mussolini's idea – which he had developed during the fighting on the Isonzo River – was of a government led by military veterans, what he called 'an Aristocracy of the Trenches'. Military exhortations and terminology ran thick through the propaganda and through Il Duce's speeches: '*Credere, obbedire, combattere*' – 'believe, obey, fight'; '*Libro e moschetto: Fascisto perfetto*' – 'a book and a rifle make the perfect Fascist'; '*Dio, Patria, Famiglia*' – 'God, Country and Family'; Fascism is a country on the march, workers who abandon the precious soil will die. There was even one that said simply, '*Il Duce ha sempre ragione*' – 'Mussolini is always right'. The themes were the purity of work and labour for the communal good, farmland and fertility, warrior virtues, such as sacrifice and bravery, and God and the family.

Under the 'Fascist Era', as the government called its tenure that had started in 1922, there was even a new calendar, as Mussolini tried to tame even time to his whims and grandiose ambitions. The starting date on the Fascist calendar was October 1922, the date of the March on Rome, and subsequent years were counted from that. '*Anno XIII E.F*', for instance, meant the thirteenth year of the Fascist Era, or 29 October 1934 to 28 October 1935. Making jokes or derisory remarks about the calendar was, of course, full justification for a report by one of the *delatori*.

Mussolini declared war on Britain and France on 10 June 1940. The Pipernos managed to survive, and keep possession of their house, while *Nonna* Clotilde kept an eagle eye on developments, gossip, rumour and the ebb and flow of the local Jewish community, and prepared to move the family north to Tuscany at any moment. She knew they were being watched, counted, informed on, but she didn't quite know the full extent of the OVRA and PolPol surveillance of the Jewish community.

Up until 1940, the Director of OVRA and the *Polizia di Stato*, the state police, was an Interior Ministry official and member of the Senate called Arturo Bocchini. Mussolini made him Chief of Police in Rome and head of all civil law enforcement across Italy. His job was simple: keep law and order across the country, and hunt for, find, imprison – and kill if necessary – the enemies of the Fascist state.

A short, jowly 60-year-old with small, round glasses, Bocchini had complete freedom of operations across the whole country and reported only to Mussolini. His personal network of *delatori*, who included every type of person from intelligence department heads to waiters and guides at the Circus Maximus, was estimated to run to over 300 people. He was a close friend and ally of the head of the SS in Berlin, Heinrich Himmler, and he had visited him in Germany twice in 1936 and 1938. The two held meetings to discuss how the Gestapo, OVRA and the SS intelligence service, the SD, could operate together across Europe.

Bocchini saw the Final Solution coming and had clear plans for how it might be implemented in Italy. Like so many powerful, ruthless men, he died not by an assassin's bullet or in battle, but of overeating, stress and a consummate lack of exercise. A massive stroke felled him in 1940, and at his funeral in Rome were three German men whose actions were going to have an enormous impact on Italy, its Jewish population and the Piperno family. They were SS-Reichsführer Heinrich Himmler, SS-Obergruppenführer Karl Wolff and the head of the RSHA, or Reich Security Main Office, who was then SS-Obergruppenführer Reinhard Heydrich.

Bocchini left behind a very closely organised and managed state surveillance system, based on informers, rigid police control, phone-tapping, arbitrary detention and internment, and a wide variety of possible offences that any individual could knowingly, or unknowingly, commit. Often it was enough that they were born in a certain type of family or educated in a certain way. Between 1926 and 1930, Bocchini had reorganised Italy's police and extended and ordered its files and archives into what became known as the Central Political Records. In the first five years of Fascism, more than 100,000 new files were added.

The Political Police, the PolPol, divided each individual's profile into a variety of different cross-matched categories, based upon a wide range of questions. Where had they been educated? Were they aristocratic or working-class? Did they know any homosexuals who frequented public gardens after dark? Did they gamble and drink excessively? Had they been observed by any reliable *delatore* attending meetings of the Communist Party when they should have been at Sunday Mass? Had they borrowed money? Were they faithful to their wife or husband? Did they have a criminal record? How, why, and how often did they travel outside of their town and commune of residence? The questions continued, anything designed to prise open a chink in an individual's personal, emotional, professional and domestic armour. Was it true their parents had once voted for the Liberal Party? And what had they done in the war?

One note from a trusted *delatore* said that someone had been spotted on two occasions attending a Fascist rally without wearing a uniform. Why? And wasn't one of their children continuing a relationship with an Eritrean, a forbidden inter-race liaison?

Into this large number of categories poured information from a wide variety of sources: *delatori*, teachers, employers, the police themselves and hospital doctors. There were denunciatory notes, files, letters, telexes, newspaper cuttings and official reports and condemnations. As Fascism spread its wings and grew from the 1920s and 1930s into the early 1940s, more and more individuals' details were to be found in the files, all stored in the basement of the imposing six-storey Interior Ministry headquarters, located in the Palazzo del Viminale in Rome.

As Jews, the Pipernos' details were not only there in the files, but they had also had to fill out a personal survey form. Were their parents or grandparents Jewish? Did they own property? Did they employ people? Were they wholly Jewish, or only partially? This became known as the Racial Survey and it drew its information from an estimated 140 different institutions, such as hospitals, lawyers' firms or parish priests, all of which was sent to the Ministry of the Interior, where it was categorised, cross-referenced and then filed. Agents from OVRA also added reports on Jehovah's Witnesses, Muslims and Pentecostals – the latter were thought to be anti-Fascists, and thus considered subversive elements, like communists and homosexuals. The presence in Italy of these two latter groups, as well as Jews, was thought by Mussolini and many in OVRA, Bocchini included, to be behind the 'genetic weakening' of the Italian population.

Fascist biological politics were a completely new area of surveillance. Pregnant women, children and even babies were monitored by a state body calling itself the National Bureau for the Protection of Maternity and Infancy. On the one hand, this provided enormous medical and personal assistance to Italian mothers from every class, including those rich enough to employ a personal physician, which meant they could deliver their babies at home. The office of the Ministry of Health helped pregnant and working mothers, built day-care centres and trained midwives and doctors, but it also monitored and registered every single baby born in Italy, its parents, grandparents and their families. In Mussolini's Fascist state, surveillance began before the cradle: it started almost on conception. In 1926 only 400 Italian mothers were assisted or documented by the National Bureau; by 1937 and 1938, this had risen to 540,000.

So as Clotilde Piperno decided whether, and when, to move north to Tuscany, so OVRA increased its surveillance of the families of 'new' enemies of the state. As the Racial Manifesto had only been introduced in 1938, Jews were the newest of enemies and had only been included in a separate category in the last national census, which had taken place in 1938. In the 1931 census, 35,000 Jews had been counted, this figure then climbing to around 42,000 from 1933 to 1938. Jews had been included in the 1931 census as a 'non-Catholic group', without reference to who they were. In 1938, they came into a separate category, meaning that this last census was the first one that could be defined as specifically racial.

Meanwhile, another 5,000–7,000 Jews arrived as temporary refugees. Visa-free travel restrictions ironically made Mussolini's Fascist surveillance state a refuge of choice for many European Jews fleeing Nazi Germany, Austria or Poland.

But if it was easy to enter Italy as a Jew without a visa, it was nigh on impossible to travel around Italy as one without an individual's identity papers – establishing them as Jewish – being checked constantly at roadblocks, hotel reception desks, railway stations and on arrival in any city, town or village where a person was intending to stay more than one night. On arrival, the first stop was always the *Questura*, the state police headquarters, to register. So, although Clotilde and her family could physically move from Rome to Monaciano, outside Siena, without any hindrance, when they got there, they would still be subjected to the same level of surveillance and gradually increasing persecution. There would almost certainly be a minimum of half a dozen identity checks in between Rome and Siena, including at least one on the train itself.

So, thought the careful, perspicacious Clotilde, if the family wanted to hide, and then to disappear, they had to get somewhere where they were not known as Jews. And that meant false identity papers, which meant not just committing a serious crime, but also finding a substantial amount of money and a friendly and sympathetic police commissioner somewhere, anywhere, who would be prepared to authorise the issue of new papers, and give official, written testimony that said that the Piperno family were people of good, nationalist, Catholic, Fascist standing – and who were certainly not Jews.

A police commissioner was the only reliable way, thought Grandmother Piperno. Otherwise, it meant using those criminal forgers and dealers of identity documents somewhere down around Tiburtina Station. And being anywhere near them would almost certainly mean that one of them – somebody unknown, invisible – would likely be a *delatore*.

Clotilde began to think about a new family name, a new future, and how to find the money required to buy this.

It was spring 1941, and across Europe both Hitler and Mussolini were expanding their respective National Socialist and Fascist empires. Poland, France, Belgium, Norway and Holland had fallen to the tanks and infantry brigades of the Wehrmacht and SS and the launch of Operation Barbarossa was just two months away.

In a fierce, competitive bid to emulate the military prowess of his German ally, Mussolini had decided to extend his Italian empire. Like the Roman emperors, Mussolini saw the Mediterranean as *Mare Nostrum* ('Our Sea') and some of the lands around it as rightfully his. These included Libya, which had been occupied by Italy in 1911 after the Italo-Turkish War and then divided into two colonies, Italian Tripolitania and Italian Cyrenaica. In 1934, these became Italian Libya. By 1941, this was the scene of heavy fighting between the British and Italian armies. To reinforce the beleaguered, outgunned and outfought

Italians, the German Afrika Korps, under General Erwin Rommel, had arrived in Tripoli in January of that year.

Mussolini saw north Africa and parts of the Balkans as something he called *Spazio Vitale*, or 'vital space'. It became the name for the policy of territorial expansionism designed to overcome the problems of overcrowding in Italy and eastern France – the Germans had adopted a similar policy in eastern Europe called *Lebensraum*, or 'living space'. The preceding winter, in October 1940, Mussolini had invaded Greece, having already annexed Albania in 1939. The invasion was a disaster, and it took the Greeks less than two months to push the 140,000 troops of the Italian Army back into Albania.

Mussolini's strategic failure opened up a hole in Hitler's crucial south-eastern Mediterranean flank, as British and Commonwealth troops arrived from Egypt to help support their Greek allies. Spurred on by Mussolini's failure, Hitler invaded Yugoslavia and then Greece in April 1941. Il Duce, smarting from his recent defeats, decided to assist Hitler by sending twenty divisions of 300,000 men to invade the western provinces of Yugoslavia, creating an Italian protectorate he called *Dalmazia* in Slovenia and parts of Croatia.

In September 1941, Italy annexed parts of the Dalmatian coast, creating the Governorate of Dalmatia. Other parts of the country, occupied when the Germans invaded the country in April 1941, became the Independent State of Croatia. As a result, the Italian Army controlled not just the whole of the Dalmatian coast and interior, but also significant parts of Slovenian territory.

The Independent State of Croatia was run by the German puppet, Croatian dictator Ante Pavelic, and its brutal anti-Serb and anti-Muslim diktats were only equalled by its fierce antisemitism. But in the parts of Croatia occupied by the Italians, the Italian and Yugoslav Jews were protected by the Italian soldiers, who found the atrocities committed by the Croatian nationalist militias, the *Ustashe*, too horrifying to tolerate.

The Chairman of the Union of Jewish Communities of Italy and the Italian Foreign Ministry said a change took place in the spring of 1942, when the first reports came in of large numbers of Jewish refugees who were fleeing Croatia, and even Serbia and Bosnia, in order to seek refuge in the sectors under the control of the Italian Army. The Foreign Ministry officials asked their army in Croatia to move decisively to solve the problem. So, an unofficial policy of protection towards Jews was adopted by Italian military commanders, governors and diplomats.

Although they were officially meant to prevent Jewish refugees from entering the Italian zone and expel any who had already arrived, they refused to do this in practice because they realised that handing over the Jews to the *Ustashe* was tantamount to sending them to a Croat concentration camp. Already, by autumn 1941, some Italian and German observers and liaison officers were spreading reports about what they had seen at the *Ustashe* concentration camps at Jasenovac.

Meanwhile, back home in Italy, Allied bombing was making life extremely difficult. Virginia Montalcini and Primo Levi's home city was, along with Milan, the centre of the northern Italian manufacturing economy. It was home to Fiat and Lancia, among others, along with banks, insurance businesses and aircraft factories. From the middle of June 1940, the city was subjected to over 100 British and American bombing attacks, carried out at first from air bases in Lincolnshire and Cambridgeshire by RAF Wellingtons, Halifaxes and Armstrong Whitleys.

The city lay in the extreme north-west of Italy, so the distance from England to Turin was little further than to Lyons or Geneva. The raids were notable for one factor above all others: their relative lack of accuracy and their tendency to destroy more civilian homes than industrial premises. This was unsurprising – the aircraft were bombing from above 15,000ft, sometimes at night, and Turin's manufacturing establishments were built in inhabited areas of the city. Consequently, civilian casualties were high – around 2,000 in all – and damage to factories and industrial plants notably low, while at least 40 per cent of Turin's homes and apartment blocks were hit in some way.

After Italy had declared war on France and Great Britain on 10 June, the first Allied air raids hit Turin on the nights of the 11th and 12th. Along with a simultaneous attack on Genoa, this was the first air raid on an Italian city during the Second World War. Nine British bombers, out of thirty-six that had taken off from bases in England, attacked the city's Fiat Mirafiori plant. The bombs, however, fell on the city, killing seventeen civilians. Mirafiori was the target again on the night of 13–14 August, when the RAF missed – again – and killed eighteen people, also wounding eighty-three. Fiat's plants in Lingotto and Mirafiori were targeted eight times in coming months and were hit only once.[1]

In summer 1941, seventy-six Halifaxes, Wellingtons and Whitleys took off in one night to attack Genoa and Turin. Five aircraft were lost and seventy-five tonnes of bombs were dropped on Turin, completely missing all of their targets. 1940 and 1941 were just the start: Allied bombing raids worsened after German troops occupied the country, and the Allies thought air attacks the most effective way to cut road and rail communications.

The strikes against Italian industry – particularly around Genoa, Turin and Milan – made many Italians afraid to stay in the cities at night and were a crucial propaganda triumph for Mussolini. The casualty figures from Allied aerial raids on the Italian cities and countryside were, ultimately, going to be huge, the bombing one of the biggest, bloodiest killers of its civilian population. And for teenagers across Italy, like Virginia Montalcini, Primo Levi and the Piperno children, the bombing was considerably more dangerous than any form of antisemitic legislation – for now.

Meanwhile the Fascist propaganda machine was not slow to communicate the Italian expansionism in Croatia. The Fascists had done their utmost to put a positive, nationalist spin on the disastrous Greek adventure, and now were concentrating on the glowing welcome received by Italian mountain troops in Slovenia, and how the combination of the Afrika Korps and the Italian Army would shortly prove more than a match for the British in Egypt and Libya. For Clotilde Piperno and many of the other Jewish families across Italy, who were worrying desperately about their future, these military operations opened wide a small and secret door to a new world away from Fascism and surveillance and persecution.

Within weeks of the arrival of the Italian Army inside Slovenia and Croatia, Jewish families from Italy decided to follow them, and see if they could settle – even temporarily – in territory the soldiers had occupied. To their surprise, this proved possible, so much so that a series of Italian generals and colonels, seeing the Jews as Italian citizens and not having any orders to do anything apart from welcome their fellow countrymen, decided to protect them. Among the ever-buzzing, almost electrical contacts of the Italian Jewish information grapevine, these territories started to be given a new nickname – 'The Promised Land'.

3

ROME, REPRESSION AND RESISTANCE

As Italy joined the war and went to fight against the British in North Africa, so the situation for the Piperno family and other Italian Jews changed dramatically and very dangerously. To escape persecution, some 6,000 of them emigrated.

Within five days of Italy joining the war, the police arrested the first Jews, who immediately were transferred to one of the fifteen new internment camps. The largest of these was called Ferramonti, built in the town of Tarsia in Calabria, far down in the south of Italy. The first prisoners arrived on 20 June, and by midsummer there were 3,800 Jews detained there: 141 of them were Italian, the remainder foreign.

Life was arduous, but there was little or no violence. This 'concentration camp' was a light-year from the German equivalents – the prisoners had a nursery, vegetable garden, library, school and synagogue. Rabbis from Italian cities visited for periods to minister to the inmates. Couples could get married, children were born, and from the surrounding fields and vineyards of the Calabrian countryside, prisoners picked corn, olives, grapes and apricots.

In a curious sleight of racial hand by the Fascist authorities, Jewish families, like the Pipernos in Rome and the Ovazzas in Turin, were not forced into these internment camps. Despite race laws that had reduced them to being the country's underdogs and despised pariahs, they were not actually imprisoned or threatened with death. Some of them took refuge from persecution in the territories occupied by the Italian Army in Greece, France and Yugoslavia, and in the latter country, some parts of the Italian military actively protected them.

Then came a development that would profoundly influence the future of the Italian Jews over the next five years. At 5.31 on the morning of 10 February 1939, Pope Pius XI died. Ambrogio Damiano Achille Ratti was 81 and had just suffered a third heart attack. Surrounded at his bedside by cardinals, his last words were, 'My soul parts from you all in peace.'[1]

His Cardinal Secretary of State, Eugenio Pacelli, who was shortly to be elected the next Pope, was present at his death. When a Pope is believed to be dead, a white veil is placed on his face and, to ascertain his demise, the cardinal who is in charge of the Vatican administration raises the veil and strikes the head of the departed Pope three times, citing his name. He then declares that the Pope is dead.

Pope Pius XI had been Pontiff since 1922, and among the memorial tributes that poured into the Vatican after his death were two, one from Benito Mussolini and another from Adolf Hitler. Flags flew at half-mast in Paris, Rome and Berlin, and the two men whose regimes had attracted the most criticism from the head of the Catholic Church waited to see what stance the new Pope would take against Italian Fascism and the Nazism of the Third Reich.

Pius XI's successor took the same name as his predecessor, and so became the twelfth pope to be called 'Pius'. In his new elevated position as pontiff, the former Cardinal Eugenio Pacelli continued to criticise Germany and Italy's two dictators. Pacelli had been opposed to both Mussolini and Hitler when he'd been Cardinal Secretary of State – and the Vatican's de facto highest foreign policy official – under Pius XI. In one way, this was ironic: Mussolini had, after all, signed the 1929 Lateran Treaty that formally recognised the Holy See as an independent state. Pius XI had also tried his utmost to stand up for the rights and religious freedoms of all the Catholics in Germany, signing a concordat (papal treaty) with them. Hitler increasingly ignored this. After Mussolini introduced the Racial Laws in 1938, Pius XI stepped up his criticism of Il Duce's regime, issuing three formal papal encyclicals, or policy statements, that Pius XI had issued against Nazism, Communism and Fascism. These were respectively entitled '*Mit Brennender Sorge*' ('With Deep Anxiety'), '*Divini Redemptoris*' (Divine Redeemer) and '*Non Abbiamo Bisogno*' (translated in full as 'We do not Need to Acquaint You'). The latter declared that Italian Fascism was a pagan movement, which 'snatches the young from the Church and from Jesus Christ ... which inculcates in its own young people hatred, violence and irreverence'.[2]

In 1942, the Vatican was the smallest sovereign state in the world, occupying 120 acres of Rome. As the war continued, it started to become one of the most intensely covered intelligence targets for its size in the expanding conflict. Before assuming the papacy in 1939, Pope Pius XII had served as the papal *nuncio*, or ambassador, in Germany for seven years, and knew exactly how Germans worked. He spoke their language fluently and understood how the Third Reich's military and diplomatic bureaucracy functioned. The Vatican was like a military hierarchy, with the Pope and his cardinals at the top, all the way down to the nuns, priests and religious brothers who ran every department of life in the Holy City, from the gardens, to the telephone exchange, to the Palatine Guard's off-duty bar.

Almost everybody in the Vatican was ecclesiastical, everybody believed in what they were doing, and everybody did as they were told by the Pope, for the simple reason that they were recruited for their devotion, loyalty and discretion. Most were highly educated, many spoke Latin, all spoke Italian, and some spoke at least two other languages. They were cut off physically and electronically from the outside world, yet they could circulate untouched with complete diplomatic immunity should they wish to travel outside their tiny city state.

From the point of view of maintaining an efficient, secure and contained intelligence network, this state of affairs functioned very well. It made the Vatican extremely hard to penetrate for outside parties, especially as the number of people who lived and worked there was so small, standing as it did at 256 in October 1942. All the intelligence that the Vatican wanted – apart from Russian – was accessible inside its walls, as diplomats who were based there, from Britain, Germany, France, the United States and neutral countries such as Turkey, all transmitted frequent updates from within its confines back to their respective countries. All of the main belligerents and neutral countries in the Second World War maintained diplomatic missions within its walls, and all the Vatican had to do to know what their diplomatic intentions were was to be able to read their codes.

From the time of the ordination of Pius XII, the Germans were convinced that the Vatican was directly sympathetic to the Allied cause – and directly hostile to that of the Third Reich. They recognised that the Pope's influence over tens of millions of Roman Catholics world-wide gave him immense power, especially within occupied countries such as Poland, with their predominantly Catholic populations. From 1939, the Polish situation was also of substantial concern to the Germans as the Warsaw government-in-exile, based in London, was in frequent contact with the Vatican, as well as with the armed resistance in their own country.

Compared to his predecessor, Pius XII quickly developed a repu-tation for being less forthright, outspoken and openly critical of the Third Reich and of Mussolini's Fascist Party. This, however, seemed to be a contradiction in terms, since when he had served as Pius XI's Cardinal Secretary of State, it had been Pacelli who had issued more than fifty written protests against the German authorities' stance on race – he had, for instance, helped Pius XI draft the 1937 encyclical entitled '*Mit Brennender Sorge*', and he was openly and deeply critical of Nazi race theory. Pacelli's stance on Christianity and antisemitism were that they could only be mutually exclusive, and he was stressing his own thoughts when he reiterated Pius XI's views on this: 'It is impossible for a Christian to take part in anti-Semitism. Anti-Semitism is inadmissible; spiritually we are all Semites.'[3]

The Germans considered Pacelli sufficiently critical that they openly voiced disapproval of his appointment by refusing to attend his coronation. Joseph Goebbels, as the Reich's Propaganda Minister, made a note in his diary in March 1939. Hitler was considering cancelling and repudiating the Concordat agreement made with the Vatican once Pacelli became Pope. 'This will surely happen once Pacelli undertakes his first hostile act,' he wrote on 4 March.[4]

What Pius XII did about the persecution of Italy and Europe's Jews, what he said, what he knew and what he could have said, could have done and could have known, has consistently occupied religious, diplomatic, judicial and historical officials and scholars since his appointment in 1939. Did he know more than he could say, without betraying and compromising intelligence sources, such as the Allied breaks into the Enigma enciphering system? Or the cryptanalytical successes of his own Vatican code-breakers? Did he say publicly less than he might, instead concentrating on supporting and facilitating the anti-Hitler resistance? Did he say and do as much as he could, without crossing a clear line in the sand, after which Himmler, Heydrich, Kaltenbrunner and Eichmann would simply declare open war on all of Europe's Roman Catholics? And how did he balance all of his religious, institutional and moral imperatives with his mandate to protect the physical and material assets of the Vatican and the Catholic Church, and keep Nazism firmly as a foe, without allowing the excesses of Stalinist communism to encroach?

The answer is that he tried to do almost all of the above, all at the same time, through statements and actions both large and small, through approaches micro and macro. Saving and protecting millions of souls was never going to be easy, especially in the middle of the world's first global conflict, and in the middle of the largest, best planned and ruthlessly implemented genocide mankind had ever seen. Looking at some of the primary examples of what he did and said, and what he knew – overtly and covertly – in the run-up to the German implementation of the Final Solution in Italy will assist in assessing his actions and words during the latter.

Among other problems that the Vatican tried to address after the imposition of the 1938 Racial Laws was the comprehensive discrimination that Jews experienced in terms of employment. So the Pope used Vatican by-laws and gave some Jewish university professors work within the walls of the Holy City. He also tried his hardest, persistently, to help Jews get hold of visas so they could emigrate to several countries, one of which was Brazil. He agreed with President Getulio Vargas in Rio di Janeiro that 3,000 so-called 'non-Aryan' Catholics could emigrate from Europe. The phrase was designed to cover the category of Jews who, for the sake of their own safety, had temporarily or permanently converted to Catholicism.

Between September 1939 and February 1941, over 1,000 visas were issued, despite Brazil's ever-changing regulations and reneging on agreements made with the Vatican. Among other incidents, they asked those applying for visas to pay for them in advance, by foreign bank transfer to the Banco do Brasil in São Paolo. They also suspected that hundreds of the visa recipients were continuing to practise Judaism, despite claiming to be Roman Catholics.

Meanwhile, Myron Charles Taylor was an American industrialist and philanthropist, who had made a fortune in manufacturing and steel both during and after the First World War. When President Roosevelt convened the Evian Conference in 1938 in France, so as to discuss the problem of the number of Jewish refugees fleeing Germany, he sent Taylor to represent the United States. In December 1939, he sent Taylor as his personal envoy to Pope Pius XII. The Vatican gave him ambassadorial status. He was to be one of the Allies' frontrunners in the upcoming intelligence war. Hundreds of thousands of European Jews were by now trying to flee the continent, and the United States was a haven of refuge many of them tried to reach. The country, however, had introduced strict quota limits on the number of Jewish refugees permitted to enter, and one of the focal points of meetings between Taylor and Pius XII involved the latter pressing the former to try and have these limits removed, or at least considerably extended.

D'Arcy Osborne was His Majesty's Envoy Extraordinary and Minister Plenipotentiary to the Holy See between 1936 and 1947. Born in 1884, he was the great-great grandson of Francis Osborne, 5th Duke of Leeds, who was Foreign Secretary in the government of William Pitt the Younger between 1783 and 1791. Refined, aristocratic and the epitome of British sangfroid, he was educated at Haileybury before joining the diplomatic service, serving in Lisbon, Rome, Washington and The Hague. He arrived in the Vatican in 1936.

When Italy declared war on the United Kingdom in 1940, Osborne, working for the Holy See but living in Italian territory, moved inside the Vatican, living in a pilgrim's hostel attached to the Convent of Santa Marta. He would mostly remain here until Rome was liberated in August 1944 and worked with Vatican *curia* and other diplomats to shelter both Jews and escaped Allied POWs, using the code name 'Mount'.

Major Sam Derry was one of these, a Royal Artillery officer and former prisoner of the Germans and Italians, who remembered clearly meeting Osborne for the first time:

> Unruffled poise … Seldom have I met any man in whom I had such immediate confidence. He welcomed us warmly, yet I found it impossible to behave with anything but strict formality. Apart from the restraining influence of my clothing [he was disguised as a monsignor] I was almost overwhelmed by an atmosphere of old-world English courtliness and grace which I had thought belonged only to the country-house parties of long ago. Sir D'Arcy was spry, trim, a young sixty, but he had spent years enough in the diplomatic service to develop an astonishing aptitude for creating around himself an aura of all that was most civilized in English life. I felt as though I had returned home after long travels, to find that royalty had come to dinner, and I had to be on my best behaviour.[5]

Ernst Heinrich Freiherr von Weizsäcker, meanwhile, was a German aristocrat, naval officer, diplomat and politician. He served as Secretary of State at the Foreign Office of Nazi Germany from 1938 to 1943, and then he became its Ambassador to the Holy See from 1943 to 1945. He was a member of the prominent Weizsäcker family, and his father would later become the German President Richard von Weizsäcker.

From joining the German Foreign Service in 1920, he served in Basel, Copenhagen, Geneva and then Rome. In 1938, he was appointed as Secretary of State, which was the second highest-ranking official after the Foreign Minister in the German Foreign Office. He was also encouraged by his superiors to join the ruling German National Socialist Party, which he did in 1938, and then he was also awarded an honorary rank in the SS. He was the German Ambassador to the Holy See, the direct duelling partner of both Osborne and Taylor.

But, together with Wilhelm Canaris and the army chief of staff, General Ludwig Beck, Weizsäcker was involved with an anti-war group in the German government, which was determined to avoid a war in 1938 that they felt Germany would lose. They were allied to another faction of conspirators against Hitler: this one was led by Hans Oster, a Wehrmacht general who was the head of counterintelligence in the Abwehr; alongside him was Hans-Bernd Gisevius, a Gestapo-turned-Abwehr officer based in Zürich, who carried out secret meetings with both the Americans and the Vatican, putting out feelers about plans to remove or kill Hitler. Weiszäcker held not just diplomatic status, but as the war began, was promoted to the rank of full colonel in the Allgemeine, or General, SS.

One of the first ways in which Pope Pius XII was involved in trying to rescue European Jews, including the Italian ones, was when he was asked by the German Catholic *nuncio* to press the Brazilian government over the issue of 3,000 extra immigration visas, on top of those it had issued. It is difficult to verify the exact number of supplementary visas that were actually given out. Only 1,000 visas were formally allocated to the Brazilian Embassy in the Vatican, and most – although not all – were probably used.[6]

In October 1939, the new Pope published his first original encyclical, entitled '*Summi Pontificatus*', which was subtitled 'On the Unity of Human Society'. Its publication coincided with the invasion of Poland by both Germany and the Soviet Union. While the Pope failed to publicly condemn the killings of Polish Catholics, as well as thousands of members of the clergy, by the Germans and Russians, the encyclical stressed disapproval of the invasions and persecutions carried out by both sides. Pope Pius could hardly claim he didn't know what was going on in Poland, and he was learning that encyclical disapproval didn't equate, in the eyes of the leaders and citizens of Europe, the United States and elsewhere, to condemnation. 'Who,' asked the pontiff, 'among the Soldiers of Christ – ecclesiastic or layman – does not feel himself incited and spurred on to a greater vigilance, to a more determined resistance, by the sight of the ever-increasing host of Christ's enemies?'[7]

When the Allied bombing raids over occupied Europe began in 1939, Wellington and Halifax bomber crews from the RAF had included tens of thousands of copies of a leaflet in their runs over Germany, containing translated extracts from the Pope's encyclical. Heinrich Müller from the Gestapo said he considered it to be so innocuous and unclear that he approved its dissemination in churches. Mussolini had no objection to it at all – he considered both Hitler and Stalin's actions in Poland and the Baltic to be bordering on the subhuman. The Polish president-in-exile in London, Władysław Sikorski, meanwhile, implored the Pope to speak out against what was happening in Poland.

The Poles also presented their information about the situation in their own country in four different reports. The principal one was called Raczyński's Note, dated 10 December 1942 and signed by Edward Raczyński, the Polish Minister for Foreign Affairs in exile in London. The Poles sent it to the different Allied foreign ministers, and it was the first official report on the Holocaust that gave precisely documented and verified information to both leaders and the public among the Western Allies. It included the names of extermination camps – Belzec, Sobibor, Treblinka – in its contents. The full report that accompanied it was entitled 'The Mass Extermination of Jews in German-occupied Poland: Note addressed to the governments of the United Nations, 10th December 1942, and other documents'.[8]

Apart from this written document of protest from one European government about the plight, not just of their people, but of European Jewry from 1941 onwards, the Polish government-in-exile also provided the Allies with three other vital early and accurate accounts of the ongoing Holocaust, and of war crimes being committed in eastern

Europe. This intelligence comprised 'The Polish White Book', 'The Black Book of Poland' and 'Witold's Report'.

The first, published by the Ministry of Information of the government-in-exile in London in 1940, documents German war crimes carried out during their invasion of Poland and immediately afterwards. The second, the so-called 'Black Book of Poland', consisted of a 750-page report documenting German atrocities in Poland between the invasion in September 1939 and June 1941, just prior to the beginning of Operation Barbarossa.[9] It was the first to detail and describe the German extermination and work programme carried out under Operation Reinhard and in the camp complexes of Dachau, Auschwitz and Mauthausen. Putnam's Publishers released the book in New York in April 1942, leading the Jewish Telegraphic Agency in Manhattan to run a headline on 8 September 1942 that read, '200,000 Jews executed by Nazis in Poland, Black Book asserts'.[10]

A third publication was 'Witold's Report', written by Captain Witold Pilecki.[11] A Polish Army officer, who volunteered to be imprisoned in Auschwitz so he could organise a resistance movement and make a report on conditions there, Pilecki escaped in April 1943. He provided the Allies with the first documented eyewitness account of conditions inside an extermination and work camp complex.

The report of 10 December 1942 and the Polish government's efforts then triggered the Declaration of the Allied Nations on 17 December 1942. Along with eleven other governments, and under the auspices of the fledgling United Nations, the United States issued a statement. It was picked up by many American newspapers, publicly acknowledging the campaign of mass murder of European Jews, describing deportations to Poland, and condemning 'in the strongest possible terms this bestial policy of cold-blooded extermination'.

On the same day, the document was presented in the British Houses of Parliament by the British Foreign Secretary, Anthony Eden:

The attention of the Governments of Belgium, Czechoslovakia, Greece, Luxemburg, the Netherlands, Norway, Poland, the United States of America, the United Kingdom of Great Britain and Northern

Ireland, the Union of Soviet Socialist Republics and Yugoslavia, and of the French National Committee has been drawn to numerous reports from Europe that the German authorities, not content with denying to persons of Jewish race in all the territories over which their barbarous rule has been extended the most elementary human rights, are now carrying into effect Hitler's oft repeated intention to exterminate the Jewish people in Europe.

From all the occupied countries Jews are being transported, in conditions of appalling horror and brutality, to Eastern Europe. In Poland, which has been made the principal Nazi slaughterhouse, the ghettoes established by the German invaders are being systematically emptied of all Jews except a few highly skilled workers required for war industries. None of those taken away are ever heard of again. The able-bodied are slowly worked to death in labour camps. The infirm are left to die of exposure and starvation or are deliberately massacred in mass executions. The number of victims of these bloody cruelties is reckoned in many hundreds of thousands of entirely innocent men, women and children.[12]

The *New York Times* printed the statement in full, under the front-page headline, '11 Allies Condemn Nazi War on Jews'.[13] The Holocaust was now public, world knowledge.

The three main sources of Polish intelligence, as mentioned above, that had formed the basis of these reports about the Holocaust and German war crimes in eastern Europe were also backed up by information coming in from other European countries. One of these was the Netherlands. At the same time as the Poles were disseminating their reports, in the Netherlands, the SS and the SD were fully occupied rounding up and deporting as many as possible of the country's estimated 125,000 Jews. One of the senior German officers running this operation was called Wilhelm Harster, a Bavarian general from the SD who had honed his skills in arrests, round-ups and deportations when he'd overseen part of the Krakow Ghetto in 1941.

By summer of 1942, operations to deport Dutch Jews were under way, when an incident occurred that would profoundly influence

Pius XII's decisions concerning any proclamations he could, or would, issue against the Holocaust, in Italy and elsewhere. On 26 July 1942, a group of Dutch bishops, who included Archbishop Johannes de Jong, issued a statement condemning, openly and widely, the German deportation of Dutch men to work in German factories and Dutch Jews to concentration camps.

The reply from Harster and his men from the SD and the SS was instant. They tracked down and arrested more than 400 Dutch Catholics who had Jewish relatives. The Germans put them on cattle cars in stations across the Netherlands. The Pope's housekeeper and secretary, a Bavarian Roman Catholic sister called Pascalina Lehnert, was to write later that the Pope's moral calculations went as follows. A protest by a conclave of Dutch bishops saw 400 Catholics disappear – what would happen if a pope made a pronouncement? How many would be deported then? Would the number deported after a pope's protest turn into 2,000, 20,000 or 200,000? She said that while politicians, generals and dictators might gamble with the lives of people, a pope could not. Pius XII often used the same words he claimed to have given to the Italian Ambassador to the Vatican in 1940, 'We would like to utter words of fire against such actions [German atrocities] and the only thing restraining us from speaking is the fear of making the plight of the victims even worse.'[14]

His dilemma increased. By 18 September 1942, both Italian cardinals and the international envoys – Taylor, Osborne and those of Brazil and France – were claiming that the Vatican's moral authority itself was being eroded by its refusal to speak out against the killings of Jews. Pius could no longer hide behind the excuse of ignorance – after all, the Americans and Poles had completed the very substantial investigatory groundwork at no small cost to themselves.

On 26 September 1942, Myron C. Taylor wrote to Cardinal Secretary of State Maglione, summarising some of the intelligence that the US State Department had received about the ongoing killings of Jews:

The following was received from the Geneva office of the Jewish Agency for Palestine, in a letter dated August 30th 1942. That office received the report from two eye-witnesses (Aryans) one of whom came on August 14th from Poland.

1. Liquidation of the Warsaw Ghetto is taking place. Without any distinction all Jews, irrespective of age or sex, are being removed from the Ghetto in groups and shot. Their corpses are utilised for making fats and their bones for the manufacture of fertiliser. Corpses are even being exhumed for these purposes.

2. These mass executions take place not in Warsaw, but in especially prepared camps for the purpose, one of which is stated to be in Belzec. About 50,000 Jews have been executed in Lemberg itself on the spot during the past month. According to another report, 100,000 have been massacred in Warsaw. There is not one Jew left in the entire district east of Poland, including Russia ...[15]

Taylor wondered if the Vatican had any information to confirm the reports and how the Pope might influence public opinion on the matter of the killings? Cardinal Secretary of State Maglione's reply, two weeks later, said little, except that information, difficult to verify, had indeed reached the Vatican and the Holy See was doing what it could to help the victims. It's hard to equate the same Pius XII who was becoming deeply involved with the resistance to Adolf Hitler, the same pontiff who said he wanted to protest in 'words of fire', with the vacillation contained in this statement. Pius XII in December then point-blank refused to match the Allied United Nations' Declaration of 17 December. And then almost instantly he performed a volte-face in his Christmas address of 1942, when he went head to head with the reality of mass death and extermination:

Mankind owes that vow to the numberless exiles whom the hurricane of war has torn from their native land and scattered in the land of the stranger; who can make their own the lament of the Prophet: 'Our inheritance is turned to aliens; our house to strangers.' Mankind owes that vow to the hundreds of thousands of persons who, without any fault on their part, sometimes only because of their nationality or race, have been consigned to death or slow extermination.[16]

After Pius XII had delivered this Christmas message in December 1942, the Third Reich answered back. The Reich Security Main Office (RSHA) was the main government department in Berlin responsible for the policing and security of the Third Reich, both inside and outside of Germany. Directly subordinated to Hitler, its first head was SS-Obergruppenführer Reinhard Heydrich from September 1939 to June 1942, and after his assassination in Prague, Himmler himself took over for six months. He then handed over command to SS-Obergruppenführer Ernst Kaltenbrunner.

The RSHA was divided into seven different *Ämter*, or offices: Amt I was Admin and Legal Affairs; Amt II Ideological Investigation, III was the internal German information-gathering service, and IV was 'Suppression of Opposition', or the Gestapo, under Heinrich Müller. Adolf Eichmann ran the subdepartment of Amt IV that dealt with Jewish Affairs, called Referat IV B4. Amt V was crime; VI foreign intelligence, under the SD; and Amt VII was 'Ideological Evaluation' – in essence, propaganda. So, in December 1942, the Amt IV Department relayed the Pope's address to the respective heads of SD delegations in occupied countries where the Holocaust was ongoing, as well as the SS, Gestapo, police and SD leaders of the various *Einsatzkommandos* operating in these countries:

> In a manner never known before, the Pope has repudiated the National Socialist New European Order. His radio allocution was a masterpiece of clerical falsification of the National Socialist Weltanschauung ... the Pope does not refer to the National Socialists in Germany by name, but his speech is one long attack on everything we stand for ... God, he says, regards all peoples and races as worthy of the same consideration. Here he is clearly speaking on behalf of the Jews ... That this speech is directed exclusively against the New Order in Europe as seen in National Socialism is clear in the papal statement that mankind owes a debt to 'all who during the war have lost their Fatherland and who, although personally blameless have, simply on account of their nationality and origin, been killed or reduced to utter destitution'. Here he is virtually accusing the German people of injustice towards the Jews, and makes himself the mouthpiece of the Jewish war criminals.[17]

Gian Galeazzo Ciano was Mussolini's Foreign Minister from 1936 to 1943, and his son-in-law. His reaction, and that of Il Duce, to the Pope's message was one of mild derision – unlike the RSHA, they didn't take it seriously. But then they, at this point, unlike the RSHA, were not carrying out the Holocaust. Mussolini is alleged to have said that 'this was a speech of platitudes which might better be made by the parish priest of Predappio'.[18]

Predappio, ironically, was his birthplace, a small town in the central Italian province of Emilia-Romagna with a population of around 4,000. Equating the head of the Roman Catholic Church with his local parish priest was Mussolini's way of belittling Pius XII's authority, and yet, suggesting that if the RSHA was going to take this speech seriously then their authority and judgement, could, in turn, be measured in reference to a small-town Italian parish priest.

Not for nothing did Heydrich, and then Kaltenbrunner, see Mussolini at best as an utterly unreliable, perpetually needy liability, but also as an arrogant provocateur. Himmler, knowing the store that Hitler placed in his temperamental, self-centred strategic ally, kept his mouth shut and knew that Mussolini was at his most useful to the German Reich by doing as he was told. Himmler called him 'our little Roman nodding dog'.

Foreign Minister Ciano, meanwhile, had already backed up Mussolini in late 1940, when deportations of Dutch Jews began, and Il Duce protested against the Vatican's stance on these operations. He said that Pius XII was 'ready to let himself be deported to a concentration camp, rather than do anything against his conscience'.[19]

Pius XII was still vacillating between silence and condemnation, as seen by the Christmas speech. While personally protesting against the arrests and deportations of French Jews in June 1942, he was also stressing to the US State Department how he preferred to stay neutral on the Jewish question. That the strength and timings of his condemnations were to coincide with the level of activity of the anti-Hitler resistance was something of which the foreign envoys to the Vatican, from Britain and the United States, were now partially aware.

By the early spring of 1943, the Germans were retreating across North Africa, and the Allies were planning an invasion of Sicily and then the Italian mainland. The Holocaust killings of 1942 were now complete.

For the thousands of Italian Jews in internment camps, living in hiding or existing in plain sight, the situation was opaque, taut, sometimes terrifying – but still tenable. Mussolini had so far refused to round up Italy's Jews and deport them to Germany; the fifteen detention centres and the stifling Racial Laws were as far as he would go to accommodate Hitler's imprecations to implement the Final Solution. Allied bombing was getting heavier, and in autumn of 1942, the head of Britain's Bomber Command, Air Marshal Sir Arthur Harris, implemented a campaign of area bombing against Turin, Milan and Genoa. In one raid on 24 October 1942, Harris, who was known by the British press as 'Bomber' but by many in the RAF as 'Butcher', designated Milan's cathedral as the focal aiming point for the area bombing of the city. British MPs, as well as other senior RAF officers, criticised Harris' decision to use a religious building as a tactical marker, and to employ bombing that effectively targeted the civilian population. During the night's bombing, 30,000 incendiary devices were dropped by 73 Lancasters: 171 Italians were killed.

For Virginia Montalcini and Ettore Ovazza and their families in Turin, the bombing was easily the most dangerous threat to their safety: part of the Ovazza family had already fled to Switzerland. Ettore and his wife and children remained in Turin. The Montalcinis, concerned at their daughter's diminishing health brought on by stress, had sent her to spend three weeks in summer 1942 at Arenzano, on the Ligurian coast. The Pipernos were still in Rome, about to move north in hiding to the outskirts of Siena. The Holocaust shuddered and crashed onwards across Europe and the Eastern Front like a vast evil dragon, its flames washing over Italy's borders. Yet for now, the country's Jews were, if not safe, then still not actually doomed.

However, Italy's Jews were already on a list, one that had been drawn up by SS-Obersturmbannführer Adolf Eichmann. On 31 July 1941 Reichsmarschall Hermann Göring had authorised Reinhard Heydrich, as head of the RSHA, to come up with a definitive plan for what he called the 'total solution of the Jewish question'. Operation Barbarossa was six weeks under way and, across Ukraine, *Einsatzkommandos* were already executing thousands of Soviet Jews and Red Army prisoners, as well as NKVD and Communist Party members, and Comintern officials. Jewish males between the ages of 15 and 45 were classified as partisans and were to be shot, but this definition had rapidly widened to all Jews, including women, children and old people. Polish Jews were being centralised in ghettos, while, in the Baltic states, German SS and police 'Aktion' squads – as the *Einsatzgruppen* were also called – were hard at work, killing by means of mass execution.

The scale of mass death was vast: on five separate days alone between October and December 1941 around 55,000 Jews were murdered in five mass executions in Latvia and the Soviet Republic of Belorussia. There were multiple mass killings throughout the second half of 1941 and the first six months of 1942 across the Eastern Front: the biggest took place at the Babi Yar ravine in the Ukrainian capital of Kiev, where an estimated 33,771 Jews were executed on the last two days of September 1941.

Now the Holocaust was about to broaden its scope – across an entire continent. On 20 January 1942, Heydrich convened a conference at a villa on the edge of the Grosser Wannsee, a lake in the south-western Berlin suburb of Steglitz-Zehlendorf. Fifteen people attended, himself included. On the invitation, it specified that the aim of the meeting was achieving a common view among the central agencies that were involved in the solution of the so-called 'Jewish question'. This was not a meeting to plan mass killings – these were already under way in Poland, Ukraine, Belorussia and the Baltic states. No, Heydrich wanted to find consensus among government and SS agencies on how the Final Solution should proceed, and to make it clear that he was laying the imprimatur of total SS authority on how all deported Jews should be treated from then on in the ongoing Holocaust.

The delegates had come both from Berlin and from places further afield, such as Poland and Latvia. Among those representing the government of Nazi Germany were the head of the Reich Race and Settlement Main Office; the Permanent Secretary of the Nazi Party Chancellery;

and officials from the General Government's administration, the Reich's Justice, Interior and Foreign Ministries and the Ministry for Occupied Eastern Territories. The head of the Gestapo, Heinrich Müller, was there, alongside such SS officials as the respective heads of the SD for Latvia and the General Government. As head of Referat IV B4 of the RSHA – the Jewish Affairs Office – Eichmann was the Recording Officer and responsible for keeping the minutes. During the ninety-minute conference, Heydrich co-ordinated all the different agencies into one focused group that was united in co-operating to 'solve' the so-called Jewish question. These focused on who qualified as a Jew, who was exempt from deportation, and the nature and regulations of Jewish mixed marriages. But predominantly, it was about agreeing a logistical and regulatory framework of how to deport 11 million Jews to the east, and then either work them to death or murder them in camps.

It was decided that Jews in German-occupied territories in Europe would mostly be deported as forced labour or to be murdered at camps in Poland. The estimated 3 million Jews in Ukraine would be taken to Siberia or, again, murdered. Heydrich talked of evacuating Jews eastwards, before what he then called the 'final solution' of the Jewish question.[20] As recording officer, Eichmann made a list of the 11 million Jews estimated to be living throughout Europe in German-occupied countries, neutral states, Axis-allied countries or in countries that would be occupied by the Germans. On 'Eichmann's List' there were two groups of countries: A, those under the Third Reich's control or occupation; and B, allied or neutral states, or those at war with Germany. List B featured Bulgaria, England (with 330,000 Jews), Finland, the Irish Free State, and then, fifth out of nineteen countries, came the Kingdom of Italy. It contained 58,000 Jews, Eichmann recorded.

As the meeting ended, the various SS officers and ministers celebrated their successful consensus on the conference's three main points with cognac. Eichmann would later recall:

> The gentlemen were standing together, or sitting together, and were discussing the subject quite bluntly, quite differently from the language which I had to use later in the record. They minced no

words about it at all ... they spoke about methods of killing, about liquidation, about extermination.[21]

After the delegates departed, Eichmann, Heydrich and Muller from the Gestapo stayed behind in the villa's summer house for another drink and to discuss the new protocol that had been agreed. Eichmann, at Heydrich's instruction, removed any direct, plain or explicit wording. Eichmann described this as editing it 'into office language'.[22]

THE PAPAL RESISTANCE TO HITLER

Don Pirro Scavizzi was a 60-year-old Roman Catholic priest from Umbria, who had moved to Rome. In the Second World War, he worked on hospital trains as a military chaplain, and with Mussolini's decision to commit Italian troops to the fighting in Russia, particularly around Stalingrad, Scavizzi made six return train trips to the front lines of eastern Europe. Four of them were to Ukraine, on hospital trains travelling via Poland.

Each trip lasted roughly between three weeks and a month, and the priest found he had an extraordinary amount of access to German operations of all kinds. He was, after all, an ally, a priest, and he was working on a military hospital train. Soldiers and their commanders trusted him. What they didn't know was that, on each of these trips, he was working informally as the eyes and ears of Pius XII, collecting any information that he could about the ongoing Holocaust.

Given that his trips took place between October 1941 and November 1942, he was physically present in Ukraine, Russia and Poland at the height of the Holocaust. He liaised with Catholic bishops in the countries he visited and wrote four confidential reports for the Pope. He witnessed and was given information about the Krakow Ghetto, the systematic killings of wounded Red Army prisoners, the concentration camps in Poland and the situation concerning the Jewish population in each country.

One of the Ukrainian towns he visited in October and November 1941, and then in June and July of 1942, was Dnepropetrovsk, on the Dnieper River in central Ukraine. These two trips coincided with the period when the Germans occupied the town and the territory around it. So, Don Pirro was there both before and after February 1942, when, in four days, *Einsatzgruppe D* massacred 29,698 of the 30,000 Jews in the city.

Don Pirro informed Pius XII in one of his reports, in spring 1943, that the murder of Jews in occupied territories was now near total and the elderly and children were being slaughtered. Scavizzi said that the pontiff broke down and cried uncontrollably.[1] These tears, as described in Don Pirro's words, were no doubt real, but much more moving and important was what Pius XII allegedly said to him afterwards:

> I have often considered excommunication, to castigate in the eyes of the entire world the fearful crime of genocide. But after much praying and many tears, I realize that my condemnation would not only fail to help the Jews, it might even worsen their situation … No doubt a protest would gain me the praise and respect of the civilized world, but it would have submitted the poor Jews to an even worse persecution.[2]

Scavizzi thus paints a portrait of a pope both resourceful and cunning enough to maximise his not-inconsiderable assets to find out, from the ground, what was going on in eastern Europe at the height of the Holocaust. He is characteristically torn between his public façade and persona and the approach he must adopt to save the lives of as many of his flock as he can, while simultaneously plotting and operating behind the scenes to provide as much material and intelligence support to the anti-Hitler resistance.

The days when the pope could deploy armies were, he knew, long gone, and the best he could do was to lull the SS and Gestapo into a feeling of complacent ignorance, while he took action unseen. He thought if he spoke vociferously, tens of thousands of Catholics would die alongside the millions of Jews. He knew that if he kept his support and strength reserved for more clandestine actions, he could achieve a much more effective, real, lasting and decisive result. It was a consummate, deadly and single-minded juggling act.

Pope Pius' decision to engage in resistance to Adolf Hitler placed him and the Vatican within the centre of a Venn diagram, made up of five constituent and overlapping circles. These were, respectively: the need to preserve and protect the religious, financial and physical infrastructure of the Holy See from external attack, be it from Allied aircraft, Italian communist politicians and partisans, German SS *Einsatzkommandos*, lack of funding, or hostile intelligence operations; the need to act against the Holocaust; the need not to provoke the Nazis into slaughtering even more people, such as Roman Catholics; the need to act in accordance with the Allied modus operandi about how to fight and win the war, while also retaining a cautious neutrality; and the need to do what the Vatican has always done well – continuance, that centuries-long campaign mentality at which it had always excelled – to look ahead to the world that would come after the war and position itself accordingly, so that it was strong and surrounded by supportive allies.

Both the Vatican and the cadre of predominantly Catholic Wehrmacht officers who sought to oust Hitler from 1940 onwards knew two things: stopping the persecution of the Jews and winning the war could only result from a military takeover of Europe, possibly involving the Soviet Union as well. Hans Oster, a colonel from the Abwehr, dispatched his first envoy, Josef Müller, to Rome in 1940.

Working on behalf of the Wehrmacht chief of staff, General Franz Halder, and code-named 'Joe Ox', Müller was an unlikely choice to liaise as an intelligence officer between the anti-Hitler resistance, the Catholic Church and the Allies. A 42-year-old former sergeant who'd fought in the trenches of the Western Front as a mortar fire controller, he was a large, bullish man. He became a lawyer, joined the Nazi Party and defended several SS and SD officers in some of the earlier court cases. He excelled at taking the wool of his true intentions and pulling it over his opponents' eyes.

Hans Oster recruited Müller into the Abwehr in 1938. His first mission to Rome was in late 1939, to pass information from Oster to the

Vatican that an invasion of the Low Countries was about to happen. Pius XII's Cardinal Maglione passed this information on to D'Arcy Osborne, who sent it by coded diplomatic telegram to Lord Halifax at the Foreign and Commonwealth Office.[3]

General Franz Halder was connected to the German Catholic Centruum political party, which Himmler and Bormann had banned, exiling it to Geneva and Rome. Their leader in Rome, Monsignor Ludwig Kaas, was a colleague and friend of the Pope's private secretary, Robert Lieber. He, in turn, had known Müller since Munich in the 1930s, when then-Cardinal Pacelli had been the papal *nuncio* to Germany.

With Generals Halder and Ludwig Beck behind him, as well as Admiral Wilhelm Canaris, Müller asked Lieber to channel information to the British. Would they help in a plot to either kill or remove Hitler? D'Arcy Osborne went to work.

In London, both Neville Chamberlain and Lord Halifax had personally backed and approved the plan. Yet, as so often happened, their plan was good, but their communications were flawed. Neither of them knew that a star code-breaking asset in the German Foreign Office's cryptanalytical department called Ursula Hagen had been among those in Berlin who'd been intercepting, reading and decrypting British diplomatic codes. In addition, the cryptanalysts from Hermann Göring's Research Bureau, or *Forschungsamt*, had been able to decipher some of Neville Chamberlain's messages between Germany and London during the 1938 Munich Crisis. The Pope, Müller and D'Arcy Osborne had an excellent plan: the problem was that the Third Reich was listening to it carefully.

Pius XII told Osborne in January 1940 that the Wehrmacht would move against France in February, but the coterie of generals involved in the resistance would suspend this if Britain was prepared to discuss peace. Chamberlain and Halifax believed the Pope. The conspirators said that they would move against Hitler in February and replace his dictatorship with a federal, democratic model. London waited for them to prove more convincing.

Pius hoped for a coup in Berlin in March 1940. By May, however, nothing had transpired, and all sides were waiting. The Vatican told the

Netherlands Ambassador to the Holy See that the Wehrmacht, Luftwaffe and SS would move into France through Belgium and Holland on 10 May 1940. The Vatican's cryptanalysts sent this information in a coded message to the papal *nuncios* in The Hague and Brussels, as well as Switzerland. The Germans intercepted and read them.

This is likely to have proved possible because the Wehrmacht's code-breakers had broken Dutch and Belgian diplomatic codes, rather than because they could read the signals of the Vatican. The Germans could only read a percentage of the three main Vatican ciphers, which were notoriously impenetrable, and which the Americans in turn had named KIA-Red, KIB-Yellow and KIC-Green, partly after the colours of the code-books' leather covers.

After the Germans intercepted the messages from the Vatican, Admiral Canaris, as head of the Abwehr, was ordered to investigate the leak of information, but as he was implicitly involved in the resistance to Hitler, this was a case of setting a snare to catch the hunter. The Germans by now regarded the Pope as equivalent to a high-ranking intelligence agent working for their enemies.

Mussolini merely thought that the Vatican had taken sides against him and one of his enemies. He was largely unconcerned – the prospect of an armed conflict in which the Italian state would take over the Vatican, and all of its material and financial assets, was not unattractive to him. Pius' cardinal secretary of state knew this. Mussolini distrusted the Vatican simply because it was a higher authority than him, with much greater call on the Italian people.

So, the Vatican prepared to put into action a plan to move some of the assets of the Institute for the Works of Religion (IWR), otherwise known as the Vatican Bank. The majority of the fixed assets of this institution were the thousands of its physical properties, the Catholic churches, old, new, big, small, all across Italy, convents, palazzos, houses and apartments – all the property owned by the Roman Catholic Church, in short. The Vatican could see the Holocaust in action and knew that it was only a matter of time before the Germans arrived in Italy and started to arrest and deport Italian Jews. So, the *curia* at the Holy See that handled the IWR started transferring money to all of its properties across Italy, so that in time of war all would be able to prove self-sustaining financially, however many unexpected guests might come to take refuge or hide.

The Secretariat of the Economy, which oversaw the handling of the $2 billion assets of the Holy See, also started making transfers of cash to regional banks in Genoa, Turin, Florence and other major cities, earmarked for sustaining churches and communities in those regions. It started discreetly moving stock assets from the Italian bourse, in banking, chemicals and shipbuilding, and moving them to Sweden, the United States, Switzerland and Brazil. The coded messages concerning this flurry of economic activity by the Vatican were encrypted in KIC-Green, the hardest of its codes to break. However, the Germans knew they didn't need to try to break it – they simply piggy-backed on the outgoing Vatican messages, and once they arrived in Berne, Basel or Geneva, they read the Swiss translations sent between their government ministries. The Swiss government used a much-simplified three-rotor civilian version of the Enigma machine, which the Germans had cracked in 1940.

In March 1940, the Pope had met in Rome with the German Foreign Minister, Joaquim von Ribbentrop. It was to be the only meeting between the Vatican and any senior official of the German authorities before the latter occupied Italy in the summer of 1943. Ribbentrop proposed an eleven-part peace plan to the Pope, which Berlin saw as the Holy See's last opportunity to ally itself with Germany before the invasion of France and the Low Countries began in summer 1940.

The main points of the plan were pan-European disarmament, the division of the continent into four zones run by the British, Germans, French and Italians, and the probable forcible disarmament of Russia and the destruction of Bolshevism, by arms. The Jews of Europe would be deported to Madagascar, Ethiopia and Palestine. Poland would be largely independent, there would be universal freedom of trade and Hitler, canny and experienced enough to avoid unnecessary dealings with the perennially antagonistic states of Yugoslavia, simply said that the 'status quo in the Balkans would be respected'.[4] Whatever the status quo may have been wasn't specified, but the message was clear: the countries of the Balkans would be left to handle their own affairs, without provocative external intervention.

In the event, the Pope was unimpressed, wouldn't be drawn into a discussion of the peace plan and berated Ribbentrop for German atrocities against the Jews. 'Jews' Rights Defended' ran the *New York Times* headline on 14 March 1940, while in the body of the article, the correspondent wrote of the 'burning words he spoke to Herr Ribbentrop about religious persecution'.[5]

The meeting proved that not only was any chance of reconciliation between the Vatican and Germany dead in the water, but Germany was determined to invade western Europe. As it did so, and as Mussolini invaded Croatian and Slovenian territory and moved into Albania and Greece, the Vatican temporarily stepped back from its involvement with the German resistance. Europe was now at war, and Germany's early and easy victories in Norway, France and Greece made the fledgling resistance movement realise they were largely outnumbered in Germany's moment of triumph.

The Axis' difficulties with Poland, meanwhile, were further compounded by the fact that the Germans who worked at OKW-Chi (the Wehrmacht High Command Signals agency), *B-Dienst* (the naval cryptanalytical section) and OKH/*GdNA* (the army's code-breaking department) knew one thing – that Polish cryptanalysts based both in France and at Bletchley Park in England had already made inroads into decrypting some of the seventeen different coded settings frequently used on the Enigma machine.

The Germans were also convinced – rightly – that the Pope had in some measure supported the resistance to Hitler. So, they knew that if they managed to intercept and decrypt signals sent to and from the Vatican, by the papacy, the Italians and Allied and neutral diplomats, they could hopefully decipher the operational intentions of all sides. Once Germany started to consider occupying Italy in September 1943, knowing what the Vatican was doing became a matter of strategic and tactical urgency. And in no area was this more so than the execution and completion of the Final Solution, one of Germany's three main operational priorities in Italy.

5

CODES OF THE HOLOCAUST

The Mogilev Police Message

At 9.51 on the evening of 16 June 1942, in the town of Mogilev in central Byelorussia, the duty radio operator at the German police headquarters sent a message. The local commander of the *Ordnungspolizei* (Orpo), or Order Police, had dictated the plain text of the dispatch earlier. It described a firefight between German police and Russian partisans earlier that day, on the road between Mogilev and the town of Babruysk. The latter was 60 miles south-west of Mogilev, and both were considerably behind the front line of the German Wehrmacht units of Army Group Centre.

That day, a unit from the 51st Police Battalion of the Orpo had been on patrol near the hamlet of Borki, which lies halfway between the two towns. Deployed behind the front lines of the Wehrmacht and SS, the police units' duties included keeping order in German-occupied territory, which primarily meant combatting partisans. They also operated as part of the *Einsatzkommandos*, the 'action groups' tasked with the rounding up and execution of Jews, Communist Party officials and NKVD (Russian secret police) personnel. Although it was a year after Operation Barbarossa had thundered over Byelorussia, there were few of these still left alive.

Part of the 51st Battalion were operating between the village of Borki and the Chigirinka Reservoir, 2 miles west of Borki. The terrain was flat and filled with woods of pine and spruce and small plots of land tilled for potatoes and maize, with the dark grey waters of the lake stretching to the north. Partisans had attacked the German police on the main road. There was a ragged, running firefight, in which the Russians killed sixteen of their opponents. As the Germans counter-attacked, the partisans withdrew into the forests, while the police unit pulled back to Borki, at the opposite side of the road.

'On the Babruysk to Mogilev road, a skirmish with partisans', ran the plain text of the message from the Orpo commander for Byelorussia, which the radio operator would encipher and then transmit in Morse code to the headquarters of the SS and the *Ordnungspolizei* in Berlin:

Sixteen men from the 51st battalion were killed, in the town of Borki weapons and ammunition were found, and it [Borki] was levelled in the usual manner. The inhabitants were liquidated.

From: Senior Officer SS and Police Chief Central Russia.[1]

The recipients of the message would be the RSHA in Berlin, which included the office of the Reichsführer of the SS, Heinrich Himmler, and also another SS official who would have almost as considerable an impact on the execution of the Holocaust: the head of the *Ordnungspolizei*, an SS-Gruppenführer from East Prussia called Kurt Daluege. He had been one of the first recruits to the SS in 1930, and by June 1942 he commanded more than 120,000 uniformed police officers, not just those deployed on operations in Poland, on the Eastern Front and in territories such as the Protectorate of Bohemia and Moravia, but also the foot soldiers of daily order in the Reich, the railway police, coastguard and traffic officers.

Daluege's commitment to the implementation and execution of the Final Solution was exemplified by one comment of his, that 'the consciously asocial enemies of the people must be eliminated by state intervention, if it hopes to prevent the outbreak of complete moral degeneration'.[2] He was centrally implicated in the Holocaust – in

October 1941, he signed deportation orders for German, Austrian and Czech Jews to camps in Byelorussia and Latvia. By June 1942, he and Himmler had met to discuss the extension of Operation Reinhard, the SS action to exterminate Jews living in the General Government area of occupied Poland.

One of his main rivals in the SS since the mid-thirties was Reinhard Heydrich, who controlled the SIPO, or Security Police, and then became head of the Reich Security Main Office, the RSHA. An original architect of the Final Solution, Heydrich despised Daluege, referring to him as 'Dummi-Dummi', or 'Idiot'.[3] But in late May 1942, the tables were turned. Czech resistance agents trained by the British SOE hurled an anti-tank grenade into Heydrich's car in central Prague. The SS officer died shortly afterwards from septicaemia, caused by pieces of horsehair from the car's upholstery being blown into his spleen.

Daluege, by then 43, was made Deputy Protector of Bohemia and Moravia in his turn, and it was he who oversaw the massacres carried out in reprisal for Heydrich's killing. This involved executing 342 men, women and children from the village of Lidice or deporting them to Chelmno and Ravensbrück concentration camps.

By the time the police radio operator in Mogilev sent the message on 16 June, Daluege had been back in Berlin for less than four days, after a trip to Prague to oversee this operation. The physical implementation of those operational parts of the Final Solution that involved German police came under his sway: the radio security surrounding these operations was another. After Winston Churchill had made public radio broadcasts the previous year condemning the persecution of the Jews, Daluege had feared as early as December 1941 that the Allies might possibly be intercepting, in an unspecified way, German police and SS radio transmissions from the Eastern Front. He was completely unaware that the Allies had captured both German signals code-books and parts of Enigma machines, and cryptanalysts at Bletchley Park had been reading into Enigma-encoded German Navy, Army and Air Force traffic. His reaction to Churchill's broadcasts had been to cease radio transmissions using Enigma encipherment, and rather to use code-books based upon an encipherment system known as a 'Double Playfair'.

But the Germans made mistakes, like everybody, and in this instance they failed to change their code-books frequently enough. So when, on 16 June, the police radio operator in Mogilev started to encode the message destined for Berlin, he reached for a code-book that had been in use for just over six months. He wrote down in pencil the five-letter groups that represented the opening words of the message: 'Sixteen men from the 51st Battalion' duly became the groups of letters ARTTN–FMXBW–OIYSU–OGILL–YVHPO–HKALE. With the callsign 'SQF', for Mogilev, attached at the top of the message, and its recipients in Berlin designated by the letters 'DQH', the operator dispatched the message, in Morse-coded letter groups, into the ether at exactly 9.51 p.m.

The Interceptors at Beaumanor

Two hours' time difference and 1,580 miles to the west, a British radio watch officer from the Auxiliary Territorial Service, the women's branch of the British Army, was on duty. Her duty shift number at dusk that June night in 1942 was A115, and she was sitting with a pair of radio earphones clamped to her head. She was in a hut in the grounds of Beaumanor Hall, a Victorian stately home outside Leicester.

The sides and roof of the large Nissen hut were painted in a colour scheme that looked like glass, as the aim was to disguise the building as a greenhouse. This was to fool any prowling German bombers who might try to destroy it or the other huts around it.

The country house was a target of considerable value. It was known by the British intelligence services as a 'Y' station, and the ATS operators sitting in the Nissen huts under the lime trees at Beaumanor had one job: to intercept and transcribe coded German messages. Most of the women – the operators were all female – could listen out for, hear and transcribe 125 Morse characters a minute:

The listening itself was not carried out in the main hall, but in cold huts in the grounds. Joan Bradshaw was 22 in 1942 ... she was in J Hut.

As soon as the shift started, they were handed a list of wavebands to listen to. They would then sit at their machines, put their headphones on and adjust the radio knobs to find one of the right frequencies and pick up signals. They would sit listening to the Morse code – a series of dits and dahs [dots and dashes] – and interpret the individual letters, which were recorded on grids in blocks of five on a 'W/T Red Form'. The recordings would of course mean absolutely nothing to them, as they were simply letters from the alphabet. The operator's ears had to be 'trained' to pick up these signals through interference from different frequencies, some loud and some quiet.[4]

A War Office architect had worked as part of the staff at Beaumanor and he designed the huts and other buildings that were used to house the wireless intercept teams. They had to look like buildings that might be found in the grounds of any country house – potting sheds, gardening huts, cricket pavilions, greenhouses, stables and conservatories. One military architect said that this disguising was unique to Beaumanor and there are no current records of any other buildings the military used during the war being disguised in this way. The huts were built on the 20-acre field north of the hall: the main priority in terms of spacing was that the huts should be placed far enough apart so that, if a German bombing raid occurred, the buildings were distant enough to minimise possible damage. Blast walls were built first, and then the outer camouflage architectural covering.

Hut J was disguised to look like a cart shed with a barn, H & I looked like cottages, Hut K was a mock-up of a stable, Hut M resembled a greenhouse, and the sixth, Hut G, was a replica of a cricket pavilion complete with a clock tower. H, I, J and K housed the radio intercept rooms. The cables and electronic wires were passed underground and each hut had a pneumatic tube for sending handwritten messages.

The ATS women had to be alert and focused at all times during their long shifts. They lived in hotels, boarding houses, requisitioned local homes, and worked hard: those on shift at night went to work in the dark and returned to their billets as the sun came up. Rationing, mentally arduous and repetitive work, and the logistical constraints of wartime were the backdrop of their lives. But for some of them, life brightened in the spring of 1944, when the American 82nd Airborne Division arrived. Posted to a series of local air bases to train for D-Day, the American paratroopers were tough, tanned from combat in Sicily and Italy, and courteous and gallant. With teas, dances and dates, they provided a welcome distraction for the women at Beaumanor.

Once intercepted, the messages they were listening out for were passed immediately to another location, this one known as Station X, a code designation for Bletchley Park. Operator A115 concentrated hard that night in June 1942, listening for the letter groups coming over the radio net, but there was interference somewhere out in the forests and plains of Byelorussia. So, when she had finished writing down the letter groups, she added her own sign-off, 'QRM', at the bottom, indicating there had been man-made interference during interception of the signal.

The text of the message itself was sent by teletype machine directly to Bletchley. Just before midnight, when she came off shift, she also handed her intercept sheets over to the duty NCO. Along with all of the other radio signals picked up by Beaumanor that day, these were given to an army dispatch rider, who took them 60 miles down the A1 highway to Bletchley.

The French Intercept Station

There was another Allied monitoring station intercepting German police and SS communications that night. At a small castle on the outskirts of the town of Uzes, in unoccupied south-western France, there was a radio intercept station run by the Allies. It was code-named 'P.C. Cadix', or *Poste de Commandemgdent Cadix*. French military intelligence had set up the site in 1939, and among its code-breakers and intercept experts there were three Polish scientists who had fled their own country in 1939, as the Germans invaded. These three men had brought the secrets of Enigma to Cadix.

They were among the small group of Poles who had not only worked on designing its military adaptation to encipherment, but also used this to start breaking into German messages encrypted on the machine. Their knowledge and expertise at Cadix – which they extended to Bletchley Park – was immense.

From September 1940 until November 1942, when the Germans occupied the Vichy zone of France, P.C. Cadix intercepted German high-frequency communications from occupied France and elsewhere. Because of the peculiarities of the way in which radio signal transmission worked, both high- and low-frequency bands 'propagated', or stretched, at night. So, the French chateau could monitor German radio traffic from the Russian front at night, and in daylight, the return signals sent from Germany back to the Eastern Front. As a result, Beaumanor and P.C. Cadix divided up the work on German Police traffic: the British copied on even days of the month, the French on odd ones.

Among the messages they had intercepted since summer 1941 had been some 3,000 dispatched from Ukraine and Byelorussia, in which SS and police units dispatched daily reports of their mass killings. Cadix would send the messages it had intercepted directly to Bletchley, rather suitably using a Polish Enigma machine. So, on that even-numbered night in June 1942, it was the turn of Beaumanor to intercept German police messages coming in from the east.

Alongside these signals coming in from the Eastern Front, there was another series of messages that both Beaumanor and Cadix had been intercepting that summer. They originated with the German Foreign Ministry and the Reich Security Main Office in Berlin, and the recipients were the German Embassy and its diplomats and military staff in Rome.

The Germans suspected the Vatican was sympathetic to the Allies and directly hostile to the Third Reich. They recognised that the Pope's influence over tens of millions of Roman Catholics worldwide gave him immense influence, especially within occupied countries such as Poland, with their predominantly Catholic populations. So, the Polish situation was of substantial concern to the Germans particularly as the Warsaw government-in-exile, based in London, was in frequent contact with the Vatican, as well as with the armed resistance in their own country.

The German code-breakers who worked at OKW-Chi, B-*Dienst*, OKH/*GdNA* or Pers Z S, the Foreign Office, suspected one thing – that their refusal to rely on code-books, as well as on machines, meant that some of their encryption systems were vulnerable and potentially compromised. As mentioned above, this included Enigma. The army, navy, High Command and Foreign Office cryptanalysts suspected that their non-Enigma systems, such as the cyphers used on the Lorenz teleprinter, and SD and Abwehr codes were also open to exploitation by the Allies. Their superiors, however, refused to do anything about it.

The Germans were also convinced – rightly – that the Pope had in some measure supported the resistance to Hitler. So, they knew that if they managed to intercept and decrypt signals sent to and from the Vatican, by the papacy, the Italians, and Allied and neutral diplomats, they could hopefully decipher the operational intentions of all sides. The Allies, in their turn, knew that deciphering the German signals would give them excellent intelligence, as it would enable them to 'piggy-back' on the information the Germans had gleaned from their allies and neutral countries. It was matrix of electronic chess, played out across the ether of wartime Europe.

Breaking the Codes of the Holocaust at Bletchley Park

By the spring of 1942, Churchill and Roosevelt were aware of the general existence of the enormous German operations to persecute Jews and other minorities. In his speech to Allied delegates on 12 June 1941, at St James' Palace, Churchill talked of 'concentration camps being overcrowded'. By this point, the reports from inmates who had escaped Auschwitz were yet to come, and the United Nations Declaration of December 1942 was six months away.

The Polish government-in-exile was meanwhile presenting accounts of what was occurring in the General Government area inside Poland, around Lublin. In another speech broadcast from London on 24 August 1941, with reference to mass killings carried out in the wake of Operation Barbarossa, Churchill stated, 'We are in the presence of a crime without a name.'

But, despite knowing that a mass persecution of Jews was under way, Allied leaders were not yet competely aware of the full nature of the Final Solution – its details, plans, objectives and methodology – nor of the network of concentration camps designed to help achieve it. Indeed, by early 1942, the RSHA was still actively formulating many of these plans itself. However, in Britain, Bletchley Park and its code-breakers were to go a substantial way towards providing crucial, accurate information about the ongoing Holocaust and what was happening inside the concentration camp system.

It was not just U-boats, Atlantic convoys and such operations as the offensives in Russia and north Africa that were occupying Bletchley's cryptanalysts in 1941 and 1942. Messages were being intercepted and read from inside the *Konzentrationslager* (KL) system, the concentration camps. Every day, each primary camp would send a status update to Berlin – the Germans gave each of their main camps a recognition code, based upon a letter. The resultant daily, weekly and monthly camp reports were marked 'ZIP' by Bletchley, implying they'd been Enigma-encoded. Some of them hadn't and were encrypted on other systems.

The recognition codes given by the Germans to the main extermination camps (Belzec, Auschwitz-Birkenau, Majdanek, Sobibor, Chelmno and Treblinka) and the labour camps system (Dachau, Mauthausen, Sachsenhausen, Neuengamme, Ravensbrück, Flossenburg, Bergen-Belsen and Buchenwald) were based on letters. These included 'F' for Auschwitz and 'D' for Buchenwald, with the specification that no camp designation letter could be its own initial, for instance Treblinka couldn't be 'T'.

When, in early April 1942, Bletchley's code-breakers came to crack the details of some of the daily signals of the KL system, they began to discover the uncompromising, horrific numerical reality of the Holocaust. For by decryption, mathematical analysis and calculations of some of the German status messages, information emerged which began to show such details as how many inmates were arriving or dying inside some of the camps, each day. Bletchley achieved this breakthrough

through a piece of technical wizardry by their staff – and a piece of immense cryptological stupidity by the SS.

Oliver Strachey, ISOSICLE and ISK, and the Code Called Orange

One of the idiosyncratic, highly intelligent and imaginative British cryptanalysts working at the Government Code and Cypher School – as Bletchley Park was formally known – was Oliver Strachey. He came from a background of diplomacy, letters, science and foreign service: he was the son of the colonial administrator Sir Richard Strachey, brother of the writer Lytton Strachey and had been educated at Eton. He only spent a term at Oxford, as his parents decided to send him abroad, which among other things saw him learning to play the piano in Vienna. He then worked in military intelligence in the First World War, and in the years between the wars he was part of a team that broke a machine cipher used by the Japanese Navy. He was an excellent and perspicacious cryptanalyst. In 1942, he was 68.

By 1941 and 1942, as the German police signals were flooding out of eastern Europe, Bletchley had begun to make significant inroads into decrypting the encoding settings used on the German Enigma machine and other encoding systems. While the Royal Navy's slowness to change its cipher codes, the dexterity of German naval cryptanalysts in breaking them and the operational agility of Karl Dönitz's U-boat 'Wolf Packs' meant that the Battle of the Atlantic often hung in a daily balance, the 'Ultra' intelligence decrypted from Enigma meant the Allies could enjoy a strong advantage.

At Bletchley, Oliver Strachey worked in a section deciphering German intelligence signals, both Abwehr and SD messages. Initially code-named Pear, the decrypts then became known as ISOS, standing for Illicit Services (Oliver Strachey). This was one example of the erudite use of nicknames as code names, whereby no non-native English speaker would have an idea of what they meant. More simply, the code names that Bletchley gave to the SS codes were based on fruit, such as Orange I and II, Quince, Grapefruit and the above-mentioned Pear. As the SS's intelligence service, the SD had its own systems, but used predominantly the same codes.

The decoding of the latter, along with Abwehr traffic and all other material concerning intelligence and espionage, was handled by two teams at Bletchley. This traffic was divided into Enigma and non-Enigma.

Enigma traffic of the SD and the Abwehr was dealt with by a team under code-breaker Dilly Knox, known as 'Illicit Signals Knox' or 'ISK'. This work was based on the fact that in 1942 the Abwehr was still using a simpler version of Enigma without a plugboard, which was susceptible to manual breaking methods. Later, specialist 'bombes', enormous prototype computers capable of breaking Abwehr and SD Enigma variants, were introduced.

Then there was the above-mentioned non-Enigma traffic, dealt with by the team under Oliver Strachey, known as ISOS, and this gave rise to another code name.[5] When the Germans occupied Rome, the SD material sent from Kaltenbrunner and the RSHA in Berlin to the SS and Gestapo in the Italian capital was a subset of ISOS known as ISOSICLE. This was estimated to be derived from a hand-cipher system, although the system was confused because some SD and Abwehr traffic was also 'piggy-backed' on 'Fish,' as the Lorenz teleprinter cipher messages were called.

To add a further level of complication, from the *Konzentrationslager*, the KL system, the SS sent signals that were sometimes encoded with an Enigma encipherment, and sometimes a non-Enigma coding:

> The SS were reporting arrivals and departures at the camps via Enigma ORANGE.[6] Each message was a pro-forma list with 4 columns – start of day, arrivals, departures, end of day. Rather than use numerical digits, the messages had an additional layer of encryption whereby the numbers 0-9 were replaced by ten letters of the alphabet. These alphabetic substitutions were chosen every day by simply allocating the digits 0-9 to the letters at each end of the five plug cables in the 'stecker' board on the front of the Enigma machine [if Enigma encoding was being used].[7]

So, the SS radio operator in each given camp would have a list of four columns of numbers. In the first column was the number of inmates in the camp at the start of the day at rollcall; then there was the number of new inmates who arrived on a transport train, from another camp or from a separate detachment – essentially, from anywhere else outside the camp; followed by 'departures' – those gassed, shot, otherwise executed or who died from disease or any other cause. The combination of the figures gave the 'end of day' number in the fourth column.

The SS radio operators would know that, if they used a number-based code, each digit in the four columns of figures could only have a maximum possible series of ten encryption permutations, 0, 1, 2, 3, 4, 5, 6, 7, 8 and 9. If, however, letters of the alphabet were used, this gave a far greater possible number of permutations per letter, from the twenty-six letters of the alphabet. If an Enigma encoding was used, this was twenty-five, as the Achilles heel of the device was that no letter could ever be encoded as itself and any letter deciphered in a message had to be something else apart from what it was – i.e., F could not be F, J could not be J, and so forth. The allocation and choice of letters to replace numbers was a means of choosing a greater number of coding permutations.

'Rodding' was a technique developed by the British code-breaker Dilly Knox in 1937, in which a 'crib' or clue to the unenciphered message is needed to begin the process of decryption. Rodding had helped break some important Italian Enigma messages early in the war. These included ones that gave the British Royal Navy crucial information about Italian naval deployments prior to and during the Battle of Cape Matapan, in March 1941, fought off the south-west coast of the Peloponnesian Peninsula in Greece:

This (process of alphabetic substitutions) effectively embedded the stecker pluggings into the body of the message, meaning that the key could often be broken by rodding, without the need for any bombe time to work out the steckers, *and as the end of day number was always the same as the start of day number the following day, breaks could be transferred from day to day so long as continuity was maintained. A gross cryptologic error by the Germans.* [author's italics][8]

This meant, in non-technical terms, that the SS radio operators in each camp took a list entirely composed of numbers, in four columns, marked as such:

A. Start of day figures of inmates.
B. New arrivals.
C. 'Departures', i.e., deaths by execution, gassing, disease.
D. End of day number.

So, maths and common sense shows that A plus B, minus C, always equals D. This last figure would obviously be the same at the start of the following day, meaning Bletchley's code-breakers had two identical numbers that repeated on two subsequent days, giving them vital 'cribs' into the encipherment used, whether Enigma or non-Enigma. As the SS documents were composed of numbers, the camp radio operators enciphered them using both letter and number codes, as a double layer of encryption, so alphabetical letters were used to replace numerical digits, as explained above:

> The contents of 4152 Orange dealt with some of the concentration camps ... Auschwitz, Dachau, Oranienburg, and the next sensational advance connected with SS cryptography was connected with this frequency.
>
> For several months a number of non-Enigma messages had been sent out from some six to seven stations early in the morning ... in fact between 7am to 8am. The messages, known as HOR-HUG reports, from two frequently occurring code groups were short, consisting of about ten groups of letters, followed by a few more or less invariable code groups.
>
> In the message proper the number of letters in any group never exceeded four, and on any one day only ten different letters were used. The last point strongly suggested a figure code, and on this hypothesis one day's traffic was broken early in April 1942.
>
> The messages contained in tabular form the vital statistics of concentration camps, the first four columns denoted A) number of inmates

at start of previous day, B) new arrivals, C) departures by any means, D) number at end of day. Thus, A plus B minus C equals D, and for any station D on the one day was A on the next. Once this was known it was generally easy to break any individual day on its own by a series of equations, and it was, of course absurdly simple if the previous day's substitution was known.[9]

What this meant was that Bletchley, and therefore limited elements of the Allied leadership who had access to the intelligence derived from these messages, had decisive and precise new information. By April 1942, they could find out in some instances the numbers of inmates already present, arriving and dying each day inside some of the main concentration and extermination camps. Their knowledge of the ongoing operations of the Holocaust leapt as a result – they now knew far more than just the general details of what was going on in concentration camps. Thanks to their cryptanalyts, they knew many precise details.

THE CODE-BREAKERS AT WAR

The German Signal from the Reich Security Main Office (RSHA)

After the Italian surrender in the summer of 1943, and the subsequent German occupation of Rome, it became even more important for all sides to know what the others were doing and intending to do. The Allies and Germans wanted to know each other's strategic intentions, while the British and Americans, as well as the Italians and the Vatican, were extremely concerned with discovering what the Germans' intentions were towards Italy's Jews. So, before and after the German invasion of the country in September and October 1943, coded signal traffic ricocheted like electronic fireflies between London, Rome, Washington, Berlin, Berne and the Vatican. All sides were trying to decipher each other's messages and discover each other's intentions. How successful were they and who could read what? Cryptanalysis had now become a major front line in the intelligence war over the Holy City.

The Vatican's cryptanalysts could, by this stage of the war, reportedly read into a very partial selection of some German, Italian and even British and American codes. Some of the inroads into the latter were made by intercepting references to Allied signals which themselves were contained in Axis coded messages. For their part, Bletchley's code-breakers were able to intercept and read one particular encoded telegram sent on 7 October 1943, from Rome to the RSHA in Berlin. It said that instructions had been given to the SS and SD in Rome 'to seize all Jews in lightning actions' and thus gave forewarning to the Vatican about forthcoming arrest operations:[1]

> To highest SS and Police Chief Italy Ograf WOLFF. RSHA has sent SS Hptstuf DANNECKER to this end with order to seize all Jews in lightning actions and to forward them to Germany.[2]

It was the confirmation that the Vatican and the Allies were looking for of Himmler's plan for the eradication and deportation of the Jews of Italy. The orders sent from Berlin to Rome, and the acknowledgements sent back, were clear and unequivocal. Ernst Kaltenbrunner and Karl Wolff told SS-Obersturmbannführer Herbert Kappler and other officers in the SD, SS and Gestapo hierarchy exactly what they had to do: the arrest, deportation, then immediate and thorough eradication of the Jews in Italy.

The intelligence war was developing. As mentioned previously, Pope Pius XII had served as *nuncio* in Germany for seven years and had had extensive experience dealing with the Germans – he spoke their language fluently and understood, of course, how the Third Reich's military and diplomatic bureaucracy functioned. In many ways, the Holy See functioned like a small 'theo-military' state, with its command-and-control structure of the Pope and his cardinals, the economic and commercial systems, the support structures of bishops, monsignors, prelates, priests and nuns from every conceivable order, even the 100-odd men of the Pontifical Swiss Guard (recruited from Swiss Catholic males between the ages of 19 and 30, these halberdiers, in their medieval uniforms coloured orange, mustard-yellow, blue and red, were a ceremonial guard for the pontiff and the Vatican).

The German RSHA signal was just one of thousands that flashed back and forth between Germany and Italy. Through decrypting German signals that were enciphered using either Enigma, codebooks, or sent as encrypted teleprinter messages, Bletchley Park managed to read a large volume of SD messages.[3]

From the interception and decipherment of some of the German messages between Berlin and Rome and vice-versa, the Allies were aware of some of the German intentions in Italy when it came to the execution of the Final Solution. What they knew and when depended on how long it took to decrypt certain signals, of course, and then disseminate the resultant information. They forwarded a selection of carefully screened pertinent intelligence to D'Arcy Osborne, their ambassador at the Vatican. This was censored and discreetly camouflaged so that it did not reveal the secret of Bletchley Park's successes with the decrypts whose resultant intelligence they code-named 'Ultra'.

Even though the Italians and the Germans could both read some British diplomatic traffic, neither side deduced that their enemies and other neutral protagonists knew what they, in turn, were doing when it came to code-breaking. The Germans, in particular, did not work out from the contents of the British diplomatic messages they intercepted that their enemies had been able to decrypt their own messages encoded on Enigma. With the security of Ultra absolutely paramount, the British made sure that in any radio traffic they made no reference to any information that could have been gathered from decrypted German or Italian coded messages. This way there were no pieces of intelligence in British signals that the Germans could then isolate and pinpoint as having originated in one of their own messages. When, for instance, the British had deployed Ultra intelligence to help locate the Italian fleet before the Battle of Cape Matapan in 1941, they successfully convinced the Germans and the Italians that the information had in fact come from aerial reconnaissance flights which had spotted Italian heavy cruisers at sea. It was just one way in which Ultra was so carefully protected.[4]

The Gestapo, meanwhile, had received stolen Vatican code-books as early as 1941, obtained by break-in experts recruited by the Italian SIM (military intelligence service) – it benefited the Italians as much as the Germans to know what the Vatican was doing. These contained encipherments which the Germans named STA/PCZ 3858 and Code II-441.[5]

In Berlin, Foreign Office cryptanalyst Dr Otfried Deubner was the deputy chief of the Italian language desk at Pers Z S (the signals intelligence agency) and responsible for cracking the Vatican's codes.[6] Like many cryptanalysts who served in the war, his professional background had little to do with code-breaking. He had been a classical archaeologist, and in 1935 and 1936 had worked at the Italian department of the German Archaeological Institute in Rome, where he had learned to speak fluent Italian. From 1940 onwards, he was transferred to work at Pers Z S, as a linguist and then as a cryptanalyst. The work he undertook on the Vatican's codes enabled him to read some 20 per cent of one of the codes that it used to communicate with foreign diplomats.

In this way, he found out that the cover of Georg Elling, a German intelligence agent inside the Vatican working for the SD's chief, Walter Schellenberg, had been blown. He also intercepted and read coded signals sent between the British Ambassador to the Holy See, Sir D'Arcy Osborne, and Pius XII's Cardinal Secretary of State, Luigi Maglione. Other German cryptanalysts from the Pers Z S agency could therefore read some of the other signals sent to Whitehall by Osborne.

The amount of solid information in existence was extremely finite – the intentions of the SS, German military deployments across Italy, what the Pope had said, when the German arrest operations would commence – but where effective cryptanalysis and subsequent intelligence deciphering came into its own was by allowing each protagonist a head start in predicting each other's operational intentions. The British, for instance, knew the Germans were committed to the execution of the Final Solution in Italy. However, short of invading the country and backing partisan groups (which they'd already done, beginning in September 1943) or bombing Holocaust transports (which they couldn't), one of their most effective options was to persuade the Pope to protest to the Germans as vociferously as possible. This would slow down the German operation, as the Vatican's protests would have to be transmitted via diplomats and generals to Berlin and back. It would buy the Vatican time to warn Jews and also time to advise Catholic seminaries and convents to prepare to hide them.

The information flow based on cryptanalysis was like a three-dimensional chess game, where half a dozen countries' intelligence services – the Vatican, Germany, Britain, the United States, Italy and Switzerland – could variously read none, a few, most or all of each other's messages. The amount of information in this equation of knowledge was then squared or cubed. If, say, Italy could read the British and Vatican's encrypted messages, that gave it an insight into what they were doing or planning to do; if Germany could read Italy's messages, in which Rome was transmitting details of British and Vatican information, then the Germans were now in possession of three of the protagonists' information. But if the British were simultaneously reading German traffic – and not revealing what they were discovering from it – they were ahead of the other protagonists, even though their messages were, in turn, being read.

It was a case of who was playing the game and who was being played. Fundamentally, however, the flow of information was governed by one absolute: the Germans didn't know the British had cracked Enigma, and the British didn't let on. Ten German signals intelligence agencies often duplicated each other's information, making it easier for their enemies to intercept and decrypt them, and the Third Reich's cryptanalysts were often more nervous of antagonising their harsh superiors – Hitler, Himmler, Eichmann – than they were keen to provide effective intelligence. Working for a dictatorship meant they largely couldn't keep a secret. The British, working for a democracy, largely could.

Meanwhile, the Germans could read Italian military and diplomatic messages sent on their C-38 device, which itself was a modification of the American M-209 Hagelin. This was the United States armed forces' answer to the Enigma machine, and the Germans had captured two of these rotor-based devices in Tunisia in 1942, worked out their encryption settings and consequently had been able to read some of the US Army's messages both in north Africa and in Sicily.

This had proved strategically vital at two particular moments. The first was when American paratroopers from the 82nd Airborne Division had landed on their drop-zones in Sicily on the night and morning of 9–10 July 1943. It told the Germans that a major airborne and amphibious assault was in progress, and it wasn't a deception operation. The second instance was when German troops were crossing back from the island of Sicily to the Italian mainland, across the Straits of Messina, as they pulled out of the fighting. By intercepting signals sent between the US Army and Navy, Albert Kesselring could work out the proximity of Allied naval ships to his own troop taskforce.

The Americans had been working hard to break into Vatican codes as well. How did they do this? Since Pearl Harbor, the Vatican had been sending and receiving a large volume of messages to and from government agencies in the United States. The Holy See wanted to know, would America join the war? What financial assistance could the Vatican continue to receive from the US State Department in time of conflict? What would the policy of the United States be to the reception of Jewish refugees? Would the Vatican co-operate with the Germans in the event of an invasion of Italy?

US cryptanalysts at Arlington Hall in Virginia, along with the British at Bletchley Park, could read a percentage of the three main Vatican ciphers, which they had named KIA-Red, KIB-Yellow and KIC-Green, partly after the colours of the code-books' leather covers. The American work to crack the Vatican's codes was shrouded in an extra level of domestic secrecy. There were a lot of Catholics in America – a lot of Catholic voters, Catholic congressmen and senators, and Catholic constituencies. If it became public knowledge that the US forces were intercepting the codes of the Pope, it could easily result in strongly negative political and social consequences. So, the word 'Vatican' did not appear in any documents, messages or governmental and military correspondence.

How did the Americans circumvent this problem? The department at the US code-breaking headquarters at Arlington Hall that handled the Vatican's codes was called 'Gold Section'. When it came to decrypting the codes of other countries, such as Germany, Italy or Spain, the system a particular analyst was deciphering would be referred to by what was known as a trigraph. The first two letters of this, for instance 'GE', 'IT' or 'SP', indicated the country of origin of the code – Germany, Italy, Spain – and the last letter referred to where the extract of coded text came from in any given message.

Messages emanating from the Vatican, however, were given the formal digraph, or two-letter indicator 'KI', which bore no resemblance to any known country. So, the three main Vatican codes, and the colours of the covers of their respective code-books, led to the names KIA-Red, KIB-Yellow and KIC-Green. The first was a straightforward code used for low-level Vatican communications: movements of clerical staff between apostolic delegations, logistics and diplomatic conferences.

KIA-Red simply consisted of 12,000 groups of three letters, each representing a word in Italian. It stood to reason that a larger number than normal were connected to clerical matters. The code was solved by a simple substitution table, and the British, Americans and Germans all cracked the code, only to discover that the highest level of confidentiality of any message written in the code concerned the bedding and accommodation for a group of visiting Vatican delegates in Madrid.

KIB-Yellow was much more complicated. It was based on the Vigenère cipher, itself an encryption device that was more than 400 years old, having been invented by an Italian cryptologist in 1553. It had resisted almost all efforts to break it. It was based on polyalphabetic substitution and the use of what are known in cryptology as 'Caesar ciphers'. In this coding format, an alphabet of twenty-six letters is laid out in order, horizontally. If the Caesar 'Shift Keyword' becomes 'three', for instance, each letter of the alphabet is moved along three spaces, so A becomes D, C becomes F, Z becomes C and so on.

This shifting of the alphabet is then repeated on another subsequent alphabet laid beneath it, and each time an alphabet is written, the first letter – A – moves one space to the right. Then a three-letter shift takes place. This procedure was like the movement of a knight in a game of chess, two spaces forward, one to the side. In the operation of a Caesar cipher, this movement is repeated twenty-six times, until there are twenty-six alphabets laid out, vertically and horizontally, each with a different letter layout, each containing twenty-six letters, making 676 in all. This is called a Vigenère Square. A keyword is given, which enables the encryptor to know at which point in the square the first word of the message plain text should start.

If, for instance, the first word to be encrypted is 'arrest', then the key-word tells the operator where in the square of 676 different letters to begin. Once the starting point is known – line 8, letter 15 horizontally, line 9, letter 11 vertically – the operator takes that point as their start, lays the word 'attack' on it, and reads vertically downwards to encode the word.

KIC-Green was similar to KIB-Yellow, but harder to crack. Once a word was encoded it was then given an indicator of two letters at the beginning, a letter was added on at the end, and this was then enciphered into a sandwich of letters that had to be removed before the code could be deciphered. So, if the word 'agent' is encoded as 'TBXSW', it receives a two-letter indicator, becoming, say, 'EQTBXSW'. It is then enciphered with a sandwich of three extra letters at the beginning and end, becoming 'CQAEQTBXSWPHY'. This code was very rarely broken, nor was the one known as KIF-Purple.

The system group known to Arlington Hall as KIF was a one-part, three-letter code of 12,000–15,000 groups, i.e., there were 12,000–15,000 permutations of three letters that represented different words. It was enciphered with twenty-five keys, each consisting of a combination of substitution tables and random mixed alphabets, and each using different nulls, or vacant spaces with no letters in them. It was nothing if not complex:

Each papal Nunciature or embassy had a unique set of sixteen of these twenty-five keys and would use them on particular days of the month. A Vatican nuncio might begin a telegram in the assigned key for the day but then shift, as many as eight times, to other keys in the course of the message.[7]

Meanwhile, the coded messages coming out of Rome by 17 October left nobody in any doubt as to what was taking place. 'The SD is now pillaging Rome ... Himmler has sent SS men who have had experience of this work in Russia to Rome', was one Enigma-encrypted signal read by Bletchley Park on 17 October, sent by the Swiss.

While the Vatican knew the German intentions, the Germans still didn't know whether the Pope would formally and strongly object to a round-up of Italy's Jews. The pontiff was lobbying the United States to receive Jewish refugees. The Germans feared Italy's Jews would escape, while Italy's Fascist Republic said it would assist the Germans in the execution of the Final Solution. All of this had given the Vatican vital advance warning, in turn, allowing Jews to escape.

The Vatican, via both its staff and Luigi Maglione, started to pass word to its *nuncios*, and to selected Catholic convents, churches and seminaries across Italy, to put into operation plans to conceal as many of the Italian Jews as possible.

ON THE BANKS OF LAKE MAGGIORE

In the last week of September 1943, a man's body washed up on the shores of Lake Maggiore in southern Switzerland. There was a bullet wound in his head and Jewish Italian identity papers in a jacket pocket. Swiss police estimated that the corpse had been dumped in the lake in Italy and then it had drifted over into Swiss waters. So, their colleagues in military intelligence tipped off the British Special Operations Executive (SOE) in nearby Lugano. It confirmed what the British knew, from their 'Ultra' intercepts of Enigma-encrypted signals sent by an SS division, the *Liebstandarte Adolf Hitler*, which was operating across the frontier around Lake Maggiore. Killings of Jews had started. The Holocaust in Italy was under way.

Betrayed by their former Italian allies who had signed an armistice with the Allies in July, by September 1943 German divisions were pouring south into Italy to occupy the country and disarm its forces. They had another, secret, agenda: the round-up and deportation of Italy's 40,000 Jews. Some of these had fled towards Lake Maggiore, heading for safety in neutral Switzerland. Among them was Ettore Ovazza and his family, the rich Jewish bankers from Turin and loyal supporters of the Italian Fascist Party. Their brutal murder by the SS was to send a clear message to Italy's Jews: whatever laws and considerations existed under Mussolini are now obsolete. The Germans have arrived.

The man's body that washed up on the shores of Lake Maggiore, inside Swiss territory, had come from further south. The bullet wound in his head and the identity papers confirmed that. Over 40 miles long, the lake lies north-west of Milan in the shadow of the Swiss and Italian Alps, with two-thirds of its length lying in Italy and the remainder in Switzerland. It's one of the five large lakes bordering the two countries, the others being Lakes Lugano, Como, Varese and Orta. At certain times of spring and summer, the current moves predominantly northwards.

Swiss police estimated that whoever had shot the man had then dumped the corpse in the lake in Italy and it had drifted over into Swiss waters. A Swiss newspaper from the nearby city of Lugano reported what was beginning just across the dark blue waters of the lake. 'Anti-Jewish persecution in Italy', ran the headline in the 23 October edition of the *Libera Stampa*, the newspaper of the Socialist Party in Lugano:

> The first days of the German invasion have seen numerous acts of violence, conforming to a preordained plan to spread terror, directed against anti-fascists, against Jews, and against those Italian citizens who have no predisposition to support the Nazis. During this period many Jews have been killed ... and the killings were particularly dreadful in the Piedmontese communes on the shore of the lake, in Arona, Meina, Stresa, Sunda, Pallanze, where all the Jewish families were arrested ... many of them were barbarically slaughtered, and numerous tortured bodies have been found in the surrounding countryside and in the lake ...[1]

Hitler felt betrayed by the surrender agreement that his former Italian allies had signed with the Americans and British on 3 September, so he launched Operation Axis, or *Fall Achse*. German divisions poured south into Italy to occupy the country, neutralise its armed forces by taking away their guns, boats and aeroplanes, and disarm a million of its servicemen en masse. Simultaneously, the Germans occupied the Italian-controlled zones in both Croatia and the south of France.

They were looting too, hunting for art, gold, statuary and jewellery from museums. Hitler and Göring wanted the art for the Führer's Aryan cultural centre in Linz, Austria. Himmler wanted gold, especially, for the coffers of the SS private economic machine. There was another secret agenda too, obviously: the round-up and deportation of Italy's Jews. Many of those living in northern Italy were from in or around Milan or Turin – like the Ovazza and Montalcini families – and on hearing about the impending German arrival, some of them had fled north towards Lake Maggiore, heading for safety in neutral Switzerland. Among them was Ettore Ovazza and his extended family, seeking refuge across the border to the north.

Before Italy had even surrendered on 8 September, German divisions had begun crossing into Italy. One of the first to arrive was the 1st SS Panzer Division, the *Liebstandarte Adolf Hitler.* The SS unit had just fought at the Battle of Kursk on the Eastern Front, going head to head with T-34s from the Red Army in July. After losing some 450 men killed and another 2,250 wounded or missing, the division pulled out of the line. They left their tanks where they were, to be used by two other SS units.

The men embarked on troop trains and crossed south-west towards Romania and Hungary. They arrived on the Italian border with Austria at the beginning of August and began crossing into Italy. The division spread out, with its regiments moving towards Verona, Parma and along the valley of the River Po, which bisects the north of Italy from west to east, before running into the Adriatic near Ravenna.

Italy was in chaos, as its entire army of more than 1 million men surrendered, swore allegiance to Fascism and to their newly arriving German allies, or simply took off their uniforms and fled. The Allies announced the armistice on the radio on 8 September, and the majority of troops in the Italian Army were taken by surprise by the news. Most of them had no idea what to do.

On the island of Corsica, a regiment of the Royal Italian Army, the *Regio Esercito*, immediately changed sides and tried to prevent an SS division from manoeuvring southwards to join up with other German units, arriving on the southern tip of the island from Sardinia. Other units were heading to defend Rome from the Italian-occupied area in the south of France, around Nice. They ran straight into German units, which had set up roadblocks in the mountainous western part of the region of Piemonte. The roads to and from France and western Switzerland ran through and across the Alps, which form the north-western border of Italy.

To the south, King Vittorio Emanuele III and the royal family left Rome on the night of 9 September in a convoy of cars, guarded by *carabinieri* who were loyal to the monarchy. They reached the port of Brindisi, on the south-eastern Adriatic coastline, and waited for Allied troops to arrive.

The British and Canadians had already landed on 3 September in the far south of Calabria, after crossing the Straits of Messina from Sicily. On the day after the announcement of the armistice, the British and Americans landed at both Taranto, on the eastern seaboard of the country, and Salerno, on the west. The Germans established control of Rome by 11 September.

The roads, railways, towns and countryside were swarmed with flee-ing Italian soldiers: few put up a fight against the Germans. Most found whatever civilian clothes they could and tried to blend back into the molten, ricocheting chaos of their country, as it started falling apart like a jigsaw puzzle upended from a table. Partisan groups erupted out of nowhere: thousands of soldiers took what weapons they could from their barracks and retreated into the countryside.

The men from the 1st SS Division headed for Milan, Turin and the city of Cuneo, lying in the shadow of the Alps, controlling access to the roads crossing into France. Other units drove towards Aosta, in the far north-west of Piemonte, to control access routes into Switzerland.

The men of the *Liebstandarte Adolf Hitler* were under strict instructions from their commanding officer, Paul Hausser, not to commit any acts of violence against Italian civilians. Hitler was keenly aware that if he was going to occupy two-thirds of Italy in the face of an enormous Allied invasion, he desperately needed, if not the support of the Italian civilian population, then its tacit acceptance of the German presence. Otherwise, the country would descend into immediate civil war, leaving the Germans facing the Allies on two fronts, partisans behind the lines and the civilian population everywhere. Hausser also told his men that arresting any Jews and sequestrating – looting and stealing, put more bluntly – were also out of the question. Himmler and Ernst Kaltenbrunner in Berlin had made it clear that both of these tasks were to be the sole responsibility of the SS intelligence police, the SD, and the Gestapo.

One regiment of the *Liebstandarte Adolf Hitler* broke this ruling almost immediately. On 19 September, a unit under the command of Joachim Pieper, who'd been highly decorated for gallantry on the Eastern Front, was on operations along the western Alpine border near the city of Cuneo. It was trying to intercept columns of surrendering Italian soldiers, crossing back into their homeland from the area of occupation in southern France. Unofficially, Pieper's men were trying to stop an estimated 1,000 Italian Jews from fleeing to France. In the small town of Boves, south of Cuneo, they ran into a band of Italian partisans.

A scrappy, fast-running firefight broke out and the partisans captured two German soldiers. A film and photo image from that day shows an SS officer in peaked cap, shorts and field jacket by an artillery piece and some half-tracks, ordering men to open fire on the town. The parish priest from Boves managed to negotiate the successful release of the two German soldiers, but it didn't stop Pieper's men turning on the town. Twenty-three civilians were killed, dozens of houses burnt and shelled. The message to the Italians was clear. Whatever regulations and edicts existed under Mussolini's regime had gone out of the window. The Germans had arrived.

Ten days later, in Turin, Ettore Ovazza and his wife had finished selling or giving away their remaining property. The only possessions they retained were those they were taking with them in a series of suitcases – clothing, some food, cash in their pockets, jewellery in small pouches hung around their necks or in money belts around their waist. They drove north to the skiing town of Gressoney-Saint-Jean, which lies in the Alpine Aosta Valley, 20 miles south of the Matterhorn, on the Swiss frontier. They arrived at the Hotel Lyskamm, where they discovered a group of other Jews, some of whom had arrived from Croatia. Their previous refuge across the border of Yugoslavia had been in the zone occupied by the Italian Army: after the armistice, the Germans had occupied this.

Nella, Ettore and their son Riccardo and daughter Elena were going to try to cross the border on foot into Switzerland, but Riccardo suggested that he go first to see if there were German patrols on the border, and to see how receptive the Swiss border police were to Italian refugees crossing into their territory. Riccardo discovered the answer to the first question when he set off with a small group of the Croatian refugees and walked north. They saw no German troops.

However, by the time they crossed into Switzerland, they ran into a patrol of Swiss border police, who were not welcoming at all. Their guide, it turned out, had betrayed them for money. They took Riccardo to the railway station in the town of Brig, 25 miles north-east of the border crossing point, which lay in the shadow of the Matterhorn. The Swiss police put him on a train back to Italy.

The railway line from Brig that heads southwards sways and swoops through a long Alpine valley, green and pastoral in the early autumn light. A tunnel goes through the Alps and the first stop inside Italy is at Domodossola. At the station, with its waiting rooms and offices laid out in a long, timbered building like a huge chalet, the German field police were waiting. They arrested Riccardo Ovazza and took him to the small town of Intra, which sits among elegant tropical gardens and Victorian holiday villas on the banks of Lake Maggiore.

They handed him over to the SS, who'd commandeered a girls' primary school as their local base. By this time, the *Liebstandarte Adolf Hitler*'s 2nd Regiment was patrolling the eastern and western sides of the lake, disarming Italian troops and trying to prevent refugees – Jews, most particularly – from trying to escape into Switzerland. On 9 October, the SS men beat Riccardo until he told them where the rest of his family, and the group of Jews with them, were hiding – Gressoney-Saint-Jean, he said. The 2nd Regiment's commanding officer sent a jeep and a truck to Saint-Jean to find them.

The SS men then put Riccardo up against a wall and shot him. They fed his body into the furnace in the cellar of the girls' school, which fuelled the building's heating system.

Ettore Ovazza hadn't heeded the constant imprecations and warnings of his extended family, to flee Italy much earlier, before the Germans

arrived, and come to Switzerland. He was too convinced that his earlier
devotion to Fascism would save him. 'They'll never touch me, I've done
too much for fascism,' he kept saying.[2]

The SS arrived in front of the hotel on 10 October and walked into
the reception area. They put Ettore, Nella and Elena into the truck, along
with their suitcases. On arrival at Intra, they took them to the girls' school,
robbed them of everything they had that was of value and then formed a
firing squad. The SS men fed their bodies into the heating furnace.[3]

Ten miles south of Intra, on the same side of the lake, lie the small towns
of Arona and Meina. Like many of the hamlets and villages that sit by
the lake, these are dotted with semi-tropical, Mediterranean gardens,
with palm trees and umbrella pines, botanical collections, arboretums
and elegant parks. Rows of large, expensive villas, some the size of small
castles, dot the shore and the islands in the lake. Since the seventeenth
century, the five lakes, including Maggiore and Como, have been the
places where the wealthy and the noble of northern Italy have built their
homes. Hotels for the tourists who head here in the summer season are
strung along the shores, looking out over the blinking sunlight reflected
off the dark blue and cobalt of the lakes' surfaces.

In the town of Meina sat the hotel of the same name, although some
local people called it the Hotel Victoria. The owner was a Turkish Jew
called Alberto Ottolenghi Behar, and he, his wife Eugenia and four children, including daughter Rachel, had moved from Belgium to Italy in
1934. The climate around Milan and Lake Maggiore, said doctors, would
be better for Mrs Behar's health.

Rachel – she was unanimously nicknamed Becky – was 13 in 1943.
She went to school in Milan, and then to the Meina elementary and secondary schools, and learned to speak Italian. Her father spoke Turkish at
home with his wife and children. Eugenia, who was from Brussels, spoke
French sometimes, while the whole family also spoke Spanish.

Like the children in the Piperno family, Becky and her siblings were
taken out of school in 1938 after the introduction of the Racial Laws.

She remembered leaving in tears, not remotely understanding what she or her family could have done wrong.[4]

At first, the family had moved to Milan, but after Italy entered the war in 1940, the Allies started bombing the city, as it was not just the country's second-largest railway and logistics hub, but the centre of Italian economic production. So, when Alberto Behar heard that the Turkish vice consul from Milan, Niebil Hertog, was moving to the shores of Lake Maggiore, he considered following suit. He discovered that the proprietor of the Hotel Meina wanted to sell it, and so he put in an offer. The family moved north to the lakeside town in January 1941.

By summer 1943, the hotels along the lake had a considerable number of long-term guests who were Jewish, from Italy, Croatia and Thessaloniki, in Greece. However, Italian municipal officials from the local Fascist Party were selling information to the Germans about the hiding places of the Jews in the neighbouring towns of Meina, Arona and Stresa. Within two days, they had located forty-one people.

The first company of SS men from the *Liebstandarte Adolf Hitler* arrived in Meina on 13 September under the command of a captain. They installed themselves in another lakeside property nearby, the Hotel Beau Rivage in Baveno. On 15 September, a group of officers and NCOs from the same company commandeered the Hotel Meina and locked Becky, her family and three other Jewish families into a series of rooms on the top floor:

> It was room 410, up on the top floor. There were six of us: my parents, my sister, my brothers. They pushed us in and there were sixteen other hotel guests, they bolted the door with a sentry behind it. We gave the mattresses to the old people. There were those who cried, those who prayed, the grown-ups tried to make us be courageous. Outside we could hear shouts, orders, a lot of Germans coming and going. After two days an SS man, not even twenty years old, took me aside and asked me: What's your name? Becky, I answered. And he said: 'You're Jewish, one day you'll get married, have Jewish children and they'll all be enemies of the greater Germany.'[5]

On two occasions, the Germans tried to kill Behar Senior, and twice the Turkish Vice Consul saved him, explaining forcefully to the SS men that the family were Turkish citizens, with Turkish passports, and not to be touched. It was their identity papers that saved their lives.

On 19 September, the officers of the 2nd Regiment of the 1st SS Division who were stationed in and around Meina held a meeting and decided what to do with the imprisoned Jews. On the nights of 22 and 23 September, the SS released the prisoners from their hotel rooms, took them to a small forest outside Meina and shot them. They took the bodies back to the edge of the lake in hessian sacks, which they also filled with rocks, and put the bodies into a small boat. Two SS men rowed out 100m from the shore and rolled the bodies into the water.[6] The SS also shot other Jews and buried them in the neighbouring woods – in all, they killed sixteen Jews in Meina and another thirty-four in seven towns and villages on the shores of the same lake.

Saved by their passports, Becky Behar, her mother, father and siblings were accompanied by the Turkish Vice Consul, with his wife and family, towards the Swiss border in two cars. Yet none of them knew that between them and safety lay another line of Germans and Italian Fascists, determined to let no refugees, Jewish or otherwise, flee into Switzerland.

8

THE *RETATA* OF ROME

Herbert Kappler had had plenty of practice in round-ups and deportations. In Italian, the word for the former was '*retata*', meaning 'a netting'. He had started life as an electrician from Stuttgart and had joined the SS in 1933, and then the Gestapo in 1936. By the time of the Austrian *Anschluss* in 1938, he was already overseeing the deportation of Austria's Jews to concentration camps. Gestapo postings followed – Stuttgart and Belgium – and work on an *Einsatzkommando* in Poland.

By spring 1943, he had been posted to Rome as a liaison officer to Mussolini, in which position his fluent Italian proved a vital asset. He'd been a favourite of Reinhard Heydrich, and was also on good, though measured, terms with his overbearing and often brutal successor, Ernst Kaltenbrunner. Following Kappler's service with Mussolini, the scar-faced head of the RSHA promoted Kappler. He made him the head of both the Gestapo in Rome and the SS intelligence arm, the *Sicherheitsdienst* or SD.

Kappler knew what he had to do. In July 1943 the Allies had landed on the island of Sicily, and then in September the British 8th and American 5th Armies disembarked on the beaches at Salerno, south of Naples. The Cassabile Armistice, signed between the Allies and the Italians, had then seen Mussolini overthrown and the country's armed forces surrender or change sides.

To Hitler, this double-crossing by his erstwhile allies had obviously confirmed his worst fears, that the regime of his Fascist counterparts had been undermined, the monarchy and its supporters had switched sides and the alliance with Il Duce had collapsed. His entire southern flank on the Mediterranean was now dangerously exposed. He dispatched ten divisions of the Wehrmacht and SS into northern Italy with strict instructions: occupy the country and disarm the Italian Army. These units had included the SS *Liebstandarte Adolf Hitler* division, which had already gone into action around the French border and carried out the murders of Jews on the lakes north of Milan and at Boves, near Cuneo (see the previous chapter).

Just as the American 5th Army was landing at Salerno, the first SS and Wehrmacht troops had already entered Rome. Kappler was among them, and he got to work. One of his first priorities was following an order issued by Himmler on 9 September, to ensure the safety of all German personnel in Rome and to liberate Mussolini.

The British had called on all neutral countries to refuse asylum to Mussolini or other war criminals and said that any such country that provided asylum would be contravening the principles of the United Nations, for which Britain was fighting. But Italians loyal to the king had taken Mussolini into hiding inside Italy. Kappler, using a network of informers, bribes and harsh interrogation methods, had persuaded some of the prisoners at the Gestapo headquarters in Rome to release information about Mussolini's whereabouts.

Once the Germans moved into the country in September and October 1943, coded signal traffic flashed between London, Rome, Washington, Berlin and the Vatican, with all sides trying to decipher each other's messages and trying to discover each other's intentions. The Vatican's cryptanalysts could, by this stage of the war, read a selection of German, American, Italian and British codes. The British had, crucially, also intercepted the encoded telegram sent in early October to Rome from the RSHA in Berlin, instructing the SS and SD in Rome 'to seize the city's Jews' and this gave forewarning to the Vatican about the forthcoming arrest operations. The British had passed this on to their Italian partisan allies, the Swiss, Americans and Russians.

When the Fascist Council had deposed Mussolini in July, 200 *carabinieri*, police officers allied to King Pietro Badoglio, had taken him into custody, first to the island of Ponza, in the Tyrrhenian Sea, then to the north-east coast of Sardinia. The Germans found him, so he was moved again, this time to a hotel in a skiing resort on the Gran Sasso plateau in the Apennines.

By the middle of September, SS and Luftwaffe commandos had freed *Il Duce*, who was taken to Vienna and thence onwards to Berlin and to Hitler's headquarters at Rastenberg in East Prussia. Field Marshal Albert Kesselring, the German Supreme Commander in Italy, then ordered that the entire population of Rome should be disarmed as soon as German troops arrived in the capital.

Meanwhile, Cardinal Maglione at the Vatican had written to the British and American ambassadors on 15 August, saying that he hoped that, after the bombing of Rome on 19 July and 13 August, from now on any bombardments of Rome, including the Vatican, could be avoided and the capital could essentially become an 'open city'.

As Kesselring gave his instructions, there were four principal Italian partisan groups operating in the capital: when the disarmament order arrived, they simply ignored it. Partisans were bringing weapons, ammunition, medical supplies and radios into Rome, either on foot or hidden in vehicles. One partisan group operating north of the city in summer 1943, allied to the Christian Democrat Party, numbered 200 men and women in its ranks. They were armed with captured German and Italian weapons, such as Mauser K-98 rifles, MP 40 Schmeisser and Beretta MAS38 machine pistols, and British Bren and Sten guns, which were airdropped in operations co-ordinated by the Allied SOE.

The partisans had three operational priorities: attacking roads and railway lines used by German troops advancing to reinforce the capital, or alternatively withdrawing northwards; helping escaped Allied POWs who were moving southwards towards the safety of Allied lines; and operating with and taking supplies to partisan groups operating in Rome itself.

The Allies obviously wanted to know what the Germans were going to do in the city. Burn it down? Expel its inhabitants? Defend it? Arrest all of its Jews? Or, much more probably, use it as their operational head-quarters from which they would co-ordinate their defence of Italy against the Allied advance, until the time came to withdraw northwards?

The Allies knew that the arrest and deportation of Rome's Jews was a German priority. To find out the operational and logistical details of the daily situation in Rome, the British and Americans depended on partisan groups and Allied agents to transmit radio messages with this informa-tion. Although the Allies could intercept, decrypt and then read a variety of signals sent by the Germans, Fascist Italians and neutral countries, like Switzerland and the Holy See, the time taken between the dispatch of the message, its interception, decoding in Britain, translation and onward dissemination to Allied headquarters in southern Italy was sometimes longer than the time it took for a partisan group in Rome to send a coded radio message directly.

On 15 September, Mussolini had dinner with Adolf Hitler, Himmler and Foreign Minister Joaquim Ribbentrop at Hitler's headquarters at the Wolf's Lair in East Prussia. How, wondered Hitler and Himmler, was the Final Solution – then in its third year – to be implemented in newly occupied Italy?

As the Wehrmacht and SS occupied the streets of Rome in September of that scorching summer, then disarmed the population and set up defensive positions on the main roads leading in and out of the city, Himmler met with Ernst Kaltenbrunner. On the agenda were the logistics and operational details for the Final Solution and the ongoing handling of the Jews of Italy.

Himmler told the RSHA to devise, implement and execute a plan. SS-Gruppenführer Karl Wolff, one of Himmler's former aides, was ordered to fly south and put the plan into action. Its aim? The arrest, deportation and ultimate liquidation of Italy's Jews.

There were by now around 10,000 German troops in Rome, work-ing alongside Fascist troops and militias from the Fascist puppet state of the Italian Social Republic. Concerned that the Vatican was trying to assist Jews in escaping, Herbert Kappler noted on 24 September that the

Vatican was selling some Spanish, Argentinian, Mexican and Portuguese visas to Jews who were trying to leave Rome on a train arranged for Spanish diplomats.

One of the Germans' first priorities was to seize the gold bullion held in the National Bank of Italy – the *Banca d'Italia* – and move it north to safety. On 21 September, German troops arrived outside the headquarters of the Bank of Italy in Rome, which sat on the ornate Palazzo Koch, fronted by palm trees on the Via Nazionale. They forced their way into the building at gunpoint. The Italian *carabinieri* guards put up no resistance.

Inside the vaults the Germans found 2,338kg of 'monetary' gold – i.e., gold coins and ingots – and seized it all. They loaded it onto trucks waiting outside in the late summer heat. Much of the gold was, in fact, from the National Bank of Albania in Tirana, seized by the Italian Fascist authorities. Italy itself had held a reserve of 500 tonnes of gold in 1925, which had fallen to 420 tonnes by 1930, then to 240 tonnes by 1935, leaving the country with only 122 tonnes in 1940.[1]

The Germans wanted to move the gold to Berlin immediately, but the Italian Fascist government in northern Italy insisted that the bullion be stored, in the interim, inside Italy itself. So the Germans put 100 tonnes of the gold onto a series of freight cars at Tiburtina Station and took it first to Milan, and then to the nineteenth-century Franzensfeste Castle in the town of Fortezza in the south Tyrol. This is located 25 miles south of the Brenner Pass. Then, 70 tonnes of the gold were moved northwards again, across the border into Austria and to the Reichsbank in Berlin.

Before the beginning of October, the RSHA was ready to put into action the plan to round up Rome's Jews. But first, Kappler wanted a bribe. On the morning of 26 September, the Gestapo chief asked the two most senior representatives of Rome's Jewish community to come to his office in the Via Tasso, in Rome's San Giovanni district. Set on a sloping cobbled street of sand-coloured apartment buildings, the building was part of the German Embassy and also functioned as the Gestapo headquarters and prison. Rooms inside had been converted into ad hoc cells, by bricking up the windows, leaving prisoners locked up in the stifling heat and near darkness. In the basement was the room where Kappler and his Gestapo colleagues carried out their interrogations.

Kappler was in a forthright mood when Ugo Foa, the Head of the Jewish Community in Rome, and Dante Almansi, President of the Union of Italian Jewish Communities, arrived at the door in Via Tasso. Kappler told the two men that the Germans considered the Jews the greatest enemy they were fighting and although they didn't need their lives – for now – they did need their gold. He gave them thirty-six hours to deliver 50kg (110lb) of gold to Via Tasso, or he would deport 200 of their menfolk.

The two Jewish community leaders immediately convened a meeting of Rome's Rabbis. One of these, Israel Zolli, went straight to the Vatican for help. A secretary dutifully made a note of the extraordinary meeting:

> Monsignor Antonino Arata, secretary of the Congregation of the Western Church, says that the Grand Rabbi of Rome, Israel Zolli, was called in by the German police, who told him that by 1pm tomorrow he had to deliver 50kgs of gold.[2]

Jews and non-Jews, meanwhile, streamed into the main synagogue to give watches, rings, coins, cigarette cases and money. Even those who could afford almost nothing came forward. Elda Della Riccia was one woman who went on 27 September to the synagogue and gave 50 lire, the equivalent of 50 US cents. Exact in their accounting, the Jewish community gave her a receipt, number 2930, signed by one Signor Ottolenghi.[3] A Roman-Jewish writer, Giacomo Debenedetti, was there:

> Cautiously, as if afraid of being refused, uncertain whether to offer gold to the rich Jews, some 'Aryans' presented themselves. They entered the hall adjacent to the synagogue full of embarrassment, not knowing if they should take off their hats or keep their heads covered, according to Jewish custom. Almost humbly, they asked if they could – well if it would be all right to … Unfortunately, they did not leave their names.[4]

Thirty-six hours later, the community had collected 80kg of gold and 2,021,540 lire. Thirty kilos of gold was hidden, and then Foa and Almansi took four of the synagogue's guards, each carrying pistols, and delivered the required 50kg of gold to the Germans at Via Tasso. They thanked the Vatican, too. The Holy See's administration wrote:

> The Jews of Rome have found the gold the Germans were demanding. Yesterday at 2pm Dr. Zolli told me that they found 15kgs from the Catholic Community, and that they didn't need our help. But they humbly asked that the door should not be closed for the future.[5]

Yet it seemed that it was not only bullion in which the Germans were interested. Three days later, on 30 September and 1 October, two men arrived to visit the Jewish Community Library, the *Biblioteca della Comunita Israelitica*. It contained some 7,000 rare books and manuscripts and was certainly the most important Jewish library in Italy, and de facto one of the most important in the world:

> The Community's library was made up of the priceless works collected even before the sixteenth century and until the nineteenth century, in the five synagogues and the thirty confraternities located in the ghetto. It included manuscripts, incunabula, soncinati, as well as works of the sixteenth century printed by Bomberg, Bragadin and Giustiniani.
>
> It is known that on September 30th and October 1st 1943 two men in uniform appeared, one of them introducing himself as a teacher of Hebrew at a Berlin Institute. They inspected the Jewish Community's library as well as the one of the Italian Rabbinical College, located on another floor of the same building. A second visit and inspection of the two libraries followed, resulting in their declaring the seizure of the material. A transport company was ordered by telephone to withdraw and load the collections on railway wagons. On October 14th 1943 the whole Community's library and part of that of the Italian Rabbinical College were taken away.[6]

On 5 October, Kappler received a coded signal from Berlin from an official at Amt VI – the SD – of the RSHA. It was either encoded on Enigma in the SS Orange encryption, or in one of the non-Enigma encipherments that Oliver Strachey at Bletchley Park had code-named ISOSICLE. Either way, the British code-breakers intercepted and read it, 'Ref: transport of gold. Your W/T message of 5/10 without number is not clear. Are the 50kgs of gold actually being sent to CDS? HOETTL'.[7]

SS-Sturmbannführer Wilhelm Hoettl worked for the SD in Berlin under Ernst Kaltenbrunner and was already, in 1943, making his own preparations for what might happen after the war. Notes in an American intelligence file held on him described the SS Colonel as a 'fanatic Nazi', 'believed to be cooperating with the Allies to save his own skin'.[8]

The gold sent from Rome was destined for the Economic Affairs Office of the RSHA, but Kaltenbrunner himself had other designs on it. Two days later, it had still not arrived in Berlin. The SS officer mentioned in the following signal, Erich Priebke, was one of Kappler's deputies in Rome: 'PRIEBKE'S trunk not arrived. Said to be still at the Embassy in Rome. As only hand dispatches are sent to this end. HOETTL.'[9]

However, whatever concerns Kappler had about the fate of the 50kg of gold that was heading for Berlin, the next signal he received from Kaltenbrunner superimposed itself. Its contents were simple, the definitive set of instructions for the beginning of the Final Solution in Italy, 'Take the 8,000 Jews living in Rome, and transport them to the north of Italy. They are to be liquidated.'

The example of what had occurred further north was now held over the heads of the SS and SD officers in the capital. SS-General Paul Hausser, commanding the division responsible for the killings on Lake Maggiore, was furious with his officers when they had arrested and killed Jewish prisoners and stolen their property. The orders of SS-Gruppenführer Karl Wolff, the Supreme SS Commander in Italy, were made clear. They came straight from Himmler himself: the killings and arrests of Italian Jews and confiscation of their property were to be the sole preserve of the Gestapo and SD.

Wolff was Himmler's former chief of staff and was deeply involved in the execution of the Final Solution in Poland and Ukraine. He was now tasked with implementing it in Italy. Intercepted by the British, the message was passed to the American Office of Strategic Services:

TREATMENT OF ITALIAN JEWS

On October 6th 1943 the following recommendation was made to high German sources by a German official in Italy.

Orders have been received from Berlin by Obersturmbannführer KAPPLER to seize and to take to northern Italy the 8,000 Jews living in Rome. They are to be liquidated. General Stahel, the city commandant of Rome, will permit this action only if it is consistent with the policies of the Reich Foreign Minister. It would be better business in my opinion to use the Jews as in Tunis, for work on fortifications. Together with KAPPLER, I will present this view through Field Marshal General Kesselring ...[10]

One of the senior SS officers whom Wolff intended to bring with him was SS-Hauptmann Theodor Dannecker, who was now made head of the Italian *Judenreferat* for Amt IV B of the RSHA. This was the Jewish Affairs Office of the SD for Italy. He'd held the same post in Paris until he was sacked for stealing confiscated Jewish property, then he'd failed a second time in Bulgaria, allowing huge numbers of Jews to escape deportation. Kaltenbrunner, Adolf Eichmann and Wolff now gave him a third chance, dispatching him and an *Einsatzkommando* into central Rome to join Kappler from the Gestapo. Together, they would spearhead the Final Solution and clear out the Italian capital's Jewish ghetto.

Luftwaffe General Reiner Stahel had been appointed as the German Military Commander of Rome, taking his orders directly from Berlin via Karl Wolff. Warned by German clergy inside the Vatican that Pope Pius XII could fiercely condemn any arrests of Rome's Jews, he urged both Dannecker and Herbert Kappler to delay the round-up operations until mid-October. The first obstacle to the execution of the Holocaust in Italy had thus been put in place by the Germans themselves. Adolf Eichmann later wrote in his diary that 'the objections given and the excessive delay in the steps necessary to complete the implementation of the operation resulted in a great part of Italian Jews being able to hide and escape capture'.[11]

While the Germans were delaying, Karl Wolff and Hitler were allegedly at loggerheads over a plot to kidnap the pontiff, forcing the Vatican to move to Liechtenstein or Portugal. The beleaguered Holy City was looking for diplomatic support from Washington: all sides, including the British and the Americans, were desperate to know what would happen next. The Allies had just invaded the Italian mainland at Salerno and were trying to work out what the German plans were to defend Italy. What would they do with Italy's Jews, and what did the Pope know in advance of these German plans?

Meanwhile, how did Ernst von Weizsäcker, Germany's Ambassador to the Vatican, help fuel the anti-communist fears of Pius XII and work with Karl Wolff to oppose Hitler's plans to occupy the Holy City? The Vatican diplomatic corps had made it clear they were united behind the Pope. If the Germans tried to kidnap him, take over Vatican territory or detain him as their prisoner, 'all the heads of diplomatic missions in the Holy City will see it as their duty not only to protest against this violence, but to demand to accompany the Holy Father'.[12]

By late on 6 October, Kappler realised his team was being strengthened by the arrival of Theodor Dannecker and informed Kaltenbrunner that the Gestapo and SD team in Rome were now in a stronger position and could manage to deport the Italian Jews to Germany. However, he noted cautiously that Kesselring might still insist on the Jews working as civil defence labourers:

> To Highest SS and Police Chief Italy, Ogruf Wolff RSHA has sent SS Hptstuf DANNECKER to this end with order to seize all Jews in lightning actions and to forward them to GERMANY.
>
> Because of the attitude in the town and uncertain conditions, action could not be carried through in NAPLES. Office preparations for action in Rome have been concluded. Kesselring has been informed whether taking into consideration the limitations of the general political situation … carrying through of measures against Jews possibly for employment on defensive works.[13]

But neither Dannecker nor Kappler could start their round-up operations without the explicit go-ahead of both Himmler and the Foreign Minister, Joachim von Ribbentrop. Fearing that if they arrested Rome's Jews, the Pope would effectively mobilise the entire Italian civilian population against them, the SS hesitated and waited for orders. A delegation of senior German officers and diplomats had suggested, in the above intercepted OSS message, that the Jews could be used for forced labour in Italy itself, instead of being transported to concentration camps. But both Von Ribbentrop and Ernst Kaltenbrunner, head of the RSHA, were adamant. Put them on trains to Auschwitz.

Virginia Montalcini. From an
Italian Jewish family in Turin,
she was captured while trying to
escape to Switzerland in January
1944, then murdered in Auschwitz.
(CDEC Milano)

Riccardo Pacifici, Chief Rabbi
of the Genoa Jewish Community
from 1936 until he was deported
to Auschwitz in December 1943.
(CDEC Milano)

Wanda Abenaim, arrested by the SS in Florence and taken to Auschwitz on the same train as her husband, Riccardo Pacifici. (CDEC Milano)

Italian Jewish banker Ettore Ovazza and his wife Nella, murdered by the SS while trying to flee to Switzerland in 1943. (CDEC Milano)

The Convent of Santa Brigida in the
Piazza Farnese in Rome; the nuns hid
Italian Jews here after the German
occupation. (Author's collection)

The Fatebenefratelli hospital, set
on an island in the Tiber River.
(Author's collection)

The former Jewish Ghetto in Rome, the scene of the October 1943 roundup of some of the capital's Jews. (Author's collection)

QUI HA STUDIATO
VIRGINIA
MONTALCINI
NATA 1920
ARRESTATA 23.1.1944
DEPORTATA 30.1.1944
AUSCHWITZ
ASSASSINATA 6.2.1944

The *pietra d'inciampo*, or memorial plaque, to Virginia Montalcini, set outside her former high school in Turin. (Author's collection)

Classical carvings adorn the entrance to a house in Rome's Jewish quarter. (Author's collection)

The interior of the synagogue in Casale Monferrato, east of Turin. (Author's collection)

At Via Rasella in Rome the walls still bear the blast marks from the 1944 partisan ambush of SS policemen. (Author's collection)

Herbert Kappler, head of the SD and Gestapo in Rome, after his capture by the Allies. (ARCHIVIO GBB / Alamy Stock Photo)

Obergruppenführer Karl Wolff, Supreme SS and Police Leader in Italy. (AF archive/Alamy Stock Photo

SS–Obergruppenführer Ernst Kaltenbrunner. (Sueddeutsche Zeitung Photo/Alamy Stock Photo)

Italian champion cyclist Gino Bartali, who helped rescue Italian Jews. (INTERFOTO/ Alamy Stock Photo)

Pope Pius XII. (Everett Collection Historical/Alamy Stock Photo)

Sir D'Arcy Osborne, British diplomatic envoy to The Holy See. (Keystone/ Stringer/Getty Images)

ARREST AND DEPORTATION

The British at Bletchley Park, meanwhile, decrypted a much longer and more detailed message sent on 10 October from Kaltenbrunner to Kappler. This was passed on to the British Ambassador, D'Arcy Osborne. The Germans encoded it, naturally, but as it was sent to Italy both by SS signals analysts and then again, in its entirety, by crypt-analysts from Pers Z S at the German Foreign Office, it meant that Bletchley Park's code-breakers had two identical 'parallel texts' from which to work, making its decryption much easier. The signal made clear the intentions of the SS:

> … precisely the immediate and thorough eradication of the Jews in Italy which is the special interest of the present internal political situation and the general security in Italy. To postpone the expulsion of the Jews can no more be considered … the longer the delay, the more the Jews who are doubtless reckoning on evacuation measures have an opportunity by moving to the houses of Jewish Italians or disappearing completely … Italy has been instructed to proceed with the R.F.S.S [Reichsführer SS] orders to proceed with the evacuation of the Jews without further delay.[1]

The German Military Commander of Rome, General Reiner Stahel, was extremely wary that any action against the Jews of Rome would draw condemnation from the Pope. This had been confirmed by a warning from an Austrian bishop, Alois Hudal, who was Rector of the German Church in Rome. This condemnation would never actually materialise, as all parties, Allied, German, Swiss, Italian and German, would testify.

Stahel decided against ordering the deportation without official authority from the German Foreign Ministry. Mussolini's Fascist state-let in German-controlled northern Italy was called the Italian Social Republic, or the Republic of Salò. Germany's Deputy Consul General there was Eitel Friedrich Mollhausen, and he went so far as to write a signal to Foreign Minister Joachim von Ribbentrop, with instructions on the top of it that it be read by the minister himself. This signal contained the key word 'liquidation'.

Ribbentrop was allegedly furious, as it put him in a position where he had to either approve the signal, and be further complicit in the Holocaust, or clash, head to head, with Himmler and Kaltenbrunner, which was even more dangerous. He wanted to suggest to the RSHA that the Roman Jews be interned in Italian camps rather than be deported, and he wanted to change Himmler and Kaltenbrunner's minds, but ultimately Ribbentrop never dared to act against the SS and SD, from whom Stahel received his orders.

Meanwhile, Karl Wolff was allegedly under orders to carry out a plan to kidnap the Pope and take him to Liechtenstein. Karl Wolff said that he had been ordered by Hitler to co-ordinate a plot to kidnap Pius XII and remove him to a castle outside of the country. Both Rudolph Rahn and Eitel Möllhausen, respectively the ambassador and deputy ambassador to the Salò government, reported that they heard about this plan too. They were backed up in this by Eugene Dollman, who was an SS officer who liaised between Wolff and Albert Kesselring.

At his end, D'Arcy Osborne thought that the British Political Warfare Office considered it was good propaganda to disseminate the rumour that Hitler was just about to kidnap the Pope. The British propaganda office therefore made up least two German wireless broadcasts in support of the theory. First, on 9 October 1943, the British released a fake German broadcast claiming that all preparations had been made for such a kidnapping. Then, two days later, another falsified transmission stated that Liechtenstein Castle in Württemberg was ready to imprison the Pope and his cardinals.[2] Osborne allegedly thought that it was highly unlikely that the Germans would carry out such a kidnapping, as the Pope's very presence in the Vatican prevented the British from bombing the key communications centre of the German Army in southern Italy, which was close to the Holy City.

Karl Wolff claimed that on 13 September 1943, Hitler gave the directive to 'occupy Vatican City, secure its files and art treasures, and take the Pope and Curia to the north'. Hitler, said Wolff, allegedly did not want the Pope to 'fall into the hands of the Allies'.[3] Wilhelm Canaris told his Italian counter-intelligence counterpart, General Cesare Ame, about the plot, and allegedly it was shelved.

The Jewish ghetto in Rome, meanwhile, sat on the edge of the River Tiber, around Piazza Giudea. At a quarter past five in the morning of 16 October 1943, 300 soldiers from three different SS police battalions surrounded the four cramped city blocks. Kappler had decided that Italian soldiers and police would not be involved, as they were considered unreliable and would leak details of the operation.

At half-past five that morning, Speranza Sonnino, who was 13, awoke to the sound of somebody hammering on her door and a voice shouting for her mother. The Germans were coming for the men, and her mother, Elisabetta, had to get their father, Umberto, into hiding.

Speranza had assumed that the Germans would only arrest adult men, but a quarter of an hour later, the same voice called at the door again and screamed that the Germans were taking the old people and the children too – everybody. The family were saved by their poverty. Being too poor to own suitcases, they clutched the few belongings they had and walked down to their front door, which opened onto the Via del Portico d'Ottavia. A woman from a restaurant next door told them to get back inside as four SS men were in the street nearby. Without suitcases, however, they did not look like refugees or people trying to flee.[4]

The prisoners who had been arrested were rounded up into a large group and herded into the front of the ancient arch of the Portico d'Ottavia, which ran through the centre of the ghetto. It had been built by the first emperor, Augustus, for his sister. For nearly 1,000 years it had been a fish market, with a church behind it. The SS arrested 1,259 people in the raid, of whom 363 were men, 689 women and 207 children. The Germans discovered that over 200 of them either came from mixed marriages or weren't Jews and so released them.

On the afternoon of 16 October they took the remaining 1,023 prisoners to a military college in Trastevere and locked them in. The building was very close to the Vatican, and the detention operation prompted Ambassador Weizsäcker to write that the arrest and confinement operation took place 'under his [the Pope's] very windows'.[5]

On 15 October, Heinrich Müller (head of the Gestapo) and a German Foreign Office official discussed how difficult it was to arrest Jews in countries with limited police manpower. He was unsure about Hitler's order to round up the Jews of Rome.

Kappler wanted to deport them immediately on the 16th, but another dozen Jews were then added to the list of arrestees. They had been found hiding very close to one of the SD officials. The porous nature of SS security, and the ease with which Jews could conceal themselves from the Germans, was demonstrated by the fact that at least six of these Jews were discovered staying in the same Rome hotel as Theodor Dannecker. He had only discovered this when Kappler, mockingly, informed him of it.

The Vatican had had forewarning that the operation would take place and knew what the almost certain fate of the detained Jews would be. It is also certain that while the Vatican began a laborious process of written and verbal complaints to the German diplomatic and military authorities, hundreds of other Catholic clergy took the arrests as a green light to begin their rescue operations of Italy's Jews.

On 16 October, Kappler reported to Kaltenbrunner that German forces had managed to seize 1,259 Roman Jews despite the unreliability of the Italian police and opposition from the Italian public itself. Although the German police had to release the part-Jews, foreign Jews and families in mixed marriages, they still had 1,029 people they could deport on 18 October. These included those at the military college and the twelve found in and near Theodor Dannecker's hotel.

Meanwhile, the coded messages coming out of Rome by 17 October left nobody in any doubt as to what was taking place. 'The SD is now pillaging Rome … Himmler has sent SS men who have had experience of this work in Russia to Rome', was one Enigma-encrypted signal read by Bletchley Park on 17 October, sent by the Swiss diplomatic legation in Rome to their Foreign Ministry in Berne:

```
7868    GROUP XIII/52                                            V
        ROME TO BERLIN
        RSS 305, 306/16/10/43; 81/17/10/43
        ? on 5404 kcs.                  2110-2125, 2208 GMT 16/10/4?
        CT 1610/1930/GR 81, 95, 164

        Action against Jews started and finished today in
        accordance with a plan worked out as well as possible
        by the office. All available forces of the
        Sicherheitspol. and the Ordnungspol. employed.
        Participation of the Italian-police was not possible
        in view of unreliability in this respect, as only
        possible by individual arrests in quick succession
        inside the 26 action districts. To cordon off
        whole blocks of streets, in view both of (ROME's)
        character as an open city and of the insufficient
        number of German police, 365 in all, not
        practicable. In spite of this 1259 persons were
        arrested in Jewish homes and taken to assembly
        camp(s) of the military school here in the course
        of the action which lasted from 0530 to 1400 hours.
        After the release of those of mixed blood, of
        foreigners including a Vatican citizen, of the
        families in mixed marriages including the Jewish
        partner, and of the Aryan servants and lodgers,
        there remain 1002 Jews to be detained. Transportation

   7658  on Monday, 18[?]/10 at 0900. Escort by 39 men[?]
   Contd. of the Ordnungspolizei[?]. Attitude of the
         Italian population was unequivocally one of
         passive resistance, which in a large number of
         individual cases has developed into active
         assistance. In one case, for example, the police
         were met at a house-door by a Fascist with an
         identity document and in a black shirt, he having
         undoubtedly taken over the Jewish house only an
         hour before and alleged it to be his own [45
         letters missing or corrupt] of German police
         into the house ... in neighbouring appartments ..
         were observed the whole time and [75 letters
         missing] part of the population did not make an
         appearance during the action, but only the broad
         masses, who in individual cases even attempted
         to keep single policemen back from the Jews,
         ... by the pistol .. [rest of message missing].
```

```
7458    GROUP XIII/52
        BERLIN to ROME
        RSS 256/11/10/43                         ✓
        GL on 6556 kcs        1902/15 GMT    11/10/43        V
        1955/156

/in     To KAPPLER.  It is precisely the immediate and thorough
        eradication of the Jews in ITALY which is/the special
        interest of the present internal political situation and
        the general security in ITALY.  To postpone:the expulsion
        of the Jews until the CARABINIERI and the Italian army
        officers have been removed can no more be considered
        than the idea mentioned of calling up the Jews in ITALY
        for what would probably be very improductive labour under
    (   responsible direction by Italian authorities.  The longer
        the delay, the more the Jews who are doubtless reckoning
        on evacuationmeasures have an opportunity by moving to
        the houses of pro-Jewish Italians of disappearing
        completely [is corrupt] ITALY [has been] instructed in
        executing the RFSS orders to proceed with the evacuation
        of the Jews without further delay.
                            ⟍ KALTENBRUNNER. Ogr.
```

While the Vatican knew the German intentions, the Germans still didn't know whether the Pope would formally and strongly object to this round-up of Rome's Jews. The pontiff was lobbying the United States to receive Jewish refugees and the Germans feared Italy's Jews would escape, although Italy's Fascist Social Republic now said it would assist the Germans in the execution of the Final Solution. The Vatican had received vital advance warning, which in part had allowed Jews to escape: the most crucial warning it had was the intercepted German message from the RSHA.

❖

While the SS in Rome and Berlin were simultaneously rounding up Rome's Jews and playing a muscular game of diplomacy with the Vatican, the Supreme Commander in Italy, Albert Kesselring, was busy. He was desperately trying to work out where the Allies would strike next. The Jews of Rome were, for him, a matter to be handled by Kaltenbrunner and Himmler.

He was trying to fight a defensive war against the largest army that had ever set foot on the territory of Italy, or the Roman Empire, in its entire history. The American and British armies, along with Canadians, New Zealanders, Poles and fifteen others, were now firmly established on the beachheads around Salerno and on the Adriatic coast. Their air forces could now fly in towards German-occupied territory from Sicily, Pantelleria, southern Italy, north Africa and Corsica. Messages were rushing in: 'hold the line', his orders said. 'Keep the Allies as far south of Rome as possible.' Berlin, he knew, was fighting on every front possible.

In Rome, a new Italian government had sworn allegiance to the Allies and declared war on Germany on 13 October. This new government was formally totally separate from, and at odds with, the Fascist government of Mussolini's new Social Republic.

And at home? The Reich was burning. Five days before, nearly 300 American Flying Fortresses had tried to bomb the ball-bearing factories at Schweinfurt in Bavaria. Losses had been high among the attackers, but it showed that every part of Germany, day or night, was now likely to be targeted.

One of the most extraordinary bits of news Kesselring heard came from the RSHA. There had been a mass break-out at Sobibor concentration camp in Poland: 300 prisoners had escaped and killed eleven SS officers. Kesselring's strategic world seemed to be shuddering.

So when, on 19 October, he heard from Herbert Kappler what the Vatican was doing, it only added further problems. Well, not so much the Vatican, said Kappler, as an Irish priest called O'Flaherty. The Gestapo chief had sent a signal to Berlin, saying that O'Flaherty, in the guise of the head of the American Red Cross at the Vatican, had been spreading information about the probability of further Allied landings in Italy. On the mainland east of Rome, to be precise:

> The representative of the American Red Cross at the VATICAN, the Irishman Monsignor O'Flaherty who is a friend of the envoy Osborne, told a reliable informant during a discussion today, among other things, that, in addition to four to five Italian divisions, there were now also two American divisions on SARDINIA. As a landing by the Anglo-Americans in the BALKANS was not desired by the Russians, the former (he said) were obliged to make progress in ITALY their objective. O'FLAHERTY declared that there was a probability of an

imminent landing from SARDINIA between CIVITAVECCHIA and LEGHORN.

OBS and BDS informed. KAPPLER.[6]

The Pope, meanwhile, was also circulating instructions and secret letters via his staff and via his Cardinal Secretary of State, Luigi Maglione. These were sent and hand-delivered, not just to Vatican *nuncios,* but to selected Catholic convents, churches and seminaries in Rome, to put into operation plans to conceal thousands of the capital's Jews. Cardinal Montini noted on 18 October that the Vatican was doing everything in its power to help the Jews. Among the requests for help received from members of their community was one note dated the 17th, which was addressed to the Pope. The sender had included no address and so it proved impossible to reply:

> From Madam X, 65 years old, in precarious state of health, she has been arrested unexpectedly on the 16th October, in the roundup of Jews, with consequent indescribable damage to her health and morale. So she prays to his Eminence [the Pope] to somehow intervene so as soon as possible she can regain her freedom.[7]

Meanwhile, almost nobody had been allowed into the Military College where the Germans were holding the people they had arrested. One man who did manage to gain access, however, was a priest called Father Igino Quadraroli, from the 2nd Section of the Vatican's Secretariat of State. On the morning after the '*razzia*', he went into the Palazzo Salviati in the Lungotevere:

> Thanks to the prayers of good people, I was able to enter the military college, where many poor Jews of humble condition are staying. They wouldn't let me talk to any of them, but I was able to leave a package of food with the names of the recipients, among whom is an 80-year-old man. The person who sent me told me that these poor people could not get any food or drink yesterday. I saw them in the classrooms from afar, then queuing up to get bread. I noticed

a poor woman signalling to an SS sentry that her child needed to be
left alone. I saw the sentry flatly deny it. I also saw a car leaving with
some doctors from St Spirito [hospital] who had gone to treat the
poor people who had been beaten. Inmates are not allowed to have
clothing, but are only allowed to provide food, and even a few lines of
correspondence, which one understands, can be a trap.[8]

The Vatican now estimated that if it issued an extra-territorial order of
immunity over its properties in Rome, this would prevent the Germans
searching them, and so Jews might be able to conceal themselves inside
these buildings. The SS, however, was another quantity entirely:

General Stahel will probably respect the extra-territorial buildings,
convents, etc. ... but certainly not the SS, which, as is well known,
acts under the orders of its own commanders. The attitude of the
church seems to him [Stahel] to make it easier for Jews, deserters
etc. to enter convents – this is because of the fact that the ecclesiastical authorities are guided by their good hearts and by the principles
of Christian charity ... but when up against the SS it is necessary
to be guided above all by prudence so as not to compromise the
interests of the Church and the refugees themselves by an act of mis-
guided charity.[9]

The Vatican was thinking on its feet, exploring multiple different
methods of hiding the Roman Jews, often in plain sight. On
18 October, two days after the round-up, the Holy See began asking the
Commissioner of Police in Rome if the number of men serving in the
Corps of the Palatine Guard could be increased. This organisation was
akin to a local police force that patrolled and safeguarded the dozens
of Vatican properties – churches, convents, houses, palazzos – that lay
outside of the actual walls of the Holy City itself.

Up until the arrival of the Germans, there were 150 of these men in
the ad hoc police unit. Now the Vatican asked to increase this number
to 2,000. It was looking for 1,850 extra officers. The Pope's Secretary of
State had made the first request to Italian military and police authorities

on 16 October, while the *retata* of Jews was progressing.[10] Nearly 2,000 extra men to be recruited meant the Vatican could, potentially, find a place to hide Jewish men. It was an attempt to protect Jews, the Vatican was to claim later.[11]

The Germans, however, tried to block the plan, demanding to have baptismal certificates, ages and dates of birth for all of the men. The Catholic priests in charge of the scheme paused while they investigated the possibility of new, fake documents for these new 'policemen'.

As they were doing this, on 20 October SS-Brigadeführer Wilhelm Harster, the Commander of the Security Police and SD for Italy, reported that the first transport of Jews had left Rome:

> Request express W/T dispatch to BDS Vienna and BDS Prague. Transport of Jews from ROME left ROME on 18th at 0900 hours with transport No.X70469 and is travelling via ARNOLDSTEIN to AUSCHWITZ. Since the Orpo (Ordnungspolizei) detachment is urgently required at this end, please find out times of passing through and arrange relief of the escort detachment by ORPO from your area.
> Dr. Harster SS Brigadeführer.[12]

The Vatican also received a fragment of news about the deportation convoy that had left Rome on the 18th. On 25 October, a Bishop Agostini sent a message to Cardinal Maglione from Padua. Several days previously, he said, a deportation train of Jews had passed through the city, which lies 15 miles west of Venice, in north-eastern Italy. The messages that had reached Agostini from the train, which he, in turn, had passed on, indicated that the deportees were in a deplorable condition, and they wanted to let the bishop know that they'd passed through Padua. Could the Holy Father do something? Even with just prayers and benediction?[13]

By 28 October, Maglione had more news. The train had now reached Vienna. The prisoners were demanding water. One of them, a 70-year-old former admiral from Venice called Augusto Capon, had managed to sneak a message out at Bologna Station, an hour south of Padua. The news he was trying to get to his family was brief: we're going through

Bologna; the situation's secret; we're worried the prisoners are being taken somewhere with a poor climate, and many of them are only wearing the light clothes they had on when arrested.

The message got to the Vatican via a circuitous route, through a conversation which had taken place on 25 October in Rome between an unnamed Jewish man and the Argentinian Ambassador to Italy.[14] But by then it was too late. The train carrying Admiral Capon and the other deportees had already reached Auschwitz on 23 October. Capon was gassed on arrival. The Final Solution in Italy was now under way.

THE SS NETWORK IN ITALY

Two days after the first deportation convoy had left Tiburtina Station, Adolf Eichmann ordered the Rome *Einsatzkommando* to head north. Kaltenbrunner wanted to keep up the momentum of deportations that had begun – however falteringly – in Rome the previous week. So he ordered Theodor Dannecker to take five men and head to Tuscany, Florence and Siena. Herbert Kappler, as Gestapo chief, was to stay put in the capital and concentrate on three priorities.

First, an estimated 7,000–8,500 Italian Jews had managed to evade arrest and deportation. Where were they? Where were their hiding places? They had to be found, rounded up and transferred by rail convoy. Kappler should signal Berlin as soon as this operation was under way.

Second, within Rome there were clearly networks of churches, convents, houses and apartments where Jews were being sheltered, certainly with the help of the Vatican and the thousands of priests and nuns in Rome. He must close down these hiding places. 'Find these Jews' was the order. Who, within the Vatican, was helping them? What group of agents was Osborne operating? And there was that troublesome Irish priest called O'Flaherty, too.

Third, partisan networks within Rome were almost certainly helping the Jews as well, enabling some of them to travel outside of the capital to take refuge in the countryside. He must find, isolate and arrest these partisans. Were there British or American agents working with them? And what about Italian soldiers and police who had deserted, stayed loyal to the king and were now almost certainly helping the Allies? Herbert Kappler had his work cut out.

The Network of SS and SD Commanders in Italy

With the five men Dannecker would take to Tuscany, he would liaise with the head of the Gestapo and SD detachments, as well as with the German Consul in Florence, Gerhard Wolf. The network of SS and SD officials installed across northern Italy was now in place. SS-Gruppenführer Karl Wolff, as the Supreme SS and Police Plenipotentiary for Italy, was in overall command of this, but orders would also be incoming from Kaltenbrunner and the RSHA.

In Milan and Genoa, overall command for the execution of the Final Solution was given to SS-Standartenführer Walter Rauff, a former naval officer who had joined the SS and then become a protege of Reinhard Heydrich in 1937. He returned to the navy and then joined the RSHA as Head of Technical Affairs in 1940, heading up the SD operations in newly occupied Norway.

It was during Operation Reinhard in Poland, however, that Rauff had turned his technical skills to the logistical problem of disposing of Jews, communists and Polish Catholics. He invented what became termed 'mobile gassing vans'. With these, the exhaust fumes from the engines of specially modified trucks were diverted into a chamber above the back of the chassis, in which twenty-five to sixty prisoners could be carried at one time.

In 1942, Rauff was posted to Tunisia, then controlled by Vichy France, where he set up a special SS execution squad, which was meant to follow behind Erwin Rommel's Afrika Korps as it advanced. Up until May 1943, Rauff led this SD *Einsatzkommando*, which killed an estimated 2,500 Jews in Tunisia. He also began an operation to loot gold, jewellery, silver and Jewish religious artefacts as the German front line withdrew.

After the Allies took over Tunisia and then invaded Sicily, Rauff's next command was in Milan, with responsibility given for Turin and Genoa as well. The arrest and deportation of Jews and the appropriation – theft, in other words – of their property was his remit. One of his SS superiors described his work in these three cities as 'a superb achievement'.[1] A later assessment of Rauff made by the British found:

> Rauff has brought his organisation of political gangsterism to stream-lined perfection and is proud of the fact. By nature cynical and overbearing, but cunning and shifty rather than intelligent, he regards his [past] activities as a matter of course.[2]

Under his command in Turin, Milan and Genoa, Rauff had two officers who were to become intricately implicated in the arrest and deportation of Jews in those cities. The first of these was in Milan and Turin, where he was the head of the Gestapo and the Italian Fascist Police – he was an SS-Hauptsturmführer called Theodor Saevecke. He joined the SS in 1938, and after the invasion of Poland, worked as a member of an *Einsatzkommando* there. He had served in Tunisia with Rauff, and in northern Italy his main operational remit was, not just the arrest operations of Italian Jews, but the logistical arrangements for their onward deportation into Austria and Poland.

In Genoa, SS-Lieutenant Guido Zimmer was in charge, although his operational area also included working under Rauff in Milan. Zimmer, in his turn, had joined the SS in 1938, and was posted to its foreign intelligence service, the SD. By 1940, he was working in the German Embassy in Rome under a diplomatic cover. He spoke Italian and spent his time setting up a network of contacts from among Italy's diplomatic community and Italian Fascists who controlled business interests. One evening, Zimmer was at a diplomatic reception where his cover as a German diplomat was blown by an Italian Fascist intelligence officer who had also had dealings with him in his alter-ego with the SD. Berlin called Zimmer back to work at the RSHA.

Wilhelm Harster, meanwhile, had joined the SS in 1933, and the SD in 1935. He was almost alone among his group of SS peers in Italy in that he had served in an infantry, artillery or cavalry unit on a front line, in an active service operation. During the invasion of France in 1940, Harster had been a machine gunner in an infantry company, before re-joining the SD. This short spell of front-line service ended when he moved to join the SD office in the Netherlands, after the invasion. For three years, from July 1940 to August 1943, he ran this operation and was an integral part of the SD and SS arrest and deportation operations, which saw 104,000 Dutch Jews transported to Auschwitz and Sobibor. Among them was Anne Frank.

When he arrived in Italy in summer 1943, he set up his headquarters in Verona, east of Milan. To liaise between him, Dannecker, Saevecke and the Italian Fascist government in Salò, Wolff appointed another *Einsatzkommando* veteran. Willy Tensfeld was an SS colonel who came from a small town south of Kiel in Schleswig-Holstein, and like his other colleagues in Italy, he had experience working with an *Einsatzkommando* in Russia. Between August 1941 and May 1943, he had served in Kharkov as the SS and police leader there. As liaison officer with the Salò government, Tensfeld was based in the city of Bologna, sitting in the shadow of the Apennines between Florence and Milan.

The SS and SD central offices in the country thus stretched in a line from south to north – Rome, Florence, Bologna – and then from west to east, from Genoa to Turin, Milan, Verona and Bolzano. These eight cities and towns, set in the shape of a diagonal 'T', dictated the layout of the main railway system and the subsequent routes that deportation trains would take.

From anywhere in Italy, from the principal cities and German deportation camps, these trains would be heading for the Italian and Austrian border at Tarvisio and Arnoldstein, which lay in the far north-east of Italy in the traversal gaps between the Dolomite mountains. These two towns lay on either side of the intersection of the frontiers of three countries – Italy, Austria and the adjacent Slovenian territory, then the Kingdom of Yugoslavia.

Anybody trying to smuggle or transport goods or human beings from north-eastern Italy into south-eastern Austria, and vice versa, legitimately or illegitimately, by road or rail, had four possible routes to choose from. Running from west to east, the first was the road that crossed into Austria at the intersection of that country's border with Italy and Switzerland, in the shadow of the Ötztal Alps. Moving east, the next was the main road and rail crossing at the Brenner Pass, north of Bolzano – the railway line that adjoined the road connecting Innsbruck with Verona. Forty miles south-east from the Brenner Pass there was the third road that led from Italy into Austria, at San Candido Innichen.

The most easterly of all was the road and railway line that crossed into Austria, 2 miles north of Tarvisio. This was the railway route that led to eastern Austria, Villach, Klagenfurt and Vienna, after which connections in three possible directions westwards, east and northwards would eventually lead to the camp complexes of Mauthausen and Auschwitz-Birkenau. On 18 October 1943, when the first deportation train carrying Italian Jews had left Rome, it was along this line that it had travelled. From Verona and Treviso, outside Venice, the railway line branched north-east towards Udine and then to Tarvisio, and the border.

From the south-east, any train coming towards Austria from the port of Trieste, on the border with Yugoslavia, would also cross the border at the Tarvisio frontier point. The SS was just beginning to use this line to transport Italian, Croatian and Slovenian prisoners. It had centralised these people in the Risiera di San Sabba detention centre and concentration camp in Trieste and was sending them from there on the journey towards Auschwitz and Mauthausen. The transport links went the other way, too. In summer and autumn 1943, the SS and Wehrmacht divisions arriving by rail into Italy from Hungary and Austria had also thundered down this route via Tarvisio, as well as across the Brenner Pass from Austria.

Across the Italian border lay the eastern Austrian state of Carinthia. Its regional capital was the city of Klagenfurt, 40 miles north-east of Tarvisio. Officers at the Gestapo headquarters there were also centrally involved in the planning for the Final Solution in Italy.

That August, SS-Sturmbannführer Kurt Christmann had arrived in Klagenfurt to take over the Gestapo contingent and to lead part of the planning. He had extensive experience in arrest and deportation operations, having commanded an *Einsatzkommando* in the Crimea in 1942.

By summer 1943, this Bavarian Gestapo officer was involved, along with his colleagues across the border, in the logistics of how to get the Jewish population of Italy out of the country once arrest and deportation operations had begun and the Jews had been physically put onto trains.

Klagenfurt – and Christmann's operation there – was important because of its geography. To get to the camp systems of Auschwitz and Mauthausen, which lay in north central Austria and southern Poland respectively, Klagenfurt, Tarvisio and their marshalling yards and the railways connecting them were a crucial transport hub. The Germans knew they had to protect these towns and railways as best as possible, both from partisan sabotage and from Allied air attack, so that cattle trucks carrying thousands of Italian Jews could run safely through them.[3] If the Allies could destroy the railway lines at Tarvisio – and the RAF and USAAF were flying raids solely with this aim – it was possible to block all rail transport out of Italy.

By summer 1943, the Brenner Pass railway route was still functioning, and provided one other way out of north-eastern Italy for Holocaust transports. The third possible railway route out of the country ran along the Italian Riviera, from Liguria into France, but this was clearly not a feasible option for any transport trying to reach Austria, southern Germany or Poland.

The SS, Gestapo and SD teams in Rome, Milan, Genoa, Turin and Verona were operational by late October 1943. Far to the east, on the border with the Slovenian territory of Yugoslavia, was the important port city of Trieste. Mussolini had annexed some of the western parts of Yugoslavia, including the coastal territory of Istria, and parts of northeastern Slovenia and Croatia when his armies moved into Croatia in 1941. He claimed the area as part of Italy. The fiercely independent Croats and Slovenes, both communist and Catholic, formed partisan groups, which were prepared to fight bitterly to prove otherwise.

When Italy surrendered in July 1943 and its Fascist troops relinquished control of the area, the Germans swiftly took over. They formed parts of these coastal regions, along with the adjacent Italian territory of Friuli Venezia Giulia, into a separate administrative zone. They called it the Operational Zone of the Adriatic Littoral, or the *Operationszone*

Adriatisches Küstenland (OZAK). The headquarters was in Trieste, and to run it, Hitler appointed the *Gauleiter*, or governor, of the Austrian state of Carinthia. This Reich Defence Commissioner of OZAK was SS-Obergruppenführer Friedrich Rainer, who had joined the SS in 1933 and had, since then, been involved in the provincial government of Carinthia, in Klagenfurt. As Governor of the Adriatic Littoral, he was responsible for the now-annexed parts of Yugoslavia and the whole Italian area of Friuli Venezia Giulia, which included Venice. To implement the Final Solution in this area, Rainer brought with him to Trieste a former deputy, Odilo Globocnik.

The network of SS and SD officers who were installed across Italy by autumn 1943 – Wolff, Kappler, Rauff, Dannecker and their colleagues – were all men experienced in the logistical organisation and ruthless implementation of racially oriented mass murder. Fierce antisemites, every one of them had commanded or held rank in an *Einsatzkommando* or national Jewish deportation programme. Hundreds of thousands of men, women and children had been murdered under their remit. Yet, even by their standards of atrocity-broking, Globocnik was more extreme.

He stands as a highly illustrative example of the kind of SS official involved in the implementation of the Holocaust in Italy. On the one hand, an accomplished functionary in the administration of mass death; on the other, a small-minded, socially insecure and deeply racist criminal, whose principal personal aim was stealing as much money, gold and jewellery as possible from his victims. The combination of the two – along with the extraordinary daily pressure brought to bear from superiors in Berlin in every signal, every coded message, at every personal meeting – made men like Globocnik behave with a totalitarian ruthlessness. And that trait, as well as adherence to the orders process, lay behind the high number of Jews murdered in the areas under their control.

An Austrian Nazi who had been a member of the SS since 1933, Globocnik was originally from Trieste. His father had been a cavalry lieutenant in the Austro-Hungarian Army, and was, crucially, a Slovenian. Bitterly ridiculed on account of his Slavic surname, both at school and when he became involved in Austrian politics in neighbouring

Carinthia, the lumbering, resentful Globocnik claimed his family roots were, in fact, truly Aryan. In 1933, he was involved in a bomb attack on a Jewish jeweller's shop in Vienna, one of the first antisemitic murders in the country.

The insecure former railway porter now soared through the ranks of the Austrian SS, becoming a deputy governor in Vienna and Carinthia, and chief of staff of the national Nazi Party. When the *Anschluss* came in 1938, Hitler made him *Gauleiter* of Vienna. Globocnik used his increasing power to take revenge on both Austrians and Slovenes who had previously stood in his way or victimised him and his family – and also to implement a programme of substantial, dishonest, personal enrichment.

When Himmler discovered that his loyal apparatchik was deeply involved in illegal currency trading, he demoted him to corporal and transferred him to the Waffen-SS, with which Globocnik served in the invasion of Poland. But the capricious Himmler, who liked Globocnik and admired his bitter, brutal ruthlessness, then swiftly pardoned him, promoted him overnight to SS-Brigadeführer (brigadier general) and sent him into occupied Poland. It was there that he seemed to come into his own.

In November 1939, Himmler appointed him SS and police leader in the Lublin district of the General Government in Poland. Along with an SS colleague, Christian Wirth, who would later also operate in Trieste, Globocnik oversaw the development of the industrialised programme of mass murder in Poland, code-named Operation Reinhardt. Along with the construction and daily functioning of camps at Belzec, Sobibor, Treblinka and Majdanek, he helped put into action the rest of the secret plans to murder the Polish Jews in the General Government District. Ultimately, some 1.5 million Polish, Czech, Austrian, French, German and other Jews would die in these camps under Globocnik's extermination programme.

Then, in 1943, after the Italian Armistice, he and Christian Wirth arrived in Trieste. He code-named his team operating in the coastal city *Einsatzkommando Reinhardt*, or Einsatz R. He brought with him ninety-two members of the Ukrainian SS, both men and women, who had worked with him in Poland. They took an old rice-processing plant in the southern outskirts of Trieste, called the Risiera di San Sabba, and converted it into an ad hoc concentration camp. Erwin Lambert, a building foreman who had overseen the construction of the crematoria at Sobibor and Treblinka, travelled to Trieste to install a crematorium at San Sabba, the only one in the whole of Italy.

Globocnik brought something else with him to Italy. When the Jews had arrived at the four concentration camps in Poland, they brought with them a substantial quantity of gold coins, bullion, jewels and other valuables. Operation Reinhardt collected 4,700kg of gold alone, which was shipped back in trains to Berlin, to the RSHA's coffers.[4] But Globocnik, playing with scalding fire by breaking strict SS regulations, took his own cut, and when he arrived in Trieste, he brought it with him. It included gold coins, small gold ingots, gemstones, gold-covered Russian religious icons, an eighteenth-century silver Jewish Torah case and a pair of silver-mounted flintlock pistols.

With him also came three former deputies from Poland, all SS Sturmbannführers: Ernst Lerch, Georg Michaelsen and Hermann Hofle. The latter had been second-in-command on Operation Reinhardt. Globocnik knew them and trusted them all – he had been best man at Lerch's wedding to a female Gestapo officer. Like their SS and SD colleagues in their zones of command across Italy, the Trieste team now got to work.

As they did so, the Vatican was searching desperately for the Jews missing from Rome and sending protests to the Germans about the situation in Trieste. The Vatican had sent an initial report to the German Embassy in Rome about the 1,000 or more persons who had vanished, containing the names of people who were classified as 'non-Aryan', 'semi-Aryan' and 'related to non-Aryans'. Families of those missing had made a huge number of requests for help and a pile of reports had accumulated, said the Vatican:

> In a conversation that the German Ambassador had with one Vatican official, Von Weiszacker had himself made it clear that there was little or nothing he could do to interest himself in [the fate of] these poor people, even if only to get news [about them].[5]

In Trieste, meanwhile, the situation for the Jewish population deteriorated fast as soon as Rainer and Globocnik arrived. The ancient Adriatic port had a sizeable community living in and around it, second only in size to that of Rome. The Archbishop of Trieste had made a desperate intercession to the Vatican on behalf of Jews from the region of Friuli Venezia Giulia, who were now threatened with deportation. Cardinal Maglione, in turn, protested to Ambassador Weizsäcker again on 26 November. It seemed that, despite the introduction and application of stricter racial rules and regulations, the Germans in the Adriatic Coastal Zone, under Friedrich Rainer and Odilo Globocnik, were now simply arresting all and any Jews and taking their property, regardless of whether they were baptised, non-baptised, married to a Catholic, or fell under any of the particular clauses for special treatment. For the Jews in the Adriatic Zone, the OZAK, there was now no way out.

The Vatican, with no real means to stop what was happening up on the top of the Adriatic, had protested yet again to the German Ambassador. The Archbishop in Trieste had already written to Friedrich Rainer. 'He had pointed out, among other things, how providential it would be to show some mercy to these unfortunate people.'[6]

II

DETENTION AND FIGHTING BACK

The arrival of Theodor Dannecker in Tuscany coincided with four vital developments in the progress of the Holocaust in Italy. The first was the announcement by the Italian Fascist government in Mussolini's self-appointed Social Republic that it would hold a political congress at which its approach to the execution of the Final Solution would change drastically. The second was the operational establishment of German detention camps in Italy designed to hold Jews, members of the Roma population, political prisoners and captured partisans before they were transported onwards to Auschwitz or Mauthausen.

There were four detention centres, the first of which was at Bolzano, in the foothills of the Alps in the Sud-Tirol region, close to Italy's border with Austria. The other three camps were at Fossoli, Borgo San Dalmazzo and at the aforementioned Risiera di San Sabba at Trieste.

The town of Bolzano was the headquarters of Karl Wolff and the SS and SD administration of Italy. The first prisoners at the camp were captured British and American agents from SOE and OSS, as well as Italian partisans. Jewish arrestees quickly followed.

The camp at Bolzano was constructed to house some 4,000 prisoners, and these were soon made up of Jews and Italian political detainees. Its main function was detention, as the time that the average Jewish prisoner spent there was often less than a week, depending on the timetable of deportation convoys. The camp came under the control of the SS office in Verona, directed by Wilhelm Harster, but with its daily functioning run by German and Ukrainian guards, commanded by an SS lieutenant, Karl Friedrich Titho, who had originally been Harster's driver during the time both men had spent working in the Netherlands.

Borgo San Dalmazzo detention camp was bigger and was constructed before both Bolzano and the conversion of the Trieste rice-processing plant to a concentration camp. It sat south-west of the city of Cuneo, a regional administrative centre in the west of Piemonte, lying in the shadow of the Alps that run along Italy's north-western border with France. The Germans established the camp on 18 September 1943, just after the British and Americans had landed at Salerno.

Cuneo and Borgo San Dalmazzo made perfectly situated locations for German units hunting Jewish refugees who were moving into or out of the Italian-occupied zone in the south of France. Units of Paul Hausser's *Liebstandarte Adolf Hitler* division based themselves in Cuneo and also further south, on the Italian Mediterranean coast at Ventimiglia. In this way, they could monitor all movements across the French border, both over the Alps and along the coast. Within a month of the units' arrival, they had succeeded in rounding up some 600 Jews, of both Italian and French origin, as well as some who had originally fled to Italy as refugees in 1941 and 1942 from Austria and Poland.

The German Strategic Plan for the Defence of Italy in Autumn 1943

By the end of October 1943, the German Supreme Commander in Italy, Field Marshal Albert Kesselring, had persuaded Adolf Hitler to agree with his strategic and tactical strategy for the defence of Italy. Essentially, it consisted of a simple plan: conducting a fighting retreat up Italy as slowly, effectively, methodically and ruthlessly as possible. Based upon establishing a successive series of defensive lines that stretched across the country, each centred around a series of strongpoints – such as Monte Cassino – which were simple to defend and a nightmare to attack.

Kesselring intended to deny the Allies every inch of terrain that he could, for as long as he possibly could. This strategy focused on the simple expedient of conducting the defence of Germany as far away as possible from the country itself. This would achieve five main objectives. First, by maximising the defensive use of Italy's mountainous terrain, criss-crossed by seemingly endless rivers and watercourses, in combination with its wet, foggy winter and autumn weather that turned roads to mud, the Germans could slow the Allies down and hold them south of Rome until spring 1944.

A side-effect of this strategy was that the Allies would take longer to capture air bases from which they could launch bombing raids over northern Italy, Germany, Austria and Romania. In addition, keeping the main body of Allied troops contained south of the capital until spring 1944 meant that any possible invasions of either the Balkans or the south of France would be impossible, although the Allied Desert Air Force, flying off air strips in Sicily, Pantelleria and Sardinia, could still reach central and northern Italy and deny tactical dominance of airspace to the Germans. This, in effect, meant that the Allied fighters and fighter-bombers would control the roads and rail networks of central and northern Italy, flying hundreds of miles ahead of their own troops, denying the Germans vital freedom of movement.

The other thing the Germans needed was time, space and logistical stability in which to put into action their Holocaust plan. Implementing the Final Solution was almost impossible in a country actively at war. When the RSHA had put their round-up, deportation and arrest operations into action in countries such as the Netherlands, Austria and Poland, the Germans had already invaded, occupied, pacified and stabilised these territories. A programme of genocide was almost impossible to put into practice when you were simultaneously fighting for a country.

Finally, the fifth benefit for the Germans of fighting the war in southern Italy was that it gave them space, time and liberty to loot central and northern Italy of art, religious artefacts, gold and statuary. By the end of

October 1943, the British and American 8th and 5th Armies were a long way short of Rome. With their French, Polish, Canadian, Indian and South African allies, they were still three months away from the attacks on Anzio and Monte Cassino, each of which would bog them down for another five months.

Kesselring had formed two series of defensive formations right across Italy, running south of Rome, named the Winter Line and the Gustav Line. The Allies were nowhere near them yet. So, for now, the Germans still had limited time and freedom of movement to execute their plans to arrest and deport Italy's Jews.

The First Resistance to German Arrest and Deportation Operations

From the moment the German arrest operations began in Rome on 16 October, the SS, SD and Gestapo were operating on the back foot, hampered and hamstrung by seven primary factors:

1 There were an estimated 43,000–50,000 Jews to arrest – nobody had an exact number – and they had all had advance warning. The raid on the Rome ghetto targeted 9,800 people, many of them the elderly, women and children, all living in a tightly confined geographical area of ten city blocks, amounting to under a square mile. Nearly 400 SS men were deployed but nearly 90 per cent of the Jews escaped. How would the Germans fare trying to arrest the Jews across the mountains, valleys and plains of half of Italy?
2 The geographical space in which the Germans were forced to operate was insecure for them, and it couldn't deliver any form of logistical stability. The Allied air forces controlled the skies, and by extension, the freedom of movement on roads, rivers and railways, and the presence of tens of thousands of partisans made the entire area behind any given German front line effectively insecure.
3 The Italian Jews could blend into the population – they were, after all, Italian – and very few Germans could either speak their language

or recognise them as physically different from the rest of the local civilian population. Everybody could see the Germans coming. A predominantly rural country, Italy was an easy place in which to hide, especially if the towns and villages were filled with a sympathetic population. Most of the German and Italian Fascist troops and policemen were caught up fighting at or supporting the front line or combatting partisans so there were relatively few who were deployable to find Jews. The Germans were thus also outnumbered. The civilian population who were hiding Jews had at their disposal very substantial residential assets – thousands of churches, convents, farms, houses, apartments – in which to hide a limited number of people.

4 The Germans were operating in a limited time frame. Yes, by October 1943 the Allies were bogged down far south of Rome, but by then, it was clear that it was only a matter of time before the Western Allies and the Soviet Union would win the war, especially after Stalingrad and 'Black May '43', as that spring month had been nicknamed by the Germans. This marked the decision by Admiral Karl Dönitz to withdraw all U-boats from the Battle of the Atlantic after the Allies – two years too late – changed their naval shipping signals codes and also developed more effective anti-submarine tactics. To add to this, Allied dominance continued in summer and autumn 1943, with the successful beginning of Operation Cartwheel in the Solomons, marking the outset of the American island-hopping campaign through the south-west Pacific. After the Red Army's 5th Guards Tank Army fought the II SS Panzer Corps to a standstill at Prokhorovka Station, outside Kursk, the Soviets had definitively gained and would now keep the strategic initiative in the fighting on the Eastern Front. In Italy, this meant there was a very finite time frame before which the Allies would advance, occupy and overtake all of the territory occupied by the Germans, from which they would be trying to deport Jews.

5 The infrastructural network that was there to support and physically hide the Jews was large – churches, farms, land – but the downside was that the Germans and Italian Fascists had the upper hand in bureaucracy. To be able to move anywhere, Italian Jews needed

convincing paperwork that proved they were someone else. The bureaucratic civil service was, at least at the outset of the German occupation, fully controlled by the Italian Fascists, but money and convincingly falsified documents would rapidly change this. Through the American Jewish relief agency and interlinked support networks the Italian Jews would have money to buy food and documents, pay bribes and travel.

6 As already described, the fact that the Allies could intercept, decrypt and read, sometimes almost in real time, the coded German signals from Berlin to Rome and Milan, and vice versa, meant the British and the Americans could deploy their intelligence and military support assets very effectively.

7 The Germans were, in some cases, their own worst enemies – or the Jews' best friends. Too many of them were double agents. At least four of the senior SS and SD officials responsible for directing the infrastructure of the Holocaust in Italy were also actively working with and for Allied intelligence, or were about to. This obviously went against the interests of Berlin and their SS oath and meant the implementation of the Final Solution in Italy was comprehensively sabotaged from within.

The Rescuers

In rural Italy, as well as in the major cities, the Catholic Church was one of the main points of refuge for Jewish escapees after mid-October 1943, when Theodor Dannecker's *Einsatzkommando* headed north from Rome towards Tuscany. One Catholic priest who was active in the escape network around Cuneo was Father Raimondo Viale. He was 37 years old, came from the mountain ski resort of Limone Piemonte and was the parish priest in the small town of Borgo San Dalmazzo, near the detention camp of the same name.

The Fascists arrested him for the first time in 1940, for giving a sermon that denounced the German and Italian invasions of France. They released him fifteen months later and he became part of a network of priests, bishops and other clergy, in Genoa, on the Ligurian coast and around Cuneo, who worked with an assistance organisation called DELASEM.

The *Delegazione Assistenza Emigranti Ebrei*, or the Delegation for the Assistance of Jewish Emigrants, had one objective – to help hide Italian Jews and prevent them being arrested and deported. Funds for the organisation came from the largest relief organisation in the United States, the American Jewish Joint Distribution Committee (JDC). The JDC had operated inside Europe before the outbreak of war led it to transfer its offices to Lisbon. By 1939, the JDC had helped 110,000 Jews to flee Europe. The money at its disposal came from the Jewish community in America, and the JDC transferred it from the United States to banks in Switzerland, where it was then withdrawn in cash. Catholic priests working for the organisation would physically carry the money across the border into Italy or assign it to one of a number of couriers.

Along with Raimondo Viale, there was another priest from Genoa called Monsignor Francesco Repetto. Educated at the Gregorian University in Rome, in 1940 he became the secretary to the Archbishop of Genoa, Pietro Boetto. At the same time, Genoa was chosen as the headquarters of DELASEM in northern Italy and Boetto asked the Vatican, quite simply, if he could blend the activities of the organisation into those of the Church. Yes, came the answer from Cardinal Maglione.

In Switzerland, the papal *nuncio* in Berne, Philippo Bernadini, co-ordinated operations in Zürich with Lelio Valobra, a lawyer whom the Germans had already deported from Italy. The two would plan activities in Switzerland and money would be couriered to Genoa, Florence, Turin and Milan, then distributed through a network of Catholic priests organised by the cardinals in those cities. Monsignor Repetto became the organisation's financier, while the physical running of the clandestine organisation's network was handled by Massimo Teglio, who was called the *Primula Rossa*, or Scarlet Pimpernel.

Teglio's father was a Sephardic Jew, one of twelve brothers and sisters who bought and canned fish. The family firm had established a trio of fish-packing plants in Britain, in Devon and Cornwall. Massimo Teglio had worked in the family business but left it as soon as he could to come home and run the Genoa Aero Club. He'd trained to be a pilot during the First World War and now, with the Second in full swing, he found himself running the covert logistics for DELASEM. To assist him, he had fifteen aircraft, principally biplanes, and some faithful pilot friends, a huge supply of regular money arriving from the Jewish relief agency in New York, the full co-operation of the Catholic Church and a network of priests. The Church was also co-operating with the Chief Rabbi of Genoa, Riccardo Pacifici, and his wife, Wanda Abenaim.

Riccardo Pacifici was born in Florence in 1904 and was a rabbi. He came from an Italian Jewish family of ancient Spanish Sephardic origins who had originally settled in Italy in the sixteenth century. He served as a vice rabbi in Venice, and then became Chief Rabbi of the Genoan Jews. Pacifici's uncle, Samuele, was the Deputy Chief Rabbi of Genoa: between the two of them, they had the full support of the Jewish community in that large port, Liguria and the foothills of the Alps around Cuneo.

On 18 September 1943, 1,000 Jewish refugees arrived through the Alps from France. On the plains around Cuneo and on both sides of the Alps, patrols from the SS *Liebstandarte* were out looking for them. The Germans captured 349 of them and imprisoned them in the Borgo San Dalmazzo camp, which they'd converted from a former barracks for Italian mountain troops. The remaining 651 Jews were scattered across the province of Cuneo, in small villages, mountain huts, and in apartments in a variety of towns. DELASEM and its network of priests and couriers made it their job to get them across the border back into France, Switzerland or onto cargo boats at Genoa that could take them to temporary refuge in Portugal.

The German decision to occupy Italy and disarm its army, navy and air force had, meanwhile, had an immediate impact on the Italian Republican Fascist Party. The residue of Benito Mussolini's Fascist administration was by now ensconced in a small area of land around Salò, in northern Italy, in effect a German puppet state. Il Duce himself was in Milan, after the SS commandos had freed him from imprisonment in September of 1943.

In November, the Fascist Party organised the Congress of Verona, ostensibly to reaffirm its broader policy towards the Allies and the war, but also to swear commitment to its German and Japanese colleagues. Berlin was adamant: Italy had to change its laws about the country's Jewish population, so Article VII of the Verona Manifesto was made clear: 'The members of the Jewish race are foreigners. During the current war they are enemies.'

This was translated into law by Police Order Number 5, which was issued on 30 November 1943 by Guido Buffarini Giudi, who was the grandly named Minister of the Interior of the Italian Salò Republic. It ordered the Italian Police to arrest Jews and confiscate their property, but it exempted two categories of Jews from deportation: those aged over 70 and those from mixed marriages. This alienated the SS and SD, which wanted to deport every single Italian Jew they could find. Italians were now fully committed to the execution of the Final Solution against their own countrymen.

Meanwhile, on noticeboards across the city of Siena, south of Florence, posters were put up proclaiming the new police order: 'All Jews, whatever their nationality, shall be sent to special concentration camps. All their property, mobile and real estate, shall be immediately confiscated.'

One man who saw them was a property agent who had an estate near the village of Monaciano, in the wooded farmland and undulating green hills 2 miles north-east of Siena. He had an entire extended clan of Italian Jews hiding in his property. It was the Piperno family: Clotilde, Giacomo, her son Giacomo Due, Vanda and Nella and the four children had been hiding at Monaciano since they fled Rome after the Germans arrived. Prior to this, the estate's agent, Ettore Bonechi, had already been sending food supplies to the family in Rome. They had become semi-prisoners in a kind of rural paradise. It was land of vineyards, of farmhouses built of old beige stone, cicadas at dusk and dusty paths and tracks that lead to the next vineyard or small crossroads.

But there was little to do: the family were highly visible every time they left the house and all it would take would be one unexpected informer. The local population in and around Monaciano were hugely supportive; but it would still only take one slip-up, one person from anywhere who might simply go to Siena and report that, just outside the village of Monaciano, there was a foreign family – strangers – behaving differently. Then the Germans and Fascists would arrive.

So, the family decided that, however they could, they would flee south, back to Rome. Better to be hiding in plain sight. And nobody, thought *Nonna* Clotilde, would be expecting a large Jewish family to be coming *into* Rome, into the heart of the round-ups and arrests. Everybody, surely, would be fleeing outwards? So, what the family now needed was to be able to get to the train station at Siena, or near it, and head to Rome. And then hide until the Allies arrived.

ON THE RUN FROM ROME TO FLORENCE

The SS teams across Italy were working under the joint direction of Karl Wolff in Bolzano and Ernst Kaltenbrunner in Berlin. Their mission was twofold – to round up and deport Italy's Jews and to seize and transport back to Germany as much art, gold, jewellery and valuables as possible. Kaltenbrunner wanted to give Hermann Göring works of looted Italian art that he could, in turn, present to Adolf Hitler for his planned, spectacular Führermuseum in Linz in Austria.

The gold and valuables would be transferred to the keeping of the SS Main Economic and Administrative Office. Yet, as the implementation of the Final Solution in Italy progressed, evidence suggests that the individual officers involved, in Rome, Milan and Berlin, were also using it as a form of criminal enterprise for their own enrichment or that of a close number of collaborators. Guido Zimmer in Genoa, Herbert Kappler in Rome, Walter Rauff in Milan and Wilhelm Hoettl in Berlin were just four of the SS and SD officers involved in this. They were all intricately linked with each other, they were carrying out the same operations, and their chain of command all ran in the same direction, straight upwards to Ernst Kaltenbrunner in Berlin and Karl Wolff in Bolzano.

This joint criminal enterprise sometimes also encompassed making and maintaining contact with Allied intelligence, both during the war and after it. Kappler and Hoettl's coded communications about the 50kg of gold confiscated from Rome's Jews were just one part of an organised system of looting and appropriation of Jewish gold, valuables and property that the SS men were running in tandem with their operations to execute the Final Solution. And in many cases, if Jewish families proved able to provide bribes or payments to the SS men, they could be spared deportation. The focus on these two criminal enterprises by the SS – ingratiating themselves with and working for Allied intelligence, and personal and institutional enrichment – sapped considerable time and energy from the daily diktats of the Final Solution.[1] And it was to prove one of several principal reasons why the operations to put it into action were to fall so far short of their targets. Another reason, obviously, was the ability of the Jews, supported by thousands of Italians, to escape arrest.

While the Germans were engaged in these covert schemes, the Jews of Italy were continuing to hide, flee and try and avoid arrest. Substantially backfooted by the comparative failure of the round-up in Rome, where only 1,100-odd out of nearly 10,000 Jews had been arrested, the SS started trying to make up for lost time. But the Jews of Italy had powerful, inventive and very varied supporters.

At the Santa Brigida convent in Rome, set in the Piazza Farnese, there was an English nun. Sister Mary Richard Hambrough was born in Brighton on 10 September 1887 and baptised as Madeleine Catherine. She would later change her name to Mary and take both of her parents' surnames to become Mary Beauchamp Hambrough (the 'Richard' was adopted later as a patron saint's name). She went to the Convent of the Sacred Heart at Woldingham, England, and excelled at singing and music. She moved to Rome in 1914, and took her vows as a nun in 1918, joining the Swedish Bridgettine Foundation.

After a year visiting Stockholm in 1923, she returned to Rome in 1924 and moved into the convent at the Piazza Farnese, where she would remain for the rest of her life. She worked closely with her abbess, Mary Elizabeth Hesselblad, who was Swedish. When they heard about the round-up of the Jews in Rome, the two of them thought that the Casa di Santa Brigida could be a good place in which to hide Jewish families.

Across Rome, another group of committed Italians were preparing to help the Jews. Giovanni Borromeo was from Rome, the son of a doctor called Pietro Borromeo. Like many others of his generation, Giovanni was conscripted into the army in the First World War, while he was in the middle of his medical studies. A two-year gap fighting against the Austro-Hungarians followed. He was only 22 when he received his medical degree, but he found that as he was not a member of the Italian Fascist Party, it became harder and harder to find a position.

After marrying in 1933, he was appointed the director of a hospital that enjoyed one of Rome's most individual locations. The Ospedale Fatebenefratelli was built on an island in the River Tiber: it had belonged to the Hospitaller Order of Saint John of God since 1892 and was theoretically not part of Italian territory. Two of the doctors who worked under Borromeo were Vittorio Emanuele Sacerdoti, who was Jewish, and Adriano Ossicini, who was Catholic and a firm opponent of Fascism. He had narrowly avoided prison sentences for his political views during the 1920s.

Vittorio Sacerdoti was a young doctor who had been working at a hospital in Ancona, on Italy's Adriatic coast. When the 1938 Racial Laws were introduced, he lost his job. His uncle then recommended him to Borromeo, who offered him a position. Sacerdoti accepted. Within three days, the Ministry of Health in Rome discovered he was Jewish, and he promptly lost this new employment. But because the hospital was outside the territorial jurisdiction of the city, a loophole in the law meant that he could practise there as a student doctor. One of Sacerdoti's Jewish uncles, Elio Ottolenghi, arranged false papers and a fake identity for him. His name now became Vittorio Salviucci.

The two young, renegade doctors, with their crusading boss, saw that immediately after the Italian Armistice and the surrender of the army, the hospital's waiting list suddenly quadrupled. Everybody wanted to hide there: its reputation as a haven and the maverick doctors gave it a reputation for concealing people. Partisans, anti-Fascists, demobbed police officers on the run, army deserters and Jews began to show up on the small bridge that led to the hospital entrance, where the umbrella pine trees stood guard over the swirling, grey-brown waters of the Tiber. The hospital also sat across the street from the external walls of the Jewish ghetto, and many of its patients came from there. Before 1943, these had been Jewish families who either were barred admission to other hospitals in Rome or could not afford the medical treatment.

Dr Ossicini said that it was Sacerdoti who originally coined the term 'Syndrome K'. The 'K', they both said, came either from the first initial of the surname of the German Supreme Commander, Albert Kesselring, or from that of the Gestapo chief, Herbert Kappler. It also cross-referenced to Koch's bacillus, or disease, a respiratory infection which was quite common then in Rome (known to us as tuberculosis). It was named after Robert Koch, a nineteenth-century German bacteriologist who discovered the causes of it.

Patients who presented themselves at the Fatebenefratelli hospital with tuberculosis were listed as having 'K' Syndrome. Perhaps, said Sacerdoti, we can have a disease named after Kesselring – Dr Borromeo is said to have agreed. The latter was a keen Catholic, and in addition to being a committed anti-Fascist, was also a strong supporter of the partisans operating in the forests outside Rome. He kept a radio transmitter in the hospital basement and, with it, was in regular communication with partisans who themselves were often sheltering Jews, whom they in turn passed on to the Fatebenefratelli Hospital for hiding.

When the round-up of Jews began, both Sacerdoti and Ossicini brought groups of them to the hospital. Dr Borromeo registered them, noting in his logbook that they were carriers of 'Syndrome K', or *Il Morbo di K*.

Jewish 'patients' were advised to cover their mouths, cough frequently, feign dementia and high temperatures, and were admitted to a separate ward which had the notice '*Morbo di K*' pinned on the door. Vittorio Sacerdoti administered to these patients, and when asked by any Italian Fascist or German visitors who the patients were in this isolated ward, he described the symptoms of the disease. On 19 October, an SS NCO and four men walked into the hospital, looking for Jews. Sacerdoti confronted them and explained that the only fugitives the hospital was holding were those patients with the mysterious disease. The Germans left promptly. Ossicini said:

Syndrome K was put on patient papers to indicate that the sick person wasn't sick at all, but Jewish. We created those papers for Jewish people as if they were ordinary patients, and in the moment when we had to say what disease they suffered? It was Syndrome K, meaning 'I am admitting a Jew,' as if he or she were ill, but they were all healthy. The idea to call it Syndrome K, like Kesselring or Kappler, was mine. The lesson of my experience was that we have to act not for the sake of self-interest, but for principles. Anything else is a pretence.[2]

A rough estimate of how many families and individuals were sheltered and saved stands at around 100, between the period of the German arrival in Rome in August and September 1943, up until the following year.

In the meantime, Dr Borromeo continued to keep in radio contact with the senior partisan commander outside Rome with whom he exchanged information, food, medical supplies and Jewish prisoners. This man, Roberto Lordi, was a former brigadier general in the Italian Air Force, decorated twice for bravery in the First World War, in which he flew artillery spotting and reconnaissance missions over the front lines at the River Isonzo. A fabulous and daring pilot, in the 1920s he flew in air races between Italy, Athens and Tripoli, and then headed up the Italian Military Mission to China.

Falsely accused by the Fascist government of embezzling funds, Lordi returned to Italy and was put under house arrest. When the Germans arrived in Rome in September 1943, Lordi, who by then had completely fallen out with Mussolini's government, walked out of his front door with a hunting rifle, saying he was going to go and attack German paratroopers. Two days later, despite being 60, he joined a partisan group. He set up a radio transmitter in his country house at Genzano, 15 miles outside Rome, transmitting to Borromeo, other partisan groups and the Jewish communities inside the capital. Via Dr Borromeo, Jews were smuggled out to Lordi's house in the hilltop town where he lived.

On 27 June 1943, Vatican Radio is reported to have broadcast a statement – or injunction – by the Pope: 'He who makes a distinction between Jews and other men is being unfaithful to God and is in conflict with God's commands.'[3] This can be interpreted as the Vatican's initial subterfuge call to Italy's Catholics to shelter the country's Jews. It came three and a half months before the interception of the RSHA signal concerning the seizure of the country's Jews. By the time Dr Borromeo had started hiding Jewish fugitives, Pius XII had already allegedly told the Catholic *curia* to open the Church's properties in the Vatican City. At that point, there were an estimated 5,750-odd Jews in the greater metro-politan area of Rome, and 2,250–3,000 in the suburbs and countryside around it, just under a fifth of the rough total of some 42,000 remaining in Italy:

> A few days earlier … he personally ordered the Vatican clergy to open the sanctuaries of the Vatican City to all 'non-Aryans' in need of refuge. By morning of October 16th, a total of 477 Jews had been given shelter in the Vatican and its enclaves, while another 4,238 had been given sanctuary in the many monasteries and convents in Rome. Only 1,015 of Rome's 5,730 Jews were seized that morning.[4]

The Vatican had made its plans to assimilate an extra 1,850 men into the Pope's Palatine Guard, while another 350 went to the Vatican summer residence at Castel Gandolfo outside Rome. When the Final Solution came for Rome's Jews in the *retata*, some 4,715 of the 5,730 total found shelter both in Church institutions like the Piazza Farnese convent and in the Vatican itself.

The Scarlet Pimpernel of the Vatican and the British Army

Meanwhile, Monsignor Hugh O'Flaherty, the Irish official in the Vatican *curia* who was D'Arcy Osborne's contact, was assembling an eclectic team of men and women, the kind that only exists in wartime. They would assist escaped Allied POWs and Jews to hide from the German occupation. The team included two New Zealand priests and a British major who was an escaped POW. He travelled in and out of the Vatican dressed in the black *soutane* and scarlet sash of a Catholic monsignor. There was also an Italian double agent whose cover consisted of working in uniform for the SS, a young Jewish couple – one Italian, one Austrian – and a ballad singer who was the wife of the Irish Ambassador.

O'Flaherty was 45 years old in 1943, came originally from Munster, and had spent three years in Rome in the early 1920s before he was ordained. He had started to work for the Holy See immediately, and for ten years travelled as a Vatican diplomat in Egypt, Haiti, San Domingo and then Czechoslovakia. The Vatican made him a monsignor in 1934. Before Mussolini's fall from power in summer 1943, O'Flaherty had already been touring Italian POW camps when he could, collecting the names of Allied prisoners, which he would then broadcast on Vatican Radio, so that their units and colleagues knew they were safe.

After the Armistice, an estimated 70,000 Allied POWs were suddenly released from prison camps by their Italian guards: these men were left in a dangerous limbo, wandering Italy – now occupied by the Germans – and trying to reach the safety of Allied lines. Partisan groups helped many, others hid with farmers and some were recaptured, only to escape again. Some managed to reach Rome and the Vatican.

One of these British POWs, who had escaped, was called Samuel Ironmonger Derry. He was 30 in 1943 and had been an officer in the Royal Artillery since 1932. The Germans first captured him in north Africa, where he had escaped and walked back to British lines. Five months later, and 200 miles away, he was recaptured near El Alamein by the same officer and unit who had been his first captors.

A boat trip across the Mediterranean took him to an Italian POW camp at Chieti, in the Abruzzo region north-east of Rome. When the 1943 Armistice saw his Italian guards dump their Carcano rifles at the entrance to the prison camp and then start to walk home, Derry followed.

The Germans captured him for the third time and he was put on a train to Germany. Accompanied by a paratrooper guard when he went to use the train's toilet, Derry jumped out of the carriage door and bounced hard and fast onto the stony rail-side turf of Italy, once again a free man. He walked southwards until he linked up with a group of British and Commonwealth POWs hiding in a forest north of Rome. He wrote a letter and handed it to an Italian courier, who took it to the Vatican. There, it reached both O'Flaherty and D'Arcy Osborne.

They dispatched a letter back to Derry, who travelled to Rome concealed under a load of cabbages in a farmer's cart. Wary that Derry might be a German spy, Osborne had sent a coded message to London, asking for confirmation that the escaped British major was who he said he was. The signal, Derry recalls from talking to the British diplomat, went to London, firstly to the Foreign Office, then to the War Office, on to MI5, and then to the Lincolnshire Constabulary in Newark, from where Derry originated. He was, it seemed, the man he claimed to be.

So, Osborne gave the burly, cheery major two things he hadn't had for fifteen months: a hot bath and a proper meal – steak with mushrooms, an Italian *dolce*, or sweet pudding, and red wine. Then he put him to work.

Derry's job, with O'Flaherty, would be administering not just Allied POWs but also fleeing Jews. The ad hoc organisation became known as the 'Rome Escape Line'. However, the Germans, through reading some of Osborne's messages, were not slow to hear about it.

The Escape Line consisted of Sam Derry, O'Flaherty, the Irish Ambassador Thomas J. Kiernan, his wife Delia Murphy, who was a ballad singer, Osborne's butler John May, and John Flanagan and Owen Sneddon, two young New Zealand priests. A Maltese widow, Chetta Chevalier, whose husband had worked in Rome for Thomas Cook Travel Agents, gave her flat in Via Imperia, near the Sapienza University in Rome's Tiburtina district.

O'Flaherty used it as a logistics base. It was one of a number of safe houses where Jews and British POWs could rest and eat for thirty-six hours, before being passed to another hiding place. Chevalier and three Maltese priests, all of whom held British passports, estimated that 4,000 separate individuals passed through the apartment.

Meanwhile, the headquarters of the escape organisation, such as it was, lay in Flaherty's rooms at the German College, inside the Vatican walls. Osborne himself had not been – formally – allowed out of the Vatican since 1940 and was living inside it in a pilgrim's hostel.

Although confined to the Vatican for a period that would become nearly four years, Osborne and his hosts saw eye to eye, despite the fact that one side was strictly neutral, and the other a belligerent combatant fighting a war on the very doorstep of the Vatican. At the beginning of

December 1942, the Vatican had presented Osborne with a papal medal. He wrote to thank Cardinal Giovanni Montini, the man who would later become Pope Paul VI:

> You've reminded me how I've always been treated here in Vatican City, with the greatest kindness and thoughtfulness. I was thinking about this as I walked home this evening, through the impenetrable darkness, that for my part I've always tried to repay this treatment by trying to cause the least amount of bother and difficulties, to my involuntary hosts.[5]

The SS could not arrest any of the selection of men inside the Vatican as it was neutral territory. Herbert Kappler was incensed by this, so he told four of his soldiers to paint a white line across the cobblestones, under the Roman colonnades, at the precise point where the Vatican territory officially ended and Italian territory began. The SS would shoot O'Flaherty, said the German Ambassador, if he stepped over this.

Further north, in Florence, the German Consul was another ally, in the form of a man named Gerhard Wolf. The diplomat had resisted every pressure and entreaty by his superiors to join the National Socialist Party in the 1930s, until he was finally told that his career could not advance unless, simply put, he became a Nazi. So, he did. But his entire subsequent career unfolded as a reaction to this forced decision. His commitment to saving the Jews of Florence became part of this, spearheading part of the unofficial and deeply covert German opposition to the Final Solution in Italy.

Wolf came from Dresden, the seventh child of a lawyer, and from his teenage years had loved history of art. He was posted to Rome in 1927, where his admiration for Italian artistic achievement merely increased, and he managed to put off becoming a member of the NSDAP until 1939.

By 1940, he was in Florence. He immediately saw that his professional, artistic and moral priorities were about to put him completely at odds with the aims and objectives of the Third Reich. He and Rudolf

Rahn, the Ambassador to the Salò Republic, and Ludwig Heinrich Heydenreich, director of the Historical Cultural Institute in Florence, fought to save both art and Jews from being deported.

Gerhard Wolf was a firm supporter not just of Italian art, but of Italian bicycling as well – especially an Italian cycling champion called Gino Bartali, who before the war had won the French Tour de France and the Italian national Giro d'Italia. He would go on long training rides between Florence and Assisi – and inside his bicycle frame he was, sometimes, carrying messages and documents on behalf of DELASEM.

A network of the organisation's couriers, often from the clergy, were moving between Switzerland, Turin, Genoa, Florence and Rome, and from September 1943 to June 1944, they moved an estimated 25,000,000 lire and helped an estimated 4,000 Jews. The hugely popular bicyclist reportedly helped them to do this.

Bartali also had another secret hidden in his Florentine cellar – a family of Croatian Jews called the Goldenbergs. The mother, father and two children spent nearly nine months in Bartali's house, until they were liberated by the Allies in August 1944. It was just one example of how thousands of Jews were hidden across Italy during the period between September 1943 and autumn 1944. The four members of the family slept on a double bed in Bartali's basement and, for nine months, their father almost never left the building.

The Goldenbergs had originally come from the coastal city of Fiume in Dalmatia, which was then part of Italy. They fled in 1940 after local Croatian Fascists threatened to kill them, and took shelter in Florence, settling in the small town of Fiesole, which sits 2 miles above the city. Until 1943, young Giorgio Goldenberg, born in 1935, would go down to Florence each day to have lessons at a Jewish elementary school, leaving behind his sister, Tea, and his parents. One evening, he came home from school and found Bartali in the living room of his parents' flat. He had no idea how he came to be there, but, as he said, 'one thing I know for certain is that he saved our lives'.

In 1943, Bartali and his cousin decided to rescue the children and their parents and Giorgio took shelter with an order of nuns at a school in the village of Settignano, which also sat on the hillside overlooking

Florence. Giorgio's parents and his young sister then hid in Bartali's basement, almost perpetually unable to go out, for fear of being seen by the neighbours. Giorgio joined them in early 1944. He recalls:

> The cellar was very small. A door gave way onto a courtyard, but I couldn't go out because that would run the risk of me being seen by the tenants of the nearby apartment buildings. The four of us slept on a double bed. My father never went out, while my mother often went out with two flasks to get water from some well.[6]

For fugitive Jewish families who were on the run and in hiding, it was often vital to have fake names and fake identity documents. These were needed to obtain ration cards, travel or stay in any hotel or boarding house. The main aim was to have a false identity card bearing the address of an area in southern Italy that had already been liberated by the Allies: this obviously made any verification or checks impossible.

But Italian Fascist policemen were aware of this, and if the person in front of them at a checkpoint, say a Jewish fugitive, carried identity documents from Calabria or Sicily, yet spoke with a strong northern accent from Piemonte or Liguria, it was instantly suspicious. In Florence, Italians from these southern regions were often employed by the secret police to strike up conversations with strangers, also claiming to originate from the south, to ascertain whether they were genuine.

Resistance couriers sometimes met in churches to hand over fake identity and ration cards: one female courier remembered passing over a large consignment of fake identity cards, claiming to prove that the bearers came from the central Sicilian town of Caltanissetta, which had been liberated by the Americans in July 1943. Too late, the female courier realised that all of the distributed ID cards had only one 's' in the city's name.

To get hold of a fake identity card, an original blank form was stolen from the municipal headquarters by anti-Fascist employees, who also borrowed, and copied, the necessary municipal stamps bearing the city's name and seal, which was then affixed to the completed document. Archbishop Da Costa in Assisi, keen to provide ID cards for Jews hiding in his parishes, enlisted Gino Bartali as one of his couriers. He would bring photographs of fugitive Jews, hidden in his bicycle frame, and return home with the ID cards two days later. Both photos and documents were hidden by the simple method of Bartali pulling off the grips on his handlebars and unscrewing his seat, so as to be able to push the ID cards down inside the frame.

Bartali's role as a courier, however, was questioned by Don Aldo Brunacci, a priest from Assisi, who was in charge of co-ordinating assistance with DELASEM in the city. He suggested Bartali was, in reality, used less frequently, and only around Florence where he lived. Bartali himself never confirmed nor denied the details of his help. However, Giorgio Nissim, a Jewish accountant from Pisa, had helped to restructure DELASEM in Tuscany in autumn 1943, after German raids saw all of its staff moved to concentration camps. Helping the archbishops of Genoa and Florence, Nissim claimed in his diaries that Bartali, along with partisans, priests, farmers and delivery drivers, helped often. He would get up in the morning in Florence and cycle 108 miles to Assisi, where fugitive Jews were hiding in convents. He would then stay there, pick up their photographs and take them back to Nissim in Florence. Two days later, he would return with the fake identities. On one occasion, the head of the SD in Florence and a Fascist official, Mario Carita, questioned Bartali. But he kept silent.

Meanwhile, 30 miles to the south of Florence, the Piperno family knew that it was going to be difficult staying in Monaciano. On 4 November they were tipped off that the following day the Germans intended to arrest Jews in Siena, so they split up among a series of secluded farmhouses. But this was still not safe enough, even when they moved to a half-abandoned house on another estate. Isolated geographically, they were also isolated in terms of communication, so when the Italian police commissioner of Monaciano was among those who suggested they move south to Rome, they agreed.

The officer was a man who had switched his allegiance against Mussolini's Fascist government following the Armistice in July 1943.

He'd always been quietly opposed to the Fascists but, fearing for his job, had said nothing. Now the time had come to be able finally to do something. He told two of his subordinates to bring their police cars to Monaciano and, along with his own car, embarked the nine members of the family and led them personally towards Rome. After this, accounts differ: the family may have travelled by rail from a station on the line between Siena and Arezzo, connected there for Perugia, and arrived in Rome, or the police officers may have assisted them as far as the capital.[7]

At first, they hid in an empty apartment whose Fascist owners had fled north – a friend of Vanda's knew and trusted the concierge. Then, one evening, she announced that she had an idea for a hiding place for the whole family. She took her brother, Piero Piperno, then 15, and his sister, who was 8, and walked to the convent in the Piazza Farnese.

They knocked on the doors. Outside there was a Swedish flag flying. A nun opened the door and took them to see the Mother Superior. Vanda explained that they were a family from the south of Italy, displaced by the fighting. They had identity papers to prove this. Could they take refuge in the convent? Was such a thing possible? The nuns took them inside. Nobody asked them if they were Jews, and they didn't say anything about their family's true origins, nor where they had actually come from. The nuns, for their part, accepted their version of events, not querying why a family with Roman accents would have documents that showed they originated in the 'meridionale', the south of Italy.[8]

It was December 1943, and the German efforts to round up and deport Italy's Jews were at their height. For families like the Pipernos, hiding in convents, church properties, farms and private houses, every day brought the same fear and anxieties. Would they be betrayed? Could they trust the people hiding them? Would they be found by the Germans? In the Piazza Farnese convent, other family members joined Vanda and Pietro, bringing the number of them hiding to thirteen.

The nuns had put them in a series of rooms in an isolated part of the convent building: the men were gathered in one room on the first floor. If German search-parties arrived, they could quickly get through into the church, where there was a secret hiding place. The men in the family group stayed inside the convent building at all times, while the women were allowed out to go shopping for food. This in itself presented a new set of dangers: what were three women doing in the marketplace, buying food for fifteen? Who was at home? Who were they hiding? All it needed was one Fascist informer, one market trader paid by the Germans, and the Piperno women would be followed.

At the beginning of January 1944, Sister Maria Elizabetta Hesselblad asked Vanda to come and talk to her in private. How come, she gently asked the daughter of the Piperno family, you have sons and daughters and cousins and parents who speak with a Roman accent, have identity documents from a town in the south, and are here in hiding? It all came out. Vanda told the whole story, trusting the Swedish nun. Yes, they were Jews, and yes, they were on the run. Hesselbald reassured her: for the sake of secrecy, nobody but she and Sister Mary Richard knew this information, and both had guessed it quickly before having the conversation with Vanda. Practise your religion, said Sister Maria Elizabetta, the one taken away from you by law in 1938. Keep an eye on our religious practices, so that if it comes to it, you won't be shown up by your lack of knowledge of Catholicism. We'll teach you Swedish and English to keep you occupied.

And if Germans come looking? On three occasions while the Piperno family were at the convent, German soldiers came and asked to search the building. On one occasion that the nuns recalled, the German security detail were told that they couldn't enter, as the convent was officially Swedish territory – de facto neutral – and protected by the Vatican's extra-territoriality rulings. For over six months, the convent in the Piazza Farnese would become the Pipernos' home. In the meantime, all they could do was to wait for the arrival of Allied troops.

For those Jews in Rome, however terrifying and overwhelming the period of hiding may have been, they did have the reassuring knowledge that the Allies were moving north to liberate them, and that there was a possible, hopeful end in sight. For the Jews in northern Italy, however, salvation seemed a very long way away.

In January of 1944, Virginia Montalcini, her mother and father were among a group of Jewish families who decided to escape from the Allied bombing raids and the SS round-ups in Turin. They packed what they could in their flat near Corso Re Umberto and walked out of the family apartment with their suitcases. They took a train to Milan and then north-east past Lakes Como and Maggiore, towards the town of Sondrio, sitting in the shadow of the Alps. They walked further up the same road, towards the Stelvio National Park on the Swiss border.

They tried to cross northwards into Switzerland, but in the mountain village of Sondalo, near the border, the Germans stopped them. Virginia and the rest of the group of Jews were taken to Milan. On 30 January, the SS and Italian Police forced her aboard a cattle car on Platform 21 at the station, from where all deportations were made. Six days later, she arrived in Auschwitz. The health of the perpetually smiling teenager from Turin had, however, deteriorated since the start of the war. In the selection line at the camp she was chosen to be gassed immediately.

13

RETALIATION

The first mainstream, countrywide demonstration against the Germans came on 1 March 1944, when partisan groups co-ordinated with trade unions and every factory in Milan, Turin, Genoa and the surrounding industrial area stopped work at precisely the same time. On the surface, the demonstration was against German mass deportations of Italian workers to provide labour, often in appalling conditions, in German and Austrian factories, and against the deportation of Italian Jews.

Both Allied and German intelligence recognised it as a tipping point in the Holocaust, when the Germans finally lost the upper hand in Italy and were forced on to the defensive, no longer able to co-ordinate successful round-ups of the country's Jewish population. The mass wildcat strike also sent a strong statement to the Germans: Italy is united against you.

By December 1943 and January 1944, Italian partisans had begun attacking German units, both north and south of Rome, as well as in the city itself. With the Allies still bogged down in the Liri Valley, around Monte Cassino, it seemed a distant thought that the capital would be liberated. In January, though, the decision was made by American Lieutenant General Mark Clark to land an army corps at Anzio, a beachhead behind German lines, south of Rome.

At first, it seemed a good idea and the taskforce made some headway. But Clark's decision to entrust the command of the landing force to a slow, hesitant and strategically unimaginative American major general, John P. Lucas, saw the Allied force bogged down in a stalemate. They were surrounded by German artillery on the high ground of the surrounding Alban hills, in a battle that seemed to many of its participants to belong to the First World War. For five months, the Americans and British remained stuck, both at Cassino and Anzio. The two competing battle areas were, ironically, meant to be the solution, one to the other. In fact, neither solved anything.

Desperate to move their fighting against the Germans onto a more aggressive footing, the Rome partisans chose March 1944 to attack. The deportation of Italian Jews across the country had slowed, as more and more German troops were dispatched south to confront the Allies and to defend Rome. Increasing partisan attacks behind the Axis front lines kept divisions pinned down in rear areas. Jews could now not just escape, hide and flee from the Germans, but they could join partisan groups and fight against them.

Lidia Rolfi was a teenage girl who did just that. From the town of Mondovi, in the south of the region of Piemonte, she had grown up wanting to be a teacher but, outraged at what she saw the Germans doing, had become a partisan. She was now fighting with an armed group in one of the areas of rolling countryside that sat between Mondovi, the regional capital of Cuneo, and the French Alps.

Augusto Segre, a rabbi from the town of Casale Monferrato, outside Turin, was meanwhile operating with another partisan group further north. The aim of both groups was to keep the Germans pinned down inside the main cities and towns by denying them use of the roads. They became masters of the ambush. On the rolling plains of the Piemonte and Lombardia countryside, the German units travelling in motorcycle and sidecar combinations, lorries and half-tracks were easy to spot from a distance. They were also easy to spot for the P-51 Mustangs, Spitfires and Thunderbolts of the Allied Desert Air Force, now operating from airstrips on Corsica and south of Rome.

The partisan groups knew that if they kept the Germans bottled up inside Turin, Cuneo, Milan and Alessandria, the groups of Jews who were hiding in the countryside were safe. Those Jews inside the cities who hadn't been rounded up and deported by the beginning of 1944 were earmarked as a priority to be moved along escape lines out into the countryside. And as the Allied fighters and fighter-bombers attacked roads, so they attacked railway lines too. The RAF, and American B-24 Liberators and B-25 Mitchells, flying off improvised airstrips on the islands of Pantelleria, Sicily and Corsica were relentlessly targeting the marshalling yards in cities like Bologna, Milan and Turin, where the train convoys – including those deporting Jews – were physically assembled.

The Attack in Via Rasella

On 23 March 1944, a company of the 3rd Battalion of the SS Police Regiment Bozen marched through the centre of Rome on its way back from a morning at the shooting ranges. They were singing, a practice designed to intimidate the Italian civilian population. They marched up the cobbled slope of the Via Rasella, which leads up to the Renaissance splendour of the Piazza Barberini. The battalion was principally made up of Italian citizens who were ethnic Germans, but who lived in the northern Italian province of South Tyrol. The men drew their unit's name from the name of their town, Bolzano in Italian, or 'Bozen' in Tyrolean German. The policemen had fought with one of the divisions that Mussolini had dispatched to the Eastern Front, and now had opted to join the Bozen Battalion as it meant they no longer had to complete another tour of duty in a sub-zero Russian winter with the Wehrmacht.

Sixteen partisans from the communist-dominated resistance organisation called the Patriotic Action Group had, meanwhile, prepared a trap. On the pavement of Via Rasella stood an iron dustcart on wheels. Inside it, the partisans had hidden a 44lb bomb, made up of TNT given to them by the American OSS. As the policemen approached, the fuse was lit and the bomb exploded, blowing twenty-eight men from the Bozen Battalion across the cobbles and into the sides of neighbouring buildings. One hundred and ten of them were wounded. The partisans fled, two of them opening fire with Sten guns as they retreated. Bodies, and parts of them, lay blasted across the cobbles: pieces of the iron dustcart were blown 3in deep into the sides of apartment buildings.[1] It was the biggest attack by partisans on German forces in Italy to date.

Within thirty minutes, Herbert Kappler arrived at the scene. He reported to the Wehrmacht regional commander, Major General Kurt Malzer, who decided that reprisals were called for. Ten Italians for each German would be a fair exchange rate, they agreed, drinking brandy later at the commander's headquarters. Malzer briefly considered burning down part of Rome, but then remembered the informal quid pro quo arrangement they had with the Vatican and the Allies. The latter wouldn't bomb Rome – and hit German units or headquarters – if the Germans themselves didn't destroy parts of the capital. General Eberhard von Mackensen, whose area of operations included Rome, approved the killing of hostages – so did Hitler in Berlin.

Both generals in Rome, and Kesselring and Kappler, took Hitler's agreement as comprising an order. Kappler believed that the deal involved the killing of ten Italians per German casualty and that the victims would be criminals, political prisoners or Jews who had already been sentenced to death. Hitler then said the executions had to be carried out within twenty-four hours.

But Kappler had only four people sentenced to death in his cells at Via Tasso. There was another group of seventeen elsewhere, and another 167 he could get from the gaol at the Regina Coeli, the central prison of the capital, called 'the Queen of Heaven'. Along with two civilians rounded up randomly in Via Rasella, that made 190. Wilhelm Harster, the SS Police Chief, checked his lists and said that there were fifty-seven Jews only, currently waiting in German custody for deportation. This gives some idea of the lack of success the Germans were enjoying in their continuing round-up operations.

The death toll from the bombing rose to thirty-three and by noon on 24 March, Kappler had a list of 271 victims. Eventually 330 people were assembled and taken in trucks down the Via Appia.

In a small wood of umbrella pine trees in the south of the city, the lorries stopped near a series of tunnels. For centuries, these had been used to mine *pozzolana*, a limestone derivative which, added to cement, makes it set harder. Erich Priebke and Karl Hass, two of Kappler's lieutenants, were among those who led the killings: many of the SS and SD men had never killed anybody before, so Kappler had brought some cases of cognac to encourage them. The Germans then shot the prisoners in groups of five – halfway through the massacre, the Germans discovered there were five extra prisoners, but Kappler decided to kill them anyway, so as to keep the location of the incident hidden. Once the prisoners were dead, German Army engineers blew up the ceilings of the tunnels, burying the corpses.

In the final count, seventy-five of those killed were Jewish. Three of the dead were well-known army officers and partisans. The first, Colonel Giuseppe di Montezemolo, was an army officer loyal to the king who had been imprisoned at Via Tasso. Kappler's men pulled out some of his teeth and nails with pliers. A second prisoner among the dead was General Simone Simoni, who had been tortured with a blowtorch.

The third was the partisan leader Roberto Lordi, the liaison officer with Dr Borromeo and the Fatebenefratelli Hospital. He had been betrayed by an informer. On 17 March 1944, the SS broke into Lordi's house in Genzano, and when he appeared at the German Embassy the following day to plead for the release of one of his friends, the Germans took him to Via Tasso.

Feigning illness, he asked that a friend of his who was a physician could come to see him. It was Dr Borromeo who arrived. Lordi had a radio, given to him by the SOE and hidden in Borromeo's basement at the hospital. He warned the doctor that if he gave in under torture and provided information to the Gestapo, he should hide the radio and flee. However, he never did give in. Herbert Kappler was later to say that Roberto Lordi died at the Ardeatine Caves, shouting '*Viva l'Italia!*'

With 335 prisoners eventually executed at the caves, the repercussions of the Via Rasella attack, and the subsequent reprisals, ricocheted and shuddered northwards. Across Italy, the massed partisan groups who now numbered some 80,000 men and women went to war against the Germans and Italian Fascists, the protection of Jews everywhere being one of their operational priorities.

14

JEWISH PARTISANS IN ITALY

The British Special Operations Executive had known about the impending start of the Holocaust in Italy since the arrival of the Germans in September 1943. By early 1944, the Allies were fighting around Monte Cassino and were bogged down in the extended beachhead at Anzio.

Following the debacle in Rome, and subsequent failures in arrest operations in Tuscany, Theodor Dannecker had been deemed inefficient by Eichmann and his other superiors at the RSHA in Berlin. In January, they replaced him with a tough, ruthless lawyer called Friedrich Bosshammer, who was now head of the *Judenreferat*, or Jewish Affairs Office, in Verona.

The Allies were aware that the majority of Jews had been able to escape round-up and deportation, but they knew that one way of both supporting Italy's escapee Jews and attacking German and Italian Fascist forces was to give support to partisan groups. Enzo Sereni was one man they chose for this task.

He was the son of the personal physician of Vittorio Emanuele II, the King of Italy, and was born in Rome. In 1927, when he was 20, he emigrated to Palestine. He worked on a kibbutz and was an ardent socialist and trade unionist. In the early 1930s, he went to Germany to organise a Jewish escape organisation and was briefly detained by the Gestapo. He then joined the British Army in 1940 and served in Iraq and Egypt, before he was recruited by SOE. He became an officer in the Jewish Parachute Unit, whose mission was to drop agents into occupied European countries.

Only thirty-three men and women actually physically made it into Europe, and Sereni was one of them. In May 1944, he parachuted into north-western Italy with a mission to link up and co-ordinate operations with two partisan brigades.

One of the men who trained Sereni was a Jewish soldier from Palestine called Oly Givon. He would shortly join the British Army and fight in Italy, but before he did this, he trained the Jewish agents of the Special Operations Executive who were about to be dropped into occupied Europe. He said:

> You have to know everything. To know the country, you have to know how to handle a weapon. Which kind of weapon. All kind of weapons. And then you have to destroy, how can you destroy roads, how can you destroy behind the lines, everything. I became a commander of the people [agents] they were born in the other European countries. And basically I was planned to go with them again to Europe or by parachute, or by underwater boat, to Yugoslavia. And I trained them. That they could walk together, fight together, and we could help them in Europe, and everywhere.[1]

Sereni's personal priority was not, however, to be attacking German supply lines or communications. He wanted to ambush and block deportation trains leaving either Milan or Turin for the week-long journey to German concentration camps. His aim was to link up with partisans east of Turin and, with the assistance of men like Augusto Segre, the rabbi from Casale Monferrato in Piemonte, who now co-commanded a partisan group, he planned a detailed operation. He wanted to ambush and capture a train leaving Turin's Porta Nuova Station, crammed with Jewish deportees.

On the night of 14 May 1944, Segre pulled on his parachute, sweating in the warm early summer night. On an Allied air base on the Adriatic coast, he received his final briefing and gathered his equipment – identity papers, Italian currency, a tweed jacket and a small collection of personal items. These were things that would be easily available in the shops and markets of northern Italy, so that if he was arrested and searched, nothing he had on him would betray him. The Halifax bomber then headed north-west, and in the early hours of the morning, Segre jumped over the rolling farmland of the Piemonte countryside, in between Milan and Turin. He then linked up with the partisans.

The SOE, and the partisan groups with which it was operating, received information about the different German transport trains leaving the major cities like Turin, Milan and Florence on the route towards Austria. The fastest and most accurate information was that which came from railway workers themselves, at the cities' stations and marshalling yards. With Allied bombing of the northern industrial centres a regular occurrence, the make-up of the cars and carriages in deportation convoys was often decided at the last moment, and for the partisans who wanted to attack any of these trains, the most reliable source of information about their movements was thus the Italian railwaymen themselves.

Bletchley Park had, by now, made significant inroads into breaking the Enigma settings used by the German railway system as early as February 1941.[2] Intelligence derived from this had also been instrumental in helping the Allies discover the exact start date of Operation Barbarossa. And now, in northern Italy, it was to help again. Sereni, Segre and their partisan group began looking for a deportation convoy on which they could stage an attack.

By now, in May 1944, the Jews of Italy had spread not just to the four winds, but to every conceivable and permissible location in the whole of Italy and its neighbours. When the Germans arrived, there had been approximately 45,000 Jews or more in the country, with groups and individuals constantly moving when possible into and back from Croatia, France, Slovenia, into Switzerland and across the Allied front line, which by May was just south of Rome. Cassino had fallen, the

Anzio bridgehead was broken and Allied troops were aligning themselves in a formation that stretched right across the country just south of
the capital.

An approximate estimate of the status of Italy's Jews on the eve of the
liberation of Rome and Florence from June–August 1944 could be laid
out in this manner:

- October 1943: 42,000–45,500 Italian and other Jews were in Italy, or
  in other Italian-occupied territories.
- The Rome ghetto deportations saw 1,259 seized and at least
  1,035 deported.
- The Vatican and other parts of the Catholic Church infrastructure in
  and around Rome and elsewhere hid some 4,700.
- Another 1,500 fled southwards from Rome towards Allied lines.
- Between October 1943 and May 1944, German deportations moved
  an estimated 3,300 Jews from Italy and its formerly-occupied areas,
  mainly to Mauthausen and Auschwitz.
- Of the 3,500-5,000 people detained in the San Sabba camp in Trieste,
  approximately 1,200 were Jews who were deported to Auschwitz,
  Ravensbruck and Belsen.
- This left some 30,000–33,000 Jews in Italy or its formerly
  occupied territories who had hidden, changed identities, emigrated
  or disappeared.

This still left 29,000–30,000 unaccounted for and helps to explain the
urgency in the orders from Kaltenbrunner, Eichmann and Himmler to
the SS, SD and Gestapo teams in Italy.

The situation for the Germans was going to deteriorate, however, as
after months of stalemate south of Rome the Allies were now about to
advance fast, far and northwards. They would tie up the Germans in a
fighting retreat and allow whole parts of the Jewish population in hiding
in Lazio, Tuscany and Emilia-Romagna to be liberated.

But the Jews who were the most at risk were those in northerly parts
of the country, in the Italian Social Republic, Genoa, Milan, Verona and
Turin. So, what Enzo Sereni and Augusto Segre wanted to do was to

stage an attack on a deportation train convoy around Turin and liberate the prisoners. They also wanted to send a clear message to the Germans that even if they succeeded in arresting Jews, it would be by no means certain that they would be able to deport them out of the country to the concentration camp system.

By 1944, the trains that the Germans and Italian Fascists were using to deport Jews were cargo and cattle trucks that formed part of the Italian railway system, as well as that of the Deutsche *Reichsbahn* inventory. German-made DRB Class 52 steam locomotives were often used as the engines of the Holocaust, and the signature cattle cars were well suited to the deportation of large groups of human beings.

Big numbers could be moved fast, far and with little supervision. The cars were locked and water and food did not need to be distributed. And because the cattle cars were windowless and closed, all the Germans or Italians had to do was guard each end of a convoy and make sure that at stations none of the prisoners escaped.

Each of the *Guterwagen* cattle or freight cars could accommodate fifty people under SS regulations, but in extremis, the Germans could push 100 into each. There was often only one bucket in each car, to be used as a latrine, and one small, barred window set high up on one side of the car. When the Germans moved prisoners from detention centres or prisons, they would fill up each car, one by one, sometimes leaving the full cars in railway marshalling yards overnight, until the requisite number of freight wagons had been filled, a convoy could be formed and a train attached.

When it came to travelling along the railway lines, the transport convoys would give priority to passing military and freight trains. This meant that at frequent points along the six-day journey from Turin, Milan or Verona to Auschwitz, the trains would be immobilised in sidings as a hospital train, or one carrying troops, tanks on low-loaders or supplies, passed by.

This was the moment that Segre and Sereni were looking for. The aim was not to blow up the railway engine, the railway lines nor, of course, the freight cars. The aim was to find the convoy at a moment it was stationary and couldn't move, then attack the railway engine and the guards who were spaced along the train.

Prisoners in Turin who were to be deported would be brought to the trains from the *Carcere Nuovo*, the 'New Prison', and driven along the wide Corso Vittorio Emanuele II (this was the boulevard along which the teenage Jewish girl Virginia Montalcini had walked to school each day). The prisoners would arrive at the station at dawn, disembark from the German lorries and then walk across the station forecourt to the cattle cars waiting in the marshalling yards.

The partisans, taking advice from the Italian railwaymen who worked at the Porta Nuova Station in Turin and in its large marshalling yards, knew any attack had to be carried out while the train was on a relatively isolated stretch of track, where it was immobile and far enough from the city centre that German troops and Italian policemen couldn't reach it in a hurry and yet not in a completely open stretch of countryside, because there, any of the Jews escaping out of the railway wagons would simply find themselves in the middle of a vineyard, rolling ploughed fields or a wood, where they could be easily surrounded and then captured again.

In 1944, the route taken by the railway lines that led out of the station at Porta Nuova went due south for 2 miles. They then swung round in a gentle, south-easterly direction through the suburb of Lingotto, past the Fiat Mirafiori factory and towards the River Po. On the edges of the suburbs of Nichelino and Moncalieri, a bridge went over the river, then the line straightened and trains speeded up and headed eastwards towards Milan.

The partisans thought that somewhere just before the bridge would be the best idea, as the deportation convoy waited in a siding for another train to pass. This was what had happened with two previous deportation transport convoys, which had left Turin on 13 January and 18 February 1944.

The partisans and railway workers were not too worried about Allied bombing either: in fact, the safest place to be during an RAF raid was in the marshalling yards themselves. Despite dozens of air attacks on Turin since 1940, only two had actually succeeded in hitting the station, one in December 1942, the other in July 1943. So, all the partisans had to do now was to wait for reliable information that a deportation convoy was being formed up and was about to leave.

In April 1944, the Education Minister of the Italian Social Republic – or Republic of Salò – addressed the Fascist Council of Ministers. By this stage of the war, with the Allies only a month away from liberating Rome, the invasion of mainland France imminent and the Germans in constant retreat in Russia, one item appeared on the agenda of the address that gave an idea of the self-delusion of Italy's Fascists. The minister said that he thought it a very bad idea to print weekly lists of looted Jewish property in the country's *Gazzetta Ufficiale d'Italia*, as one recent entry had been for 'two pairs of used socks, one national flag, a bidet and an enema bag'. If only these items had been the only things looted from Italy's Jews.

By summer 1944, the German execution and implementation of the Holocaust was flagging. The liberation of Rome and Tuscany was approaching. Thousands of hidden Jews were being freed while more fled south, behind Allied lines. The German rear areas were in a state of war with Italian partisans, and the majority of the Jews left inside German territory had long since hidden, escaped, joined partisan units or moved southwards to the other side of the Allies' ever-advancing front line.

Some, however, had not. Among them were those who were still prisoners of the Germans and Italian Fascists.

The Attack on Servigliano Detention Camp

The Italian partisan who was to lead the only documented attack on a Jewish detention centre in Italy was a bookish, scholarly man. Edoardo Volterra took after his father, who was a mathematician, and he adopted his name too, calling himself 'Vito' instead of Edoardo. Before the war, he was a teacher and specialised in the academically arcane field of Roman law, lecturing about the rules and regulations of Ancient Roman marriages.

He moved to Rome from the south of the country but, like so many other Jews, he found that the introduction of the Racial Laws in 1938 stopped his career dead in its tracks. So, the slight, cerebral man decided to become a partisan. He was one of the first recruits to a partisan group that began operating outside Rome.

The *Partito D'Azione*, or 'Action Party', found that its ranks tripled after the July 1943 Armistice. By late spring 1944, Volterra and his group were operating in the forests of Abruzzo, north of Rome, in the foothills of the wooded mountains that lead down to the Adriatic Sea.

On the one hand, the July Armistice had seen tens of thousands of Italian soldiers pledge allegiance to the Allies or desert to join partisan groups, but it had also seen thousands flock to the cause of Mussolini's Fascist Social Republic. The forests and countryside of Abruzzo were also filled with escaped Allied POWs.

German soldiers were preparing defences against the forthcoming Allied advance north, and there were thousands of civilians, many of whom had taken refuge in the countryside from the constant Allied bombing of the towns and cities on the coast, particularly the port of Ancona. Twenty-five miles south of the port was the village of Servigliano, sitting on the railway line that ran from the coast towards the Apennines.

During the First World War, the Italian Army built a camp on the outskirts of the village, consisting of forty wood and stone huts. Six thousand Austrian prisoners of war, captured in the fighting on the Isonzo River, were interned there from August 1916 onwards. When the Second World War began, the camp was first used to house a small number of foreign Jewish detainees. There were only about thirty of them, living in the almost deserted camp and mostly left to their own devices.

But when Italy moved into Albania and Greece in late 1940 and early 1941, 3,000 Greek POWs arrived. Then came north Africa, and 2,000 British and Americans. The Armistice in 1943 had an instant effect

– the Italian guards fled and the prisoners poured into the surrounding countryside. German soldiers from Ancona arrived at the beginning of October and began to try and round them up.

By now, the Italian Social Republic was housing most of its Jewish prisoners in camps such as the one at Borgo San Dalmazzo, but further across the country it also needed space near Ancona. The Fascists had by now set up a string of ad hoc camps and detention centres near all of the major towns in German-occupied territory, which by then basically meant a line north of Rome. Up near Ancona, the old POW camp at Servigliano was perfect for the Fascists' requirements. Ministry of Interior troops from the Salò Republic, dubbed the *Camicie Nere*, or Blackshirts, guarded the detention centre.

On 24 March 1944, the partisan Volterra led a raid to free the Jewish prisoners: an air raid was in progress, with the Allies dropping bombs on targets near the coast. The sky danced with explosive noise and searchlight beams. Sixty-four Jews, helped by the partisans, managed to break out.

The following morning, a German company arrived, and the partisans, along with thirty of the Jewish prisoners, fled into the forests of chestnuts and oaks, leaving another thirty-four in the hands of the Germans. They took these Jewish prisoners to Ancona Station and sent them north to the detention centre at Fossoli, the first step on the road to the concentration camp system. Satisfied with this haul of detainees, the German unit then withdrew from around Servigliano.

Some of the remaining Jews, who had been hiding with the partisans in nearby woods, decided to walk back to the camp briefly to see if they could find anything to eat. The partisans warned them how dangerous this was but the Jews insisted.

Two days later, the Germans returned yet again. This time they brought another sixty Jews with them. A week later, the partisans, in their turn, attacked, running through the forests outside the camp, firing Bren guns and Mauser rifles at the German guards and tearing through the almost deserted barracks huts to drag the remaining Jews with them.

In mid-June, the to and fro, the cat and mouse, was continuing, until the Germans finally pulled back to Ancona. Servigliano was freed and ninety Jews had been saved.

Partisan accounts of the series of skirmishes around the camps between March and June mention that Allied aircraft at one point deployed over the area, strafing the Germans in a ground attack and bombing the camp at the request of the partisans. This would stand as the only documented case in the whole of the Final Solution in Italy in which Allied airpower was directly deployed in an attack on a concentration camp, detention centre or deportation convoy of Jews.

15

LIBERATION

Herbert Kappler fled the Via Tasso Prison at dawn. He left some SS guards and all the prisoners behind him and drove north in a staff car, following a truck full of German soldiers. It was 4 June, and Kappler reckoned that if he and the men drove fast, they could manage to escape the advancing American troops who were trying to encircle the city. Keeping an eye overhead for any Allied fighter-bombers, the Gestapo chief and his colleagues headed into retreat.

The speed with which the Allies had arrived on the outskirts of the capital had taken them all by surprise. One moment, it seemed, Kappler had been planning an arrest operation for a handful of Roman Jews, the next, he was grabbing his equipment and running fast down the steps of the Via Tasso headquarters.

In one of the larger cells, he left behind him fourteen men, all with their hands tied behind their backs. There was a Pole, eight Italian Catholics, four Italian Jews and an Allied agent who, under questioning, hadn't given his name. The Germans were due to shoot them all that morning, planning to take them all in an old Spa 38 truck to a disused villa a short way outside Rome. The execution would take place in the grounds. The villa was known simply as *La Storta*, or 'The Bend', from its position on the road.

The temperature inside the Via Tasso cell, meanwhile, was over 100°F, the summer sun of Rome battering down on its shutters and outside walls. There were the mosquitoes, too, the ubiquitous *zanzare* that are such a feature of Italian summers, their high-pitched whines making sure the sweltering men could not get any sleep on the concrete floors.

Suddenly, on the morning of 5 June, the SS guards just vanished. They were replaced by a small group of Austrian soldiers, who didn't seem to know what to do with the prisoners.

The Jews had been condemned to death simply because they were Jewish, and because Kappler had thought it far more economical to take them on a truck to the garden at the villa and shoot them in the back of the head under the palm trees. Much easier than detaining them, waiting for enough Jews to be captured in round-up operations to justify a rail convoy, and then sending precious SS men to go with them as guards. These men would travel as far as Arnoldstein, and then have to come all the way back again to Rome.

The Allied agent was facing death because he worked for the Special Operations Executive, and the other eight Italians because they were partisans, or loosely affiliated to them. Early on that morning of the 5th, the prisoners could hear shellfire, the sound of explosions, the taut ripping smatter of machine guns as the Allies fought their way into Rome. Tortured half to death, starving, dehydrated and exhausted, it was as much as most of the men could do to even stand. One of the prisoners was a hunchback and, resorting to ancient, traditional beliefs as they approached their hour of death, each man took turns running a hand over his hump in the belief that it would bring them luck.[1] But all of them, in their heads, knew they were going to die. Especially the partisan agent code-named 'Eugenio'.

Then three things happened very fast. The gunfire came closer. The Austrian guards ran out of the courtyard, leaving the old Spa 38 lorry where it was parked. It had broken down, so for now the prisoners could not be taken off for execution. The men heard cheering and stumbled out into the sunlight to discover the population of the blocks of flats in the street had turned out to applaud them. The Germans had vanished. The Allies had arrived. Rome was liberated.

About a mile away, the Piperno family had been awake since dawn, like so many of Rome's other inhabitants. Clotilde, Piero, Giacomo and the others walked out of the rooms where they were hiding and down into one of the closed courtyards of the convent, which sat inside the main entrance of the building. Should they go out, they wondered? Was this the end? Was this really the liberation? Or was it just the beginning of a major street battle between the Allies, the partisans and the Germans, which could continue for weeks, leaving Rome besieged?

They decided to stay put and wait. They had survived this far, it did not make sense to die at the last moment out of stupidity. On the night of 4–5 June, they'd heard the sound of numerous trucks all around, but assumed they were German ones. But then they heard voices speaking French: it was Free French army units, which had arrived in Rome to re-occupy the French Embassy nearby.

Major Sam Derry, D'Arcy Osborne and Hugh O'Flaherty knew this was the end. Allied signals had been criss-crossing all morning as the Americans had approached Rome. The triumvirate that ran the Rome Escape Line decided that until the British and the Americans physically controlled the streets of the city, no Allied POWs and, especially, no Jews should venture outside.

And then, as they made this decision, they heard the sound of what would turn out to be nearly half a million feet, running, charging, rushing, walking, heading for St Peter's Square. In front of them, Pope Pius XII was about to thank God for having saved Rome, and the Romans:

Rome, which yesterday lay still anxious for the lives of its sons and children, for the fate of incomparable daughters, for the fate of incomparable treasures of religion and culture, with the terrifying spectre of war and unimaginable destruction, looks out today with new hope and strengthened confidence to its salvation. Therefore, with a profoundly grateful spirit, we lift up in praise and adoration our minds and hearts to the trinity of God, the Father, the Son and the Holy Spirit, on whose solemn feast day, by divine mercy, inspiring in both warring Parties intentions of peace and not of affliction, the Eternal City was preserved from immeasurable danger.[2]

It had taken the Allies four major offensives, between January and May 1944, before the German defensive lines south of Rome were eventually broken by the British 8th and the American 5th Armies. Following the fall of Monte Cassino, the British, Americans, Poles, Canadians and French focused their troops on a very narrow stretch of front that lay between the Monte Cassino Valley and the sea.

Mark Clark finally fought his men out of the Anzio bridgehead, the Allied front west of Cassino pushed forward, and the German 10th Army that lay between the Allies and Rome performed an east-facing loop around the outskirts of the capital, then headed north towards the Trasimene Line and escaped. The 8th Army was pushing as hard as it could up the Liri Valley, 30 miles to the south, and Clark saw his opportunity and entered Rome.

Rather than follow the German 10th Army and face it down in battle, Clark decided that liberating a capital was more important than destroying an enemy's forces, and in so doing, contributed to the war in Italy – and the ongoing Final Solution – lasting beyond the end of 1944. So, during the night of 4 June, the Canadian 1st Special Service Force, the American 1st Armoured Division and five other divisions then headed into the capital.

Inside Rome, in a small apartment, a 25-year-old American journalist from Georgia unbuckled a beige suitcase and took out a pair of headphones. Along with a British radio operator from the Special Operations Executive, he began to tap out a message in Morse code. It was encoded in a cipher the British called 'Monkey': 'Here is free Rome, here is free Rome, here is free Rome …'

The American was called Peter Tompkins and he was working for the American OSS. He liaised with a partisan group both inside and outside Rome and one of his radio operators had been the agent called Eugenio, then just emerging from imprisonment at Via Tasso – a former soldier called Arrigo Paladini. Eugenio's network had been instrumental in hiding Jews outside the capital. Tompkins had been in Rome, and Italy, off and on since 1940. His parents were a painter and sculptor from Savannah, Georgia, and Tompkins was completely at home in the country, having spent holidays there since he was a teenager.

Tompkins gathered information from a network of partisans and Allied sympathisers on such things as the movement of German armoured units south to Anzio and Cassino. Although Bletchley Park and Beaumanor Hall could intercept the signals sent by these units, such was the pressure on both places, at that moment, to handle all of the urgent signals traffic coming from the German armed forces in Normandy, that Italy often found itself being relegated in terms of decoding priority.

By the time Tompkins and his colleagues were sending messages from free Rome, the first Allied paratroopers were soon to emplane in their C-47 transports in southern England, ready to spearhead the airborne assault the following morning, which was D-Day. Rome fell the day before the Allied armies arrived in Normandy.

Bletchley had been running at maximum output for three months prior to Operation Overlord, and so Tompkins and his Radio Vittoria network would transmit short, coded signals to the Allies at Cassino or Anzio. This was faster and gave Bletchley some breathing space. On some occasions, Tompkins and his team also simply used traditional means, like the telephone.

The Germans, who knew about Radio Vittoria and the American spy, were determined to stamp out his network. Then, on 3 May, they got lucky. They captured Agent Eugenio, the former Lieutenant Paladini, at a roadblock in the Piazza Sante Croce. He had a transmitter in the boot of his car and a jacket pocket full of radio crystals. This time, thought the Germans, they could suffocate the radio network and lock up its agents in Via Tasso to die.

But Eugenio didn't talk, despite being beaten half to death by Herbert Kappler's men and half-starved. Lunch for him, one day in the cells, was a tin cup of warm water with flecks of soap in it. It had been used to do the washing up. It did have a very small amount of food in it, though, as attached to the rim of the cup were tiny shreds of vegetables and soggy bread, left over from the dishwashing.

That Agent Eugenio didn't talk drove Herbert Kappler mad. The Gestapo chief would have been considerably further enraged, however, if he had known that he had unwittingly met Peter Tompkins at a party previously. The two men had attended the same reception one evening in Rome in the spring of 1944, Tompkins pretending to be an Italian American businessman.

They were in a room full of German officers and Fascist Italians, while Kappler concentrated on trying to seduce two Italian women. At one point, he broke off to ask the Italian American to cook him a late evening omelette, which he drank with some grappa (Italian brandy). He never found out about the man who had made him this meal. Tompkins had by then just arrived back in Rome, in January 1944, shortly before the landings at Anzio began. Well connected, one of his sources was an NCO who worked in Kappler's prison.

None of this, however, had prevented the round-up and execution of fourteen of Tompkins' partisan colleagues at the Ardeatine Caves. The OSS agent from Georgia had hidden and lived in a small flat in Piazza Lovatelli, 300m from the nuns in Piazza Farnese, 200m from the Fatebenefratelli Hospital and close to the Jewish ghetto. Rome, in those days of war and liberation in summer 1944, was a closely sewn network of enemies, agents, double-crossing intriguers, priests, spies, rabbis and German soldiers. It was as though Kappler, Dannecker, the Jews, the Pope, O'Flaherty, Derry, Osborne, Tompkins, the SS, families like the Pipernos, nuns, priests and partisans danced a macabre waltz of necessity around each other, the prize being life and liberty. And the punishment for getting something wrong? Violent death.

As 5 June progressed, the American infantry divisions poured into Rome and quickly moved north, running into occasional battles with the German 10th Army outside the capital. Operation Diadem, the plan to advance north and capture Rome, had worked. The road to Tuscany and the Apennines now lay open.

General Harold Alexander, the Supreme Allied Commander, and the head of his 8th Army, Lieutenant General Oliver Leese, both optimistically estimated that if the Allied armies did not get bogged down north of Rome, as they had done south of it, they could reach Genoa, Rimini and the Po Valley by autumn. This would also affect the ongoing Final Solution in the country. The Allies would occupy a much larger percentage of the Italian terrain and the SS would be predominantly pinned down inside the cities of Turin, Milan and Verona. So, finding Jews in the countryside would be doubly difficult for them. Thus Allied speed in getting to the Po Valley was vital: the huge, macro-strategic considerations and developments had a bearing on each individual life of the Jews who, across *Il Bel Paese*, were now in hiding.

The triumphs of the Allied armies in Italy, culminating in the capture of Rome on 5 June, soon seemed to pale into insignificance with what had happened in Normandy. The launch of Operation Overlord took place on 6 June, the day after Rome was liberated. The invasion of Normandy was meant to have been accompanied in tandem, not just with a significant tactical advance up Italy – like the fall of Rome – but with the launching of Operation Anvil, or Dragoon, the invasion of the south of France.

But delays in reaching Rome, the quagmire south of the capital and differing strategic decisions between Washington and London now saw it postponed. Dragoon would finally be launched on 17 August, but its main effect on Italy was that it would simply reduce even further the priority of the Italian campaign, in terms of available Allied fighting men and material, as these were diverted to France.

Churchill was also interested in invading the Balkans from the Dalmatian coast. The aim of that hypothetical operation, and Dragoon, was to tie down German divisions that could otherwise be used in Normandy and north-western Europe. So, after the liberation of Rome, the 8th and 5th Armies would now have only fourteen divisions between them, facing seventeen German ones, from the 14th Army along the western coast of Italy, and with the Axis 10th Army on the Adriatic.

On 7 June, Lieutenant General Harold Alexander acted on orders from London and Washington. He set out to push the retreating Germans as hard as he could northwards to a line that ran across Italy from Pisa to Rimini. Little did he know that the Germans had already been constructing a series of defensive positions along this exact axis for six months. The Germans named it the *Gotenstellung*, or 'Gothic Line'.

It was to be the focus of precisely what the Allies most feared – a strong, in-depth series of German defensive positions across northern Italy, blocking their advance towards Austria and Yugoslavia.

So, while the 8th Army stormed up the eastern seaboard of Italy as fast as it could, heading for the port of Ancona, the predominantly American 5th Army advanced up the Tuscan coast, fighting for one seaside town after the next, with units of local partisans joining in with the fighting as the American troops arrived. Pisa, Lucca, Pistoia and the heartland of Tuscany fell to the GIs, and by the beginning of August they were approaching the banks of the River Arno, which flows through Florence. Running on a 200-mile front, the 8th Army came in from the centre, towards the Tuscan capital and the town of Arezzo.

For two months that summer, it seemed as though the Allies might well be across the River Po by September, before the winter rains swept in, the Apennine mountains became cloaked in snow and the roads and flatlands of Italy turned to muddy quagmires. On the first 70 miles of their advance north from Rome, the Allies did not encounter any significant German obstacles, and by 21 June, the 8th and 5th Armies had advanced 110 miles. Harold Alexander and his generals were suddenly talking about pushing through the north-east of Italy, into Austria and Yugoslavia.

None of them knew about Kesselring's Gothic Line. They all knew, of course, that significant German reinforcements lay north of them but, elated by the success of the advance from Rome – after the gridlock of Cassino and Anzio – they thought the war in Italy was won and forgot quite how much fight the Germans still had left in them.

By late July, New Zealand troops stormed the Pian dei Cerri hills overlooking Florence, moving into Fiesole. In Gino Bartali's basement, the Goldenberg family could hear the war – and liberation – approaching. Florence was declared an undefended open city, prohibiting further shelling and bombing in accordance with the Hague Convention.

On 4 August, the retreating Germans decided to blow up explosive charges along the bridges of the Arno, trying to block New Zealand, South African and British troops from crossing. But the German officer in charge of the demolitions had very different ideas. Gerhard Wolf, the diplomat, ordered that the Ponte Vecchio was to be spared.

And then in Bartali's basement, Giorgio Goldenberg heard shouting in the street. He and the family came out of the basement into the sunlight. 'Everyone was shouting that the British were arriving,' he said. He went outside and saw a British soldier with the word 'Palestine' and the Star of David on his shoulder insignia. He went up to him and began to hum the *Hatikvah*, the song that would later become the national anthem of Israel. 'He heard me and spoke to me in English. I understood that we were free, thanks to Gino and his cousin.'[3]

The Piperno family left the convent in the Piazza Farnese by midsummer. Rome was flooded with displaced people by then, families fleeing the fighting further north in Tuscany, or who had come to the capital simply because their homes in the south had been destroyed. There were people from Naples, Taranto, Viareggio and Florence, Jews and Catholics, all of them Italians.

As the fighting roared up the Tuscan coast that summer, and through the foothills of the Apuan Alps towards Florence, a unit of the Waffen-SS, its 16th *Panzergrenadier* Division, had been carrying out a string of large-scale massacres. From near Lucca, up to the coast by Viareggio and Massa Carrara, to a small mountain village called Sant'Anna di Stazzema, the SS had murdered nearly 2,000 civilians in a string of reprisal killings. So the civilian population of the Tuscan foothills fled west and south, towards Arezzo and Siena, and then sometimes right down to Rome – because it was bigger, there was more space and everybody said there were more American soldiers there, and thus, more money.

The sisters at the Convent of Santa Brigida, meanwhile, were worked off their feet. There was no room for families who had somewhere else to go, and the Pipernos, at least, had a home nearby, or what might be left of it. Clotilde and one of her sons had returned to their house in the Jewish ghetto three times since the Allies had arrived in Rome, and it was still habitable.

Jewish people were coming out of hiding now, inquiring desperately about those who had been taken away or those who had survived, and it seemed that the cobbled streets around the old fish market in the ghetto echoed to the sound of vast absences. The Rome they knew was flooded and choked, full and different. It was crammed with people.

Everywhere, there were displaced Italian people, with the eyes of those had seen their homes bombed or villages devastated by artillery fire. They didn't seem to care or differentiate between the different sides who were fighting in this war, only that it, the war, had done this to them. It had blown up their house, slaughtered their cows, seen their teenage son die in a reprisal killing, or their father sent off with a regiment on a train to Stalingrad, to come back with purple and blackened finger stumps across one hand from where frostbite had hit during a fighting retreat against the Red Army. He'd been one of the lucky ones, as 80,000 of the Italians hadn't made it back from Russia.

Rome was flooded, that summer, with heat and sunshine and freedom. There were no Germans, only scraps and relics of their uniforms – an SS peaked cap, a Luftwaffe tunic – spread out on the pavement for sale. Every street was just one, great, big market, with everything up to buy – bundles of pungent, brown tobacco; potatoes, oranges, lemons, apricots and cucumbers carried in from the countryside; 2-litre bottles of red wine with no label; leather pistol holsters; Luger, Walther and Beretta automatics; Lucky Strike cigarettes; and US Army mattress covers, which were perfect for making clothing, so long as the new owner cut off the stamped marking that said, 'Property of the Department of Defense'.

And then there was penicillin, the Holy Grail of all purchases, and tins of American K-Rations, the tinned, chopped pork which, when mixed with eggs and pasta, made an ad hoc spaghetti carbonara. It seemed the world was available to buy.

And along the boulevards, in the bars, on the pavements, in their Willis Jeeps, trucks and half-tracks, threaded thousands upon thousands of American soldiers with their M1 carbines and pistols, their Ray-Ban sunglasses and incessant cheeriness, apologies and thanks. Men from Iowa, Texas, New York and Nebraska, all swarming over Clotilde Piperno's city, as she tried to take her family back to a semblance of normality that summer, where every day started with the realisation that they had survived.

THE DIARY OF AN SS DOUBLE AGENT

The Allied advance gathered pace and momentum in midsummer and autumn 1944. The key Adriatic coastal town of Rimini fell in late September, the Americans fought through the towns on the Tuscan coast, up as far as La Spezia, and Indian and American troops slogged through combat up the slopes of the Apennines. By late autumn, the Allies and the Germans were facing each other across the Gothic Line and, as winter came, it became clear that the Po Valley and the flatlands of northern Italy would not be reached until the next spring.

Despite urgent encouragement from Berlin, the pace of the Final Solution slowed dramatically. The decreased pace of the Allied advance further south meant that the SS and SD in northern Italy now had less logistical leeway in which to continue their operations, as partisan operations in this confined area of land that was still under German control escalated dramatically after October 1944.

SOE and OSS support missions to the resistance groups increased, and as the availability of Allied-supplied weapons soared and the amount of territory under German control dropped, so the partisans began to dominate more and more territory outside the main cities and towns. However, the ambitious plan to capture a deportation train, which had been conceived by Augusto Segre and Enzo Sereni, had not worked.

Betrayed by Italian informers, Sereni was captured outside Turin. By November, he was in Auschwitz.

Another reason for the decrease in the arrests of Jews was that the tracking down and deportation of those remaining in northern Italy had slowed considerably because of the German officials deployed to do it. They were men who were more interested in looting and stealing Jewish property and making post-war plans for themselves than in executing Berlin's orders. One of these was the SS-Obersturmführer from Milan called Guido Zimmer.

Zimmer, as mentioned before, had joined the SS in 1936, and in 1940, as a member of the Foreign Intelligence department of the RSHA, he was posted to Rome. After his cover was blown, he moved back to Berlin, and then back to the Italian capital to work as a subordinate to Herbert Kappler. By 1944, he was the deputy head of the SD and SS office in Milan and Genoa, responsible for finding and deporting Jews and 'sequestrating' – stealing – their property. The reality was that he did a lot of the latter and very little of the former. Zimmer's villa in Milan was described by one visitor as being filled with silver, jewels and looted art, and he regularly released from detention Jewish families who paid him sufficient bribes.

Zimmer was in constant contact both with Italian Fascist businessmen with whom he hoped to work after the war, and with American OSS agents based in Switzerland. He was also, highly secretly, working alongside General Karl Wolff to negotiate a separate peace deal and early surrender in Italy between Germany and the Allies.

This plan had a variety of code names, from Operation Wool, to Operation Aurora or Sunrise. It focused on contacts between Allen Dulles, the OSS station chief in Switzerland, Karl Wolff from the SS, and their respective staffs, as well as other German, Italian, American and British personnel – military and civilian. Negotiations took place in the Swiss town of Lugano and the plans and meetings for this continuing operation went on between both sides from autumn 1944 to early April 1945. Most of the cadre of senior SS and SD officers in Italy were to be involved in it, tangentially or directly, and Zimmer's covert notes show exactly how this progressed. It was little wonder he had small enthusiasm for deporting Jews or obeying Berlin's orders. By the end of 1944 and the beginning of 1945, Zimmer, Wolff and two other SS officers were the German 'face' of this peace plan.

One crucial, covert and non-negotiable condition on which the American negotiators from the OSS insisted was that Wolff's SS office should immediately halt any operations against Jews in areas of Italy still controlled by the Germans. The Final Solution could, it seemed, finally be brought to a halt across the country.

Nobody would ever really know why Guido Zimmer kept a diary. The SS lieutenant, described in a CIA case file as 'slim, athletic, of average height, with dark brown hair and a high-pitched voice',[1] was neither noticeable nor particularly prepossessing. Unlike his SS colleagues Walter Rauff and Herbert Kappler, he bore no evident malice to those he arrested and deported, and he was not a brutal man, who relished torture and violence, like Globocnik or Hans Andergassen, a notoriously sadistic Gestapo officer at the Bolzano camp. He was not noticeably or overtly antisemitic either, like Dannecker, Saevecke and Wilhelm Harster.

The qualities that Zimmer did possess in abundance were duplicitousness, cunning, deceit and a desire to intrigue. And like all good diarists, a desire to enlighten, confess, comment and share opinions.[2] From early 1944 until after the end of the war, Zimmer was an SS lieutenant, at times serving as an acting Hauptsturmführer (captain), who was based in Milan and Genoa.

And he kept his diary assiduously. As part of Walter Rauff's SD office, his job was the tracking down, arrest, centralisation and deportation of northern Italy's Jews and the appropriation of their property and valuables. Zimmer was also, however, tasked with developing an intelligence network among Italians that would lead him to Jews and also to any Allied intelligence networks, such as those run by the American OSS and British SOE.

His diaries describe a network of individuals with whom he had dealings both legitimate and criminal, men and women who were acting for their own side or the enemy's, or both, and often at the same time. The picture painted by Zimmer's operations is the inside, covert story of what was really happening in northern Italy in the last eighteen months of the Final Solution – who was dealing with whom, why and for what, and where and when.

Zimmer's priority was making money, saving his skin, allying himself to those more powerful and taking credit for other people's achievements. That he survived unscathed is a tribute to his serpentine ability to insinuate himself into the protection of the powerful – and to extricate himself from trouble before it overwhelmed him.

He lived in a villa in Genoa, which he had requisitioned, and had an apartment in Milan, again stolen from its former Jewish owners whom he had deported to Mauthausen. He travelled frequently between the two cities and often to Turin. By March 1944, he was setting up Operations Tosca and Bertram, infiltrating French and German agents into southern France, via San Remo on the Italian Riviera.[3]

One thing that his agents needed on arrival in France were travel permits and Zimmer notes in his diary that the person to approach for these was an American captain working for the OSS, who had his headquarters in the Bergamo Hotel in Nice. Geoffrey Jones, says Zimmer, was about 45 years old, 1.75m tall, strongly built, with blond and thinning hair. He was inclined to laziness, wrote the SS subaltern, and consequently would fill out a large number of blank travel permits and leave their signature and issue to one of his NCOs. What Zimmer wanted from the agents in southern France were the addresses and whereabouts of Jews, to whom he was intending to sell stolen Spanish passports. To this end, he and an Italian Yugoslav agent he code names 'Draga' were copying the keys and security systems of the Spanish Consulate in Milan:

On the 8th of February DRAGA managed to get the vault keys to himself for about 40 minutes. With a wax [mould] set up in great haste by SS 1st Lt. ZIMMER, some impressions were made [from] which a master-key for the special locks was then prepared. Provided the keys fit, it is planned to make photographic extracts in the next few days of the most important securities. The individual implicated at the Consulate General has, in the past 4 weeks, demonstrably purloined 27 passport form-sheets and sold them with the stamp and signature of the Consul-General, for a total of 6 million Lire. 1st Lt. Z [Zimmer] has definitely ascertained to what extent the Consul-General himself is implicated in the passport sale. One of the Consul-General's next trips will be made in the company of DRAGA's wife, who has entered into a [sexual] liaison with him.

The currency exchange rate in 1944 in Italy for the Italian lira was set at 100 lira to US$1, or 1 German reichsmark to 10 lire. If Zimmer and his accomplice at the Spanish Consulate were selling twenty-seven Spanish passports for 6 million lire, then the going rate for a Spanish passport for a Jewish Italian trying to escape deportation was US$2,200 each.[4]

Along with these financial scams, Zimmer was also involved, with his SS colleagues, in setting up a 'stay-behind' radio network that would be operated by both Italians and Germans after the surrender in Italy.

It's clear in the diaries that all sides – the SS very much included – knew that Germany had lost the war, and Zimmer and the SS hierarchy around him were financing their escapes and preparing for the surrender to the Allies they knew would eventually come. In the meantime, Zimmer spent his days running an extraordinary variety of double agents and inventing intelligence schemes of any nature that would keep his superiors in Berlin happy – Himmler, Kaltenbrunner and Schellenberg. Zimmer, Walter Rauff and Theodor Saevecke come across in the pages of the diaries as being complicit with American intelligence and desperate to protect themselves from the two most feared postings – being recalled to Berlin for disciplinary action or being transferred to the Eastern Front.

The rhythm of Zimmer's day, however, often depended on the psychology and behaviour of his many agents:

The Baroness fainted in front of her mirror and fell down. Since this occurred in a hotel room, attendants are to be imagined. [The Baroness Freddy di Blasis was a Finnish-born Italian national who mingled much in German military and social circles in Italy during the war years. She was living in Genoa from November 1943 to April 1944.] She painted her relationship with the RFSS [Reichsführer SS, Heinrich Himmler] to the doctor in a harmless light.[5]

Not all of Zimmer's contacts were as ethereal or insubstantial as Baroness Freddy, who was desperate to escape to Switzerland, and Zimmer promised to arrange a visa for her, on the condition she would spy for him on the Russian diplomatic community there.

The cabal of SS officers, meanwhile, were hedging their bets and trying to set up contacts with the British and Americans in Switzerland. In the early overtures of Operation Sunrise, which saw Karl Wolff negotiate an early surrender to the war with the American OSS in Berne, Zimmer was acting as his envoy.[6] SS colonel Walter Rauff, Zimmer's direct superior, heard of the plan and requested that he be allowed to join the circle of conspirators. But Zimmer knew this would all cost money, especially travelling to Switzerland to meet with the American OSS, as well as buying forged travel documents. The whole plan must be carried out without the knowledge of Himmler or Kaltenbrunner in Berlin. If they were to discover the treachery of their subordinates, then, as Zimmer writes, it was not even worth returning to Berlin.

To raise money, Rauff and Zimmer were selling Spanish passports to Jews and appropriating as much gold and jewellery as they could – but they needed hard currency. Zimmer got in touch with a man called Gianni Welli, who lived in the small town of Luino, on the banks of Lake Maggiore. Welli was dispatched with two other agents to buy 600 gold coins, for which they were given 1,320,000 lire in cash by Zimmer. The three men arrived outside the apartment in Milan where the vendor of the gold coins lived. Welli entered alone, then disappeared out of a separate service entrance with the cash. There was only one possible punishment for him, wrote Zimmer, when the man was arrested two days later, 'It is necessary to intern him in a concentration camp.'

Before Welli was deported to Mauthausen, there was one more question to torture out of him: which Jewish politician, living in Switzerland and travelling regularly to Milan, was dealing with which SS officers with the purpose of selling or exchanging captured British pounds sterling for other currencies? All of Zimmer's SS colleagues were walking a tightrope, trying to make as much money as possible, where necessary by taking large bribes from Jews who were desperate to escape deportation, and at the same time keeping up the pretence to Berlin that the quotas of Jews being arrested and deported were those agreed between Milan, Rome and the RSHA.

Meanwhile, Zimmer, in his role as an SS intelligence officer, was ironically in charge of the fight against the black market. Twenty of Zimmer's men from the *Geheime Feldpolizei*, the Military Field Police, raided a factory. It was next to an apartment where Zimmer and three of his accomplices were running a radio station, code-named IDA, which made contact with Allied headquarters at Caserta in southern Italy, and also sent messages to American intelligence in Switzerland. The twenty military policemen raided the factory and seized thirty illegal refrigerators and 600 electrical heaters. What must be done with them? they asked the SS lieutenant. 'I fail to see why refrigerators and heaters must be seized for Germany?' wrote Zimmer. 'To the best of my knowledge we do not wage war with such articles.'[7]

In his ongoing efforts to contact the British and Americans, Zimmer was now dealing with a prominent Italian businessman and politician called Luigi Parilli. Frightened that if he travelled outside of Milan and Genoa he risked being ambushed by omnipresent partisan groups, Zimmer was reassured when a contact of Parilli's told him that the partisans, in return for 10,000 lire, or US$100, would write a certificate that stated that SS-Lieutenant Guido Zimmer was a 'friend and supporter' of the partisans. There hardly seemed to be any fixed sides any more: everything, it appeared, including loyalty, weapons, operational intelligence, documents and safety was up for sale.

Zimmer's superior in Turin, SS-Hauptmann Theodor Saevecke, wanted to join the mission to discuss an early surrender with the Allies. While Zimmer and Rauff were considering how to approach Karl Wolff on this matter, they were worrying whether Saevecke was, in fact, playing both sides of the SS against each other – in Milan, Genoa and Berlin – and therefore wasn't to be trusted. But two other matters intervened: one big and one more routine.

The SD and Gestapo's favourite local restaurant was being squeezed by local black marketeers, who were threatening to cut off the supply of food and drinks to the tavern. As the restaurant was linked to a nearby black-market supplier of petrol that Zimmer used, the restaurant owners were given money to pay off the black marketeers. Zimmer's lunch retreat was safe.

Then something much more pressing came up. One of Zimmer's key business contacts was a man surnamed Ferraro, who lived in Biella near the Swiss frontier. He was the president of a large company in Naples, and the fact that he was suspected of being partially Jewish and a financial supporter of local partisan groups didn't deter Zimmer, nor his SS colleagues in Turin and Milan – not when money was at stake. In the aftermath of the March 1944 industrial demonstrations in Turin, Signor Ferraro had been arrested on the orders of SS Sergeant Major Horngacher, who ran the SS *Ausenkommando* in Turin. Ferraro now had 'trade union troublemaker' added to his other crimes, which included being a suspected Jew and partisan supporter. And so Horngacher wasted no time putting the businessman into a cattle car at Turin's Porta Nuova Station. Convoy 639-5035 was now on its way to Linz in Austria, with the next stop being Mauthausen.[8]

Jewish or not, Ferraro's Italian colleagues offered Zimmer 250,000 lire, payable in gold or foreign currency, to get the businessman out of the concentration camp system, off the train and back to safety in Italy. So Zimmer, with his bribe at stake and his business contact dangerously near to possible execution or gassing at Mauthausen, went for broke and called in favours all the way up the SS chain of command in northern Italy. He spoke to Sturmbannführer Huegel, who contacted SS-General Wilhelm Harster in Verona. He stressed that Oberscharführer Kaspar Ringicher in Turin – who loathed partisans – had not done his job properly.

The train convoy on which Ferraro was travelling had last been heard of near Linz, in Austria. Zimmer and Harster's office sent an urgent signal to the Gestapo there:

To: STAPO, LINZ 339. On 17 March 1944 at 1400 train No. 7869 left Bergamo with transport No. 6395035 containing 307 prisoners, including 18 strikers. The train was destined for Mauthausen via Villach. The prisoners were to work in Germany. They had been arrested during the strike in Turin. There was no intention to intern them in the Mauthausen concentration-camp. Could you please find out what the ultimate destination of the transport was? At the same time, please find out where FERRARO is. He was placed aboard this transport by mistake. A prompt reply will be appreciated. ZIMMER Genoa. HARSTER Verona.[9]

Meanwhile, Lancia, the automobile and aerospace engineers, were developing new aeroplane engines for use at high altitude, and Junkers in Germany wanted to know anything it could about them. SS-Sturmbannführer Huegel suggested paying an employee of Lancia 10,000 lire to supply technical plans whenever necessary. But, who would pay the money?

In all of Zimmer's schemes, whether they were about aero engines, Jews, prisoners en route to concentration camps or black-market fridges, if money wasn't available, a profit wasn't involved, nor influence and favour with the Americans guaranteed, then he and his senior SS colleagues simply weren't interested. So, when it was discovered that one of the SS Italian agents in Milan, a Signor De Quarti, was living with a woman suspected of being partially Jewish, there was no question of what should be done – she paid up, or she'd be put on a train.

Fraulein Altmann said she was German and her parents were pure Aryans but then Zimmer's men discovered she'd been adopted. Her true birth mother was a woman from Frankfurt who was now in a prison camp in Russia – so that made Miss Altmann mixed race, first grade.

Deportation papers were prepared and investigations into her parentage continued, but her citizenship would be discontinued. The next train convoy to Mauthausen was due to leave in a fortnight, but then the SS discovered that their agent, Signor De Quarti, was on the verge of a breakthrough in radio technology, and he was about to marry Miss Altmann anyway – making her eligible for Aryan status – so she was spared.

The tempo of Zimmer's days sped up as the Allies advanced north, and it proved harder and harder to fill the increasingly demanding arrest and deportation quotas the RSHA in Berlin was demanding. The work that crossed his desks ranged from the life-threateningly urgent, to the sublime, the routine and the inconsequential.

A flower merchant from Ventimiglia called Giovanni Ribero, an ardent Fascist and pro-German, offered to supply information on 'matters of naval interest' from Marseille and Genoa to the SS. How, they wondered, was he going to do this without using his car? Then they realised that the suspect simply wanted authorisation to use his car for business purposes disguised as intelligence gathering.

Meanwhile, a Jewish radio technician called Gabbai had been arrested and was about to be deported: Zimmer stalled this and ordered that all necessary technical equipment and radio publications be placed at the prisoner's disposal in his private cell, so he could continue his research. He was worth more to the Germans alive, working and in Turin than in a concentration camp.

And then in spring 1945, Zimmer, who was looking for a house in the countryside around Turin where he could hide after the war finished, discovered that he and local Jews were now in the same boat. One of his contacts suggested that, for the right price, he had an available house in the suburb of Pinerolo, which was isolated and uninhabited. However, 100 Jews were trying to take refuge there as well, in its surrounding outhouses – Zimmer was in a queue. And when he came to try and buy Italian identity papers, he found himself dealing with a forger who was simultaneously providing counterfeit passports to Jewish refugees. Zimmer was forced to turn a blind eye. In the line for help, the SS officer was now behind the Italian Jews.

By this point, he had a covert Allied wireless operator, code-named 'Little Walter', using one of the upstairs bedrooms of the house where he lived. Walter Rauff had authorised the payment of 100,000 lire to the supplier of the radio equipment. And then, in the final pages of his diary, there was a copy of one of the last, desperate letters that he wrote. It was to a woman called Sandra in Turin, to whom Zimmer had clearly formed an attachment.

In this letter to Sandra, he apologised that he couldn't come because he was hindered by duty. He had to remain in Vercelli (between Turin and Milan) and could come to Turin only on Monday, 19 February 1945. Sandra, he said, should wait with full trust for the day – which cannot be so far, said Zimmer – on which they would live together and be happy.

THE END IN NORTHERN ITALY

By the winter of 1944 and 1945, the German front line had fallen back all the way up northern Italy. It ran north of the Apennines, south of the River Po, while Axis-controlled territory included Turin, Milan, Genoa and Bologna. The Allies had overrun most of the Gothic defensive line that ran from Rimini, on the Adriatic, to the port of La Spezia on the Mediterranean. The Wehrmacht, SS and SD were fighting a hard, hurried retreat, and as the area of northern Italy they controlled got smaller, the measures they took to round up ever-smaller and better-concealed numbers of Jews got more extreme and inefficient. The security environment in which they were operating became less and less tenable due to partisan attacks, and disruption of roads and railways meant deportation convoys functioned at a minimal level.

It was in this enclave in northern Italy that SD official Friedrich Bosshammer was still trying to implement the Final Solution. Since January 1944, he estimated that his office had found and deported around 3,400 Jews, but by late 1944 and early 1945, this had slowed to a trickle of a few dozen per week. In those first six months of 1944, prior to the liberation of Rome, Bosshammer had personally overseen the arrest operations for Jews, who had been deported on four separate convoys that left from Turin and Milan, via Verona, as well as from

Bologna. The citation for Bosshammer's War Merit Cross Second Class (with Swords), which he was awarded by Himmler, said that he had 'led the fight against the Jews in the Italian region since February 1944 ... performed noteworthy work in the service of the Final Solution to the Jewish problem and has personally distinguished himself in numerous actions against Jews'.

Bosshammer also now made the arrest and deportation operations a co-operative effort between the SS and SD, the Gestapo and the Italian Fascist authorities from Mussolini's Italian Social Republic. In this, he was assisted by a leading Fascist official from the Salò Republic. His name was Giovanni Preziosi, a man from the outskirts of Milan, born in 1881; after finishing high school he had decided to enter the priesthood, as it seemed to combine the two disciplines he found most compelling – very hard-line Catholicism and a conservative political outlook that blended perfectly with the nascent Fascism that had sprung up in the country in the 1920s. The Church eventually defrocked Preziosi for his extreme political views, however, and he became a journalist.

He quickly embraced a hard-line, antisemitic political point of view, joined the Fascist Party and, with Mussolini, marched on Rome. He blamed the Jews for Italy's lacklustre performance in the First World War, and in his journalism propagated the idea that they were behind a combination of communism, democracy, capitalism and Freemasonry. To this end, he was the first person to translate into Italian the notorious Russian antisemitic text, *The Protocols of the Elders of Zion*. By the mid-thirties, he had found a political and racial bed companion in Nazism, and wrote frequently about Italy's need to adopt an anti-Jewish stance similar to Germany's. When the Racial Laws were passed in Italy in 1938, he celebrated them by writing a pamphlet called *Ecco il Diavolo: Israele* (*Here is the Devil: Israel*).

When the Italian Social Republic was established in 1943, Preziosi moved to Berlin, where he became an adviser to Hitler on Italian policy. One of his central beliefs was that the Italian Fascist Republic should march hand in hand with the Germans in terms of anti-Jewish operations, and so when he moved back to Italy in March 1944 to become the

General Inspector on Race, it suited both Hitler and Mussolini for him to work with Bosshammer in Milan and Verona.

Both sides were convinced that a dual approach to the implementation of the Final Solution would make its operations more efficient as the war progressed from 1944 onwards. Preziosi and Bosshammer advocated much stronger round-up operations in Italy's northern cities and urged the SS and Wehrmacht to engage in more anti-partisan operations, so that the hunt for Jews in the countryside could be managed in a more logistically stable manner. But as both partisan operations and the number of resistance fighters increased in late 1944 and early 1945, and as the Allies advanced closer, this proved impossible.

In Trieste, Odilo Globocnik and Friedrich Rainer found that the outskirts of the city was one large, constantly fluid battle, a clattering series of endless skirmishes and ambushes between German troops, Italian Fascist soldiers and policemen on one side, and on the other, Italian partisans and Marshal Tito's communist fighters who were infiltrating from across the border in Slovenia and Croatia. What Jews there had been, in and around the city, had been rounded up and either killed in the Risiera di San Sabba camp or deported to Auschwitz. An estimated 2,000–3,000 of them had died. By the end of spring 1945, the updated and approximate total of Jews who had been deported could be represented like this:

- The number of Jews in Italy and in Italian-occupied territories in October 1943 was between 42,000 and 45,500.
- On 16 October 1943, the Rome ghetto operation had seen at least 1,035 deported.
- October 1943–April 1945: German deportation convoys and varied transports had moved an estimated 4,733 from northern Italy, almost all to Auschwitz.
- The Germans also took 328 Jews from the Borgo San Dalmazzo camp to Auschwitz via Paris; additionally, 500 other Jews, mostly arrested in Libya, and transported to Italy, were deported to Belsen.
- Around 1,820 Jews who had been on the Italian-occupied islands of Rhodes and Kos were deported, mainly to Auschwitz.

- In total around 8,410 Jews were deported from Italy or Italian-occupied territories.
- 7,680 perished during the Holocaust.

This left some 36,600–37,100 Jews who had hidden, changed identities, emigrated, escaped, disappeared or otherwise survived.

Karl Wolff's negotiations with the Allies meant Bosshammer was given limited operating space by his superiors, partisan attacks meant his SS men were concentrating on their own unit's security rather than round-up operations, and around him the SS and SD infrastructure was fragmenting as small cadres of men and officers desperately prepared their own escape plans. Zimmer and Walter Rauff were involved not just with Operation Sunrise, but with their own personal schemes of flight.

Any deportation convoys that could move were frequently attacked en route to Tarvisio, the Brenner Pass or Trieste, and the road from there to Austria was subject to partisan ambush. German soldiers and policemen were attacked as they arrived at addresses where Jews were suspected of being in hiding and Allied fighter-bombers made road travel highly risky.

By spring 1945, as Karl Wolff's discussions with the OSS fizzled out under diplomatic protest from Moscow to Churchill and Roosevelt, Bosshammer, along with Guido Zimmer, started to put into action his personal escape plan. But the fate of some SS and Gestapo officers was now to involve an unexpected obstacle.

The Jewish Brigade Group Arrives in Italy

On 23 August 1944, Winston Churchill had sent a personal and secret telegram to President Roosevelt, outlining his plans for the formation of a unit of Jewish soldiers who, alongside the Allies, could fight back against the Germans. Chaim Weizmann was a Russian-born biochemist from Byelorussia and a key Zionist leader who had moved to England in 1904 and become a British citizen. He was elected President of the British Zionist Federation in 1917 and worked with the British Foreign

Secretary Arthur Balfour on the seminal Balfour Declaration. Issued in 1917, this expressed British support for the establishment of a national home for the Jewish people in Palestine.

During the Second World War, Weizmann worked as an adviser to the British Ministry of Supply. His family fought for Britain, too. His second son became an RAF pilot, flying in a Coastal Command squadron on anti-shipping missions. Flight Lieutenant Michael Weizmann was shot down over the Bay of Biscay in 1942 and his body was never found. His father, at the head of the Zionist Federation, had meanwhile been trying to persuade Churchill for almost two years to establish a unit of Jewish soldiers. In 1944, Churchill agreed, and sent a telegram to this effect to Washington:

> After much pressure from Weizmann I have arranged that the War Office shall raise a Jewish Brigade Group in what you would call a regimental combat team. This will give great satisfaction to the Jews when it is published and surely they of all other races have the right to strike at the Germans as a recognizable body. They wish to have their own flag which is the Star of David on a white background with two light blue bars. I cannot see why this should not be done. Indeed I think that the flying of this flag at the head of a combat unit would be a message to go all over the world.[1]

Roosevelt's answer was straightforward, '[In reference to] Your 765. I perceive no objection to your organizing a Jewish Brigade as suggested.'

So, on 3 July 1944, the British agreed to establish a brigade of Jewish soldiers who would be recruited both from Britain and from the *Yishuv*, the existing Jewish community in Mandatory Palestine. The officers would be both Jewish and non-Jewish. The men, regardless of whether they were recruited from Palestine or Britain, often originated from Poland, Hungary, Italy, Germany or Ukraine and were well aware of what was happening to Jews in the countries from which they had fled.

The brigade formed up in Egypt in late September 1944. There were around 5,000 men, organised into the 1st, 2nd and 3rd Battalions of the

Palestine Regiment, along with a regiment of artillery, with additional engineers, medical personnel and signallers. Their commanding officer was Brigadier Ernest Benjamin, a Canadian-born British Jewish officer, who had been decorated during the British campaign to capture the Vichy French-controlled island of Madagascar in 1942.

The Jewish Brigade trained in Egypt and was then inserted into the Order of Battle of the British 8th Army. Its three battalions fought in northern Italy in March and April 1945, and they established an exemplary combat record for themselves.

On 3 March 1945, the unit moved onto the front line in northern Italy for the first time. Its area of deployment was in the province of Emilia-Romagna, along the southern bank of a narrow river, bordered by elder and willow trees, its bottle-green waters running swiftly through the vineyards, fields and orchards south of Bologna. It was called the Senio. Operation Cygnet involved crossing it and establishing firm positions on its northern and eastern bank, just part of the Allied attack on the key city of Bologna. This would accompany a massive armoured and infantry push towards the German-controlled flatlands along the River Po and would see the Allies able to deploy their enormous superiority in tanks, cross the Po and storm towards Milan, Trieste, the Austrian border and Yugoslavia.

The Allied assault in April 1945, on Bologna and the German positions on the Gothic Line, saw some fifteen different nationalities under arms. The Jewish soldiers came under the command of the 2nd Polish Corps and the other units on either side of them in the line were a cross-section of the multinational Allied Commonwealth Army, then fighting its way up Italy. There were New Zealanders, the British tank crews of the Desert Rats of 7th Armoured Brigade, Indian Sikhs, Italians and South Africans, Canadian tank crews, Scottish light infantrymen, battalions of Polish soldiers and Brazilian armoured units. In front of them, the Germans had their backs against the wall, with orders to hold every metre of ground as long as they could.

The commander of the 15th Army Group, Lieutenant General Mark Clark, told Allied war correspondents:

We are delighted to have the Jewish Brigade operating with our force on the Italian Front. I wish the Brigade all the luck and success. I am greatly satisfied that the Jewish people who suffered so terribly at the hands of the Nazis should now be represented by this front-line fighting force.[2]

A war correspondent from the Jewish Telegraphic Agency in New York arrived to join the soldiers as they went into action on the Senio:

These tough, tanned soldiers, probably more than any other in the army, have something to fight for. Some of these troops have escaped from Nazi concentration camps. Some have been tortured. Nearly half have relatives who are known to be dead, or worse, have vanished and are missing inside Europe. These soldiers are fighting an eye-for-an-eye, and a tooth-for-a-tooth war. I have never seen men so desperately determined, so grave about combat.[3]

The Jewish Brigade fought breathtakingly hard: it might have arrived on the front line late in the war, but its men were more than determined to make up for it. They carried out aggressive patrols across the Senio, running up against experienced German armoured units. On the other side of the narrow river were two German divisions, including paratrooper *Kampfgruppen* (battle groups). There were an estimated 115 tanks too, forty of which were Tigers. Yet, the Jewish battalions captured prisoners from these army and paratrooper units, overrunning defensive positions, fighting hand to hand with bayonets fixed and hurling grenades into MG-42 machine-gun positions dug into the vineyards and sodden, muddy fields.

In one attack they killed nineteen Germans and captured eleven, for the loss of two of their own dead and three wounded. The Germans had fought a hard retreat all the way across Sicily and up the mainland of Italy. They had had all winter to prepare their positions on the Senio, while the Jewish Brigade had never been in battle. But they fought like Roman gladiators taking revenge for all the fights they'd ever lost. The correspondent from the Jewish Telegraphic agency dubbed it 'the battle of the floodbanks', as both sides were dug in along the flood defences that rose alongside the canals, which intersected the flat ground lying either side of the Senio:

> The Jewish Brigade units are on one side of the canal, and the Germans are on the other. They are so close they can lob grenades back and forth. Both sides burrow mole-like in the banks, or burrow completely through, and establish positions on the waterside.[4]

The Germans would attach five-second fuses to large Teller anti-tank 'T' mines and leave them attached to tripwires – but, thrown back at the enemy, the Jewish soldiers realised they made devastating ad hoc hand grenades, capable of blowing apart a bunker.

The soldiers came from twenty different nationalities, their languages those of the old Europe from which they had fled – Austria, Byelorussia, Hungary, Poland – but among themselves they spoke Hebrew, and English with their non-Jewish officers and NCOs.

A captain from the brigade wrote a letter home, which was printed in the Hebrew-language newspaper *Davar*, published in the British Mandate of Palestine and Israel. In his letter, he wrote about a German Jewish NCO in his platoon, a Lance Corporal Levy. On attacking a German position dug into a house and kicking open the door, Levy reportedly shouted, 'Swine! Come out. The Jews have come!' Four German soldiers, terrified, with hands trembling above their heads, emerged. 'I am not a Nazi!' shouted one. 'I am a Social Democrat.'

The captain described in his letter how his men 'raced forward with fixed bayonets like a pack of wolves' in an attack, and on reaching the German positions began throwing hand grenades until they heard a German voice pleading, 'Mum. Mum. God Almighty. Help.'[5]

Private Yohanan Peltz, a soldier from the brigade who took part in that same bayonet attack, said afterwards, 'We showed the world we could fight and win.' Another brigade soldier added, 'After the Holocaust, where so many Jews went to their death without fighting, we broke a taboo, we proved to the world that we can fight.'[6]

In another action near the Senio, soldiers from the brigade went head to head with a complex of German machine-gun positions and mortar emplacements and captured and destroyed them in fifteen minutes. Battle-hardened armoured crews from the North Irish Horse, in their Sherman Firefly and Churchill tanks, roared along behind them, while above them, South African pilots from the Desert Air Force flew ground-attack missions in Spitfires and Curtiss Kittyhawks. On one sweep, the pilots flew over the men of the Brigade Group with their aircraft formed into a Star of David formation.

A British Army Artillery NCO, Acting Sergeant Major Ken Sanitt, had transferred into the unit after four years of fighting in north Africa, Mesopotamia and at Monte Cassino. He summed up the aggressive approach of the Jewish Brigade: 'The British and Indian soldiers I had been fighting with were elite troops, but they were war-weary, while the Jewish Brigade were spoiling for action. Their fighting spirit was fantastic.'[7]

The War Diaries of the 2nd and 3rd Battalions of the Palestine Regiment summarises pithily one attack and its aftermath, carried out by them and the tank crews of the North Irish Horse:

3rd March 0600 hrs. Brigade attaches to and comes under command of the 8th Indian Division. 1200 hours. Brigade infantry in counterattack supported by 12 tanks of the North Irish Horse. Successful, Prisoners taken petrified by being abused in their own language and even dialect. Softened by fear, they gave valuable information when interrogated.[8]

The unit was also highly disciplined when not actually on the front line. In two paragraphs of daily orders in March 1945, men from the brigade were urged not to cut down trees to use for heating, as the trees' owners – local Italians – would have no other source of income themselves. Soldiers were urged as well to keep discipline intact in the daily minutiae of life in Italy. When returning empty bottles to the local shop that had supplied them, soldiers were told, 'When returning beer bottles of the hinged-stopper variety, units will ensure that stoppers are left open. It is necessary to preserve the life of rubber washers which are in short supply.[9]

In early April, the soldiers stormed through Monte Ghebbio, encircling and outfighting companies of German paratroopers, and then took their place in the line-up for the final attack on Bologna. The Allies finally liberated the strategically key city, lying on the crossroads of the Apennines and the plains of northern Italy, on 21 April 1945. The Jewish Brigade advanced north-east, towards Ravenna, their bloody-minded determination to get into action undiminished by three weeks of fighting on Operation Cygnet.

Beyond the Senio and towards far north-eastern Italy lay the towns of Tarvisio and Arnoldstein, previously mentioned as the railway junctions lying either side of the Austrian and Italian borders, respectively. These four primary routes in and out of south-eastern Austria and into north-eastern Italy had been badly affected by Allied bombing by this stage of the war. From west to east, the first was the road that crossed into Austria at the intersection of that country's border with Italy and Switzerland, in the shadow of the Ötztal Alps. Repeated American bombing raids had hit this road since summer 1943, when it first came in range of B-17 Flying Fortresses and B-24 Liberators operating from Sicily, Pantelleria and Corsica.

The Battle of the Brenner Pass

Moving east, the next was the vital main road and rail crossing at the Brenner Pass, north of Bolzano. The railway line that adjoined the road connected Innsbruck with Verona and ran through a lengthy series of tunnels and across numerous bridges. The Allies knew how important the Brenner Pass route was for the Germans, both for supplying their troops in Italy and for transporting human cargo, like Jews and wounded German soldiers, out of the country and into Austria. The US Army Air Force did its best to destroy the Brenner bridges and tunnels, as well as the railway lines, in autumn 1944 and spring 1945.

The Brenner Pass is 59 miles long and the railway line and road stands at nearly 5,000ft altitude. The main targets for the US Air Force were the twenty-two tunnels and sixty large bridges built into the pass, which carried a huge volume of German military transport in and out of Austria. The pass was vital for the Germans in Italy – the Tarvisio crossing could be used, but it lay much further away and was not so centrally linked into the Austrian and Italian rail network as the Brenner Pass, which gave a direct link from Verona to Innsbruck, and thence to Germany. The Germans kept the pass heavily defended with all calibres and numbers of flak weapons, from 37mm to 105mm, which had the range to reach any American bomber. Destroying enemy activity through the Brenner Pass had thus become a prime tactical objective for the Allies:

> The simplest and most accurate route for the B-26 Bombers to fly, was a north-south axis up the pass. With a visibility of over 50 miles through the pass, all the bridges would be visible in the bomb-sights. Likewise, all the bombers would become sitting targets for the German guns. If the B-26s were to take out the bridges in the pass, they would have to fly west to east across the pass, giving the lead bombardier only 15 seconds to sight the target before releasing his bombs.[10]

On 6 November 1944, Operation Bingo began – its aim was to break the German military supply line by closing off the Brenner Pass. B-25 Mitchells, B-24 Liberators and fighter-bombers from the Desert Air Force were deployed. By January 1945, the Germans had some 475 heavy guns guarding the pass and the Americans would fly three aircraft at the head of their bomber formations, which would drop white phosphorus bombs, not just to target the gunners but to camouflage the aerial formation with smoke. The flak was intense: in forty-eight American missions, 224 aircraft were lost as a result of anti-aircraft fire.

One day in December 1944, William C. Wildman from Chapin, south Carolina, was flying a B-24 Liberator. 'Bursting anti-aircraft shells exploded into jagged steel thick as your fist and wide as a basketball at times,' he said. Suddenly, the Liberator's windshield exploded. Shards of steel nicked Wildman's flight jacket and removed much of the skull of flight engineer Joe Kelly, from New York, who was standing behind Wildman, holding on to the back of his seat. 'Half his head was gone. An eye was gone,' said Wildman, who flew thirty-two missions over Italy, Austria, Romania and Germany from autumn 1944 to April 1945. 'Frankly, I was pretty shook up. That could have been me.'[11]

Forty miles south-east from the Brenner there was the third road that led from Italy into Austria, at San Candido Innichen. Then, the most easterly of all was the road and railway line that crossed into Austria, 2 miles north of Tarvisio, where Ya'akov Hollander had first arrived in Italy (read more about him in Chapter 18). This was the railway route that led to Villach, Klagenfurt, Vienna, then east and northwards towards the camps. The SS had used this line to deport Italian Jews out of Italy and it was along this stretch of railway track, for instance, that the Italian, Croatian and Slovenian inmates, herded into the Risiera di San Sabba detention centre and concentration camp in Trieste, had travelled towards Auschwitz and Mauthausen.

But now, as the war ended in Europe, northern Italy and eastern Austria were filled with British and American troops. Germany had annexed Austria in the *Anschluss* in 1938, making it part of the Third Reich. In 1943, at the Moscow Conference, the Soviet Union, Britain and the United States declared that after the war this occupation would be declared null and void and Austria would return to being a free and independent country. The Allies and the Red Army poured over its borders in the period between the end of March and the beginning of May 1945, and in the immediate aftermath of the war, the country was temporarily divided into four different national zones of occupation.

The British area of occupation included Klagenfurt, the capital of the Austrian state of Carinthia, which is situated in the far south-east of the country, on the border with Hungary and Italy. The city lies 30 miles across the border from Tarvisio. Carinthia, as well as its two adjoining states of Styria and Ost-Tirol, or East Tyrol, now comprised the British Zone. This division and allocation of territory was to prove crucial to the future of many of the Jews, Italian and otherwise, who had survived the Holocaust and were now crossing from Austria into Italy. It was also to have an impact on the future of some of the Gestapo and SS men who had been involved in the execution of the Final Solution in Italy.

For anybody trying to move human beings or material back into Italy, instead of out of it, Tarvisio was equally vital – especially if whoever was carrying the commodities wanted access to seaports on the Adriatic, in particular, Trieste, Ancona and Bari. And now that the fighting against the Germans was coming to a halt, the men from the Jewish Brigade Group had another plan, one that involved these ports – and thousands of people.

The Jewish Brigade Takes Revenge

In early 1945, one young Jewish corporal in the Brigade Group, who had fled Düsseldorf to go to Palestine in the 1930s, summed up the desire for revenge like this:

> Gassed them. My two sisters and parents. Just like a pest control-
> ler exterminates rats and cockroaches. I can't sleep for thinking of
> them fighting for their last breath in the chambers … God, then
> into the ovens. No graves, no headstones, no prayers, no remem-
> brance. Nothing.[12]

The brigade CO, Brigadier Benjamin, as a Jew himself, was completely aware of this longing for vengeance. He knew his men were some of the very few soldiers in the Allied forces who would have had direct family, friends and relatives murdered in ghettoes, camps and deportation operations. His men would want to take revenge themselves and would also feel it incumbent on themselves to take revenge for fellow Jews who could not. This put the men of the Jewish Brigade Group in a position of extraordinary power – and simultaneous vulnerability. Benjamin there-fore stressed, as much as his authority permitted, that his men should try to respect orders concerning the treatment of prisoners.

On 6 March 1945, in the routine Part One Daily Orders, he wrote:

A. I want to impress the supreme importance of capturing alive German prisoners and sending them back quickly for interrogation.
B. I realise that there are a large number of men who have every personal justification for revenge themselves, and wish to kill every German they come across. Our object is to hasten the defeat of the enemy. It has been proved that by taking prisoners and extracting information from them more is to be gained.

C. However great the crimes committed by the Germans, I am determined that the Jewish Brigade Group shall act correctly in accordance with recognised convention.[13]

Benjamin said:

I, for one, could not blame them. As a Canadian-born Jew, whose family resided in safety in London, apart from the danger from Luftwaffe raids, when I learned of the Holocaust and saw the first documentary films of the camps, given a gun I would have cheerfully shot those responsible for the evils inflicted on my people.[14]

The aforementioned private in the Jewish Brigade group, called Yohanan Peltz, was originally a Polish Jew. He described how the sense of anger built up:

… when we heard of the extermination camps and when we found out from the survivors what the Germans in fact did, and then that in turn turned into not an anger but a fury, and then everybody began feeling that we owed the Germans something. It was something you couldn't stop, it wasn't organised, there wasn't a cry out among the brigade, we're going to form a unit of revenge, it was very secret. We didn't keep records, no written record, that was for the purpose that if nothing is written, nothing can be discovered; we had a group who were good at collecting intelligence and evaluating it. It's not a nice word, but that's what we were ... executioners.[15]

...

And secondly, because it is significant and it is important for people to know that we did these acts of vengeance that we didn't forget, that we didn't just lay down and were satisfied with what we have done at the front line. Quite rightly, many people ask themselves and ask others why the Jews didn't resist, why the Jews didn't kill their enemies and it's a legitimate question and a correct question. And I think that the fact that we did some vengeance answers in part their questions.

...

And then, look, vengeance is a very natural feeling. I don't know why some do-gooders think vengeance is bad. It's not bad. I think that vengeance is legitimate. If you have an enemy who is brutal, who murders your relatives, and he's trying to get out of it unpunished, it's legitimate to kill him. And this is vengeance. I think it's legitimate. The fact that we couldn't do very much is another story. We were serving as soldiers in the British army.

We were not masters of our own desires. And we have to do it in such a way that will not do harm to the Brigade as a whole and to us as individuals. So we formed this group ... we had a group of people who were good in collecting intelligence and evaluating it. They collected the intelligence, and they were pinpointing ... the Germans who were guilty of murder and cruelties and so on. Then we had a sort of a kangaroo court of a few men who considered the evidence, and if the evidence called for it, sentenced the men to death.

...

Many members of the Jewish Brigade went into Germany and Austria and they actually saw the camps. I was in Dachau, I saw, I saw Dachau, I saw the results. And that was a very short while after the war ended. The place wasn't cleaned up yet. It was as dirty as it was when the Germans left it. Dirty, I mean dirty by their deeds. And then of course we talked to the survivors. And they told us the stories, the terrible stories. And that, that was the point where normal anger turned into real fury.[16]

'We were looking to see where were the real Nazis, the SS, the commanders of the camps, but [they were] not easy to find,' said another member of the group, Oly Givon.[17]

The Jewish soldiers suspected that a German officer was hiding in a house in Tarvisio, and they had information that he might have been a Gestapo officer. Another soldier, Israel Carmi said:

> We went to the house and told him that if we find any weapons he's going to be shot, on the spot. We searched, found a pistol in the oven, the German officer pleading for his life, and prepared a list of other Nazis in hiding. A group went out, found the officers, and killed them. Then one officer, two [of our] military police, two more people went into Austria.[18]

Oly Givon posed as a lone SS officer on the run, who was trying to find more of his comrades. The unit had heard about a popular beer hall across the border in Austria, so Givon went there, linked up with other SS men and arranged a meeting with a fugitive Nazi officer:

> Ok, and I say to them, I'm an SS officer, and I said I was alone, wanted to link up with people. I arranged a meeting with a Nazi officer. I say, I'm a Jew, you acted against the Jews, you killed Jews, and I started to talk with him, and at the moment I am a hundred percent sure he was the man who killed Jews. Then I said in the name of the nation of the Jews, I kill you. And I killed him.[19]

These are thought to have been the first revenge killings of SS and Gestapo personnel by Jews after the war. One estimate says that there were several dozen revenge squads and as many as 1,500 executions.[20] This remains unprovable and the true figure is probably somewhat lower, although the personnel targeted were SS or Gestapo officers. Jewish Brigade Group member Israel Carmi was interviewed several times:

When we arrived at the home of our suspect we would put on [British] Military Police helmets with the white band and police armlets. Then we would enter the home and take the suspect with us, saying that we wanted him for interrogation. Usually they came without a struggle. Once in the car we told the prisoner who we were and why we took him. Some admitted guilt. Others kept silent. We did the job.[21]

'We were young Jewish soldiers,' said another. 'We knew that our people would never forgive us if we did not exploit the opportunity to kill Nazis.'[22]

The geography of borders and frontiers being formed and secured at the end of war was one reason why the revenge activities of the brigade were curtailed. By late summer 1945, it was no longer as easy as it had been to cross from Tarvisio into and out of Austria. Yohanan Peltz explained:

Then, the other reason was the physical situation in Europe changed. In 1945, the frontiers were actually open, they were fluid. Nobody knew exactly who is where and what is where; where the front is where. Things were not organized. It took a few months for the powers to get organized to determine where the frontiers are and to start guarding them properly. A few months after the end of the war, it was not easy anymore to penetrate the frontiers and to steal the frontier and to sneak into towns and to do what you had to do. And then, of course, the Brigade was dispersed.[23]

THE SELVINO CAMP

One morning in May 1945, in the first spring of peace for six years, Ya'akov Hollander woke up in a hospital somewhere in Austria. He was 15, stick thin, and weighed little more than 5 stone.

For six years he had stood barefoot, or with feet wrapped in rags, day after day, in mud, liquid coal dust, slush and dirt. He was a Polish Jew, and he had survived twelve concentration camps, detention centres and ghettoes. He was born in Krakow in 1929, one of a family of five.

There had been around 70,000 Jews in the southern Polish city when the Germans invaded in 1939 and made Krakow the capital of the General Government – the name they gave to the part of Poland that was not directly absorbed into Germany. In May 1940, 50,000 Jews were forced out of the city, and by late spring 1941 they had been interned in a huge ghetto on the city's outskirts. Ya'akov was 11 by then.

Each day consisted of avoiding starvation and German beatings, round-ups and executions. At one point, his father, mother, he and his brother hid in a basement room, with a special lock installed on the door that could not be opened from the outside. They escaped detection.

When the Krakow ghetto was liquidated in March 1943, the surviving Jews were transferred to the Płaszów concentration camp on the city's outskirts. It was a brutal centre for slave labour, supplying armaments factories and a local quarry. Ya'akov remembered, with dread, the sadistic Austrian SS camp commander, Amon Goth, 'who would walk around like a hunter shooting people'.

Next came a transfer with his parents and brother, Benek, to Starachowice, in south central Poland, where the rake-thin, starving young teenager worked in an armaments factory, slaving next to a blazing oven, helping make artillery shells. Then came work in a coal mine. Then Auschwitz.

In the winter of 1944, Ya'akov and Benek were among inmates forced to join a 200-mile death march from the camp complex in southern Poland to another one in north central Austria. This was Mauthausen, and alongside its four main camps there were nearly 100 more sub-camps spread across Austria and southern Germany.

On the march to Mauthausen, the brothers stuck together, and Ya'akov tried desperately to encourage his brother to reach their destination, and even with an injured leg he managed to stumble forward through the snow. But he collapsed on arrival, he and Ya'akov were separated and the two never saw each other again.

In April 1945, with the Americans advancing south through Bavaria and across northern Austria, the SS force-marched some of the inmates from the central complex at Mauthausen to one of its sub-camps. Gunskirchen lay some 30 miles to the west, hidden in a pine forest outside the town of Lambach. Ya'akov was among the prisoners on this march to the camp hidden in the trees – his final destination.

On 4 May, a battalion from the American 71st Infantry Division drove into the outskirts of Lambach and arrived in the village of Gunskirchen. As the division pushed south-west through Austria, it began to find the dozens of sub-camps of the Mauthausen system, containing Italian, German, Austrian and Hungarian Jews. One of these was Gunskirchen, outside Linz, and the American soldiers found hundreds of emaciated, desperate prisoners streaming down the roads outside the camp. Their SS guards, alerted to the arrival of American troops, had disappeared overnight.

The GIs noticed the overwhelming stench in the air. Major Cameron Coffman, from Fort Thomas, Kentucky, was the division's Public

Relations Officer, who went into Gunskirchen camp on the afternoon of 4 May. He typed a press dispatch the following day, from the small Austrian village hidden in the pine trees. It was one of the first eye-witness accounts written by an Allied soldier entering part of the KZ system. Several American newspapers were to publish it:

With the 71st Division of the 3rd Army in Austria, 5th May: -

Nazism at its worst was unfolded in its stark reality before Doughboys of the 71st Infantry Division when they stumbled upon a carefully-concealed concentration camp six kilometers north of Lambach, Austria, which held 15,000 people who were not true 'Aryan' or whose political opinions were contrary to Hitler's 'New Order'.

My days of reading about Hun atrocities were over. I visited that camp today. The living and dead evidence of horror and brutality beyond one's imagination was there, lying and crawling and shuffling, in stinking ankle-deep mud and human excrement … 200 emaciated corpses would be a very conservative estimate, for the most part they had died during the past two days, but there were many other rotting bodies inside the barracks beside living human beings who were too weak to move.

It is practically impossible to describe in decent or printable words the state of degradation in which the German guards had permitted the camp to fall. Located in a dense patch of pine trees, well-hidden from the highway, and from the air, the site was well-suited for the slimy, vermin-infested living conditions that existed there … the sight was appalling, and the odor that reached you a hundred yards or so from the camp site was nauseating.

Travelling into the camp along a narrow wagon-road was an experience in dodging the multitude of dazed men, women and children fleeing from the horrors of this living hell …

Coffman accompanied other American soldiers into one of the over-crowded huts that lay within the camp:

... a building which was originally built for 300, but now housed approximately 3,000. Row upon row of living skeletons, jammed so closely together that it was impossible for some to turn over, even if they could have generated enough strength to do so. Those too weak to move defecated where they lay. The place was crawling with lice. A pair of feet, black in death, protruded from beneath a tattered blanket, just six inches from a haggard old Jew who was resting on his elbow and feebly attempting to wave to us.

A little girl, doubled with the gnawing pains of starvation, cried pitifully for help. A dead man was rotting beside her. An English-speaking Jew from Ohio hummed 'The Yanks are coming', and then broke out crying. A Jewish Rabbi tripped over a dead body as he scurried towards me with strength he must have been saving for the arrival of the American forces. He kissed the back of my gloved hand and clutched my sleeve with a talon-like grip, as he lifted his face towards heaven. I could not understand what he said, but it was a prayer. I did not have to understand his spoken word.

Major Coffman's group continued to search through the buildings:

... an unforgettable drama was enacted when a sergeant of our group of five raced out of one building, his face flaming with rage. The sergeant, a Jewish boy of Polish descent had found three of his relatives, lying in the filth of that barracks. They are lying tonight beneath white sheets, for the first time in three years, in one of the better homes in Lambach. Their diet of a daily cup of anemic soup has suddenly changed to eggs, milk, and bread ...[1]

One of the American officers accompanying Coffman that day was Captain J.D. Pletcher from Berwyn, Illinois. He too wrote a long report. At the end of it, he summarised his reaction to what he had seen:

The hunger in evidence is hard to imagine. Outside the gate of the camp was the carcass of a horse that had been killed by shellfire. There was a great, gaping wound in his belly. As we passed it, one of the inmates was down on his knees, eating off the carcass. It had been dead several days … I felt, the day I saw Gunskirchen lager, that I finally knew what I was fighting for, what the war was all about.[2]

One of the prisoners who fled the camp that day was Ya'akov Hollander. He crawled under the wire and into some trees. A squad of GIs from the 71st Division found him and took him to a hospital in nearby Lambach, run by the Red Cross. Set on the scales, the nurses found that the emaciated, starving boy weighed 33kg, or 5 stone. He was to learn later that his father had died in Auschwitz, his mother in Płaszów, Benek in Mauthausen and the SS had executed his second brother Dolek in Belsen on 4 May, three days before the war was over. But Ya'akov had survived:[3]

Through all of the horrors that I endured, I don't remember ever crying. One of the most traumatic events that remains etched in my memory is from a coal mine, on Christmas. A coal-miner brought me a cake. I tried to save half for my brother Beno, who was at the camp, sick. The coal miner said that would be disastrous for him, they would put him in the camp if they [the Germans] saw that he brought me a cake. He made me eat the whole cake, and when I came back to the camp in the evening, and told my brother I couldn't bring half of the cake for him, I burst into uncontrollable sobs, my grief for having eaten the cake without sharing it with him, it was indescribable.[4]

In the weeks after the liberation, he stayed in bed in the Austrian Red Cross hospital, recovering very slowly in that first spring of peace, his only possession the pyjamas the nurses had given him. Suddenly, one morning, through the window he heard the sound of singing. He immediately recognised the tune and the Hebrew words of the iconic nineteenth-century song, *Hatikvah*. It tells of 2,000 years of Jewish yearning to return to the Promised Land of Israel. It was a little phantasmagorical, remembered Ya'akov, so, just as he was, he got up out of bed, walked out of the hospital ward, still only in his pyjamas, and headed towards the sound of the singing.

He found a convoy of military lorries that had parked at the side of the road. There were emaciated, exhausted Jewish camp survivors and refugees in the backs of the trucks. Around them were soldiers in the uniform of the British Army, who Ya'akov saw carried the emblem of the Star of David, the Magen David in Hebrew, on their left shoulder. He immediately realised they were Jews like himself.

There and then, without returning to the hospital, he asked these men to take him with them. He climbed onto one of the lorries and shortly afterwards, the convoy moved off. It headed south-east through Austria, towards the Italian border, along roads lined with pine forests and alpine fields, the abrupt towers of the Dolomites rising on the skyline. The drivers seemed to know where they were going, and between Lambach and their destination they stopped several times, the convoy picking up more Jewish refugees at each halt.

Once across the frontier and into Italy, the first town in which they arrived was Tarvisio, situated 3 miles inside the border, in the region of Friuli Venezia Giulia. There, the lorries stopped for the night. The Jewish refugees and former camp inmates were led into the long hall of a municipal building, where a Jewish soldier greeted them.

Just seeing the Star of David on the arm of his British Army battle-dress had a magical effect on the new arrivals. Several of them dropped their small bundles of belongings and embraced him and kissed him, standing there under the lights of the hall. He gestured behind him: a trestle table was laid with food, plates, knives and forks. There were tins of British Army rations, bully beef, 'hard-tack' biscuits made from flour, water and salt, and bars of chocolate. There was some macaroni, tomatoes and white bread, with tea and cold water to drink.

Many of the refugees had not eaten with knives and forks for five years. Food had often been cold, stale, rotten or wet and sometimes almost non-existent. It had brought danger, too. Hiding an extra scrap of bread in your clothing in some camps meant the guards could shoot or whip you. But, for almost the first time since the dripping, dank fog of the *Konzentrationslager* had swallowed them up, they ate well and in safety.[5]

That night, they slept on clean camp beds, the Jewish soldiers guarding them and the building. The next day, they headed south-west again, threading along the bottom of the Dolomites, until they came to a small town called Selvino, set in the foothills of the Italian Alps, north of Bergamo. And there, for Ya'akov Hollander, a new life began.[6] 'And then came the camp at Selvino,' he said. 'It became home for me in every sense of the word.'

Even during the time when the men from the Jewish Brigade were fighting on the Senio, they had begun to think what it would be like coming face to face with the survivors of the camps, the civilians and the partisan fighters.

As the end of the war approached, Moshe Sharett, who was then the head of the Jewish Agency's Political Department, met in the middle of April 1945 with Jewish Brigade soldiers in Italy. On 4 May, after the brigade had left the front, and just as Germany was about to surrender, Sharett outlined the main operational points for the men. Finding survivors and crossing the border into Austria were two priorities. Establishing displaced persons' camps was a third. He was aware that some soldiers from the Jewish Brigade had by now already crossed into Austria, discovered Jewish survivors and were bringing them back to Italy. 'Meeting with the survivors was a shock that was very difficult to describe … firstly, everybody got some information about the fate of his family, and about the story of the Holocaust.'[7]

Some Jewish Brigade soldiers crossed the border into Klagenfurt, looking for Jews:

The guys went into Klagenfurt, across the border, we saw a young woman dressed like Marlene Dietrich in the square, beret, raincoat, they thought she was Jewish, and she was, she led them to a group of survivors hiding in a ruined house. The Jewish guys said 'Shabat, Shalom,' and … it was like the coming of the Messiah, they started to physically touch us to see if we were real. You cannot imagine what it meant for Jews in Europe to see the Magen David on the sleeve of Jewish soldiers.[8]

An estimated 70,000 Jewish refugees arrived in Italy after the liberation, and one of the homes the Jewish Brigade Group helped establish was in the mountains above Bergamo, in Selvino. At first, the number of survivors in the camp was around 800, and in charge was a Jewish soldier called Moshe Zeiri. The home was a former sports centre which, under Mussolini's regime, had been a summer retreat for the children of party officials.

The camp was to exist until early 1948, when the State of Israel was declared. The Jews gave it the nickname '*Beit Aliyat HaNo'ar*'. '*Aliya*' means 'ascension', the act of returning to the land of Israel (Eretz Israel). In many ways, it was organised along the lines of a collective, similar to the *kibbutzim* that were established in Palestine. Arrival at the camp was a complete shock for most of the children, who had just emerged from concentration camps. Shmuel Shilo was 16 in May 1945:

> We had no faith in adults, because the adults we knew either wanted to kill us, or were Jews who … looked after themselves and not after us. And here, suddenly, were adults, moreover soldiers and officers, who looked after me, and wanted me to live, to learn, to get dressed, who wanted me to eat, who wanted to bring me to Eretz Israel … I don't know if it would have been worthwhile staying alive, or whether I would have stayed alive – if Eretz Israel had not existed. If I hadn't connected with the Jewish Brigade. Because my first encounter with Eretz Israel, with something totally different, was through the Brigade. I think Eretz Israel saved my life.[9]

Mordehai Braun remembers the journey from Austria to Italy:

> We were in Salzburg and the Jewish Brigade soldiers arrived with trucks to take whoever wanted to go to Palestine … They gathered us together on canvas-covered trucks … and we were on our way. Where were we going? We didn't know, but we drove … through the nights

too. We were not allowed to talk. Every time we stopped they gave us coffee and tea to drink, and also something to eat. We stopped at some base and they disinfected us with all kinds of chemicals. We stayed the night, and then we continued ... Eventually we reached Modena.[10]

For many of the children, being back in a camp brought back memories, as Mordehai Braun explained:

They housed us in a military academy in Modena. It was nice, I mean, it was not a hotel ... there were all sorts of classrooms. We slept in hallways, in rooms. Somehow they gave out blankets, and that's what there was ... Every day we heard yelling: Kapo! Kapo! They found some Jew who had been a Kapo in the camps and they lynched him with beatings. I started working in town and earned money, so I could buy all kinds of things that I wanted, and I could also go to the cinema.[11]

As the Jewish Brigade Group was slowly transferred across Europe, some of the duties at the Selvino camp were taken over by officials from the Jewish Joint Distribution Committee, who had arrived from the United States to help the DELASEM organisation. Every single one of the children and teenagers expected to be able to go to Israel. Mordehai Greenberg was 12 when he arrived in a refugee camp in Rome:

We arrived in Rome, and were taken straight to Cinecittà (film studios in Rome constructed during the Fascist era). This was the city of movies. The entire right side belonged to refugees from Naples, from all sorts of places, from the shellings. The left side was for the more distinguished crowd, all with different nationalities, foreigners who had been thrown into the war. I had friends there from Yugoslavia, France, from many different places. We also studied there. Once, we performed in some Hanukah party that the scouts in Rome organized ... We had a room, others lived in a recording studio, so they just put up dividing walls made out of cardboard ... One day they took us to the Brigade's show in Rome – 60–70 of us went there by truck. We hardly held onto the ladders. We traveled standing up.[12]

At Selvino, the atmosphere was designed to let the children and teenagers acclimatise to some form of normality. After a concentration camp, for Shmuel Shilo, a pillow fight was like a new beginning:

> After two weeks I also began to throw pillows, and I also started dancing with girls, and I also started playing football … It took two weeks, no longer, and we were restored to our original age. I think that one of the main things about Selvino … was that this house – for the time period that we were there, a little more than a year – gave us back our youth … Selvino was a colony of Eretz Israel. True, we spoke Polish, or Yiddish, or Hungarian, but cultural life was conducted in Hebrew.[13]

Moshe Zeiri, who ran the home, had served in a military engineering company, and when food ran short, he and the other soldiers simply gave the children their rations. The older children looking after the younger ones was Zeiri's abiding memory of the home. Rina Radocki was one child who remembered him:

> Moshe Zeiri received us nicely. He also started to organize a choir for us, and taught me solo songs. I sang 'Galilee Night'… There was a real atmosphere of Eretz Israel there. We started to feel good … The house was very beautiful, like a palace for us, very tidy, blue beds and clean, and there was a pool there. After everything we'd been through, we arrived at such a luxurious house …[14]

For him and hundreds of others, including Italian Jews, it was the beginning of the road towards a new life. The Jewish soldiers rescued him, and he and others were then helped on this new road by this idiosyncratic and brave group of soldiers, patriots and adventurers who had resisted the Holocaust in Italy and were now trying to do something definitive about its aftermath.

Two of the Jewish children and teenagers who found themselves there were called Menachem Krigel and Eugenia Cohen. Before the war, 11,000 Jews had lived in and around Menachem Krigel's hometown of Buczacz, then in Poland and now in southern Ukraine. Between 1941 and 1943, German troops and a Ukrainian nationalist militia killed around 7,000 Jews in the city, with another 3,800 transported to Belzec concentration camp, where almost all of them were killed. By the time the 14-year-old Menachem Krigel had spent fifteen months of 1943 and 1944 hiding in a woodshed, fleeing not just the Germans but anti-semitic Russian partisan groups, there were only about 200 Jews left, and he was one of them.

But by mid-1945, along with 60,000 other Jewish refugees, Krigel had arrived in Italy en route to a new life in Palestine. He was hoping to board a cargo ship in Trieste that would run the British blockade off Cyprus and deliver him to his Promised Land.

Eugenia Cohen, meanwhile, was a teenage girl from an Italian Jewish family which, up until 1943, had lived outside Milan. When the German round-ups started, in Pandino, on the Lombardy plains, a family called the Madonninis hid her. The family had rented rooms to her brother Alberto and the extended family until the autumn of 1943, but then he was arrested outside a tobacconist in Pandino, just after buying a packet of cigarettes. Cohen was forced to reveal his family's location and then was deported, along with his parents, to Bergen-Belsen. But Ernestina Madonnini, who had seen the police approaching their home, managed to conceal Cohen's sister Eugenia in the attic. At considerable risk, the Madonninis then organised false papers for Eugenia with DELASEM and cared for her until the war ended.

As the war finished, Eugenia heard about the children's home in Selvino and travelled to help. Speaking no Yiddish, Polish or German, she looked after the almost feral children who had survived the Holocaust in Poland and Ukraine. They had never slept on sheets, shared food, used knives or forks or worn shoes, and had learned not to trust anybody. 'She spoke to them in kisses and hugs, and in love,' her son was to later say.[15]

Eugenia herself said:

Groups of children started to arrive [at Selvino]. At first, they were Polish and Hungarian, from the camps. They would tell stories, and I didn't understand a word, they spoke either Yiddish or Hungarian. But in those two weeks I took care of them, everything, food, clothes. I loved them, it was as simple as that. I wanted to help them. I saw that they were younger than me, they didn't have mothers, they didn't have anything. I worked with my heart, not with my head. I can picture one of the little girls, she laid her head down on me, I stroked her hair, and she only spoke Polish. It was … I can't explain.[16]

In the Selvino home, the children were aware of and celebrated Jewish holidays:

And girls from one family, when it was Ros Haqqanah, or Yom Kippur, the walls shaked from that much sobbing. I touched them and kissed them all the time, I even spoke a few words of Hebrew, but it wasn't very good. This [my time at Selvino] was the biggest thing I ever did in my life, and my husband and I became so attached to them. So when we emigrated to Eretz Israel, we said they were like our children. We emigrated early, my husband in January or February [1946], me in July.[17]

The husband that Cohen refers to, whom she fell in love with, was one of the soldiers from the Jewish Brigade called Reuven Donath. She changed her name from Eugenia to 'Noga', which means 'Venus' in Hebrew, waited for Private Donath to be discharged from the British Army and travelled to Palestine with him. Her son, Nir, said that she believed it was fate, as when she was 16, a clairvoyant had told her that she would meet a Jewish man from far away across the sea with whom she would fall in love. 'It was written in the stars,' said her son.[18]

Lidia Rolfi Comes Home

Seven hundred miles further north as the crow flew, in those chaotic, breathless and extraordinary first months of peace, somebody was walking home. The roads of Europe tramped to the sound of millions of displaced people, prisoners of war, soldiers, airmen, civilians, farmers, bombed-out city dwellers, Poles, Austrians, Germans, French and Italians heading west or south-west. Everybody was fleeing the advance of the Red Army, and everybody was on the move.

As Allied soldiers moved north, west and east, as the Third Reich crumbled in on itself like a pack of tissue-paper playing cards balanced on ashes, people were going home and thinking, for the first time in six years, that the future might include being alive. One of these people was the young Italian woman from Mondovi, near Cuneo, arrested as a partisan in June 1944.

When the Germans had picked up Lidia Rolfi in June 1944, the first stop had been Cuneo Prison. Then a train to Turin, a detention centre, and another train from Bolzano to Austria. On the way northwards towards the concentration camps, she had met a young Frenchwoman called Monique, and when they found they were both destined for the women's concentration camp at Ravensbrück, the two of them stuck together. Whereas Lidia came from a working-class family of small-holder farmers, Monique was from the French bourgeoisie. Monique was a young communist, and the pair talked about food all the time.[19]

In Ravensbrück, the thrice-daily queues for food – in reality, hot water with turnips and potatoes in it, with a small slice of black bread – were interminable. So, both Monique and Lidia kept their spirits up talking about the food they would cook after the war. One recipe was for orange marmalade, and both memorised it. When the SS guards at Ravensbrück fled, and Monique and Lidia began the long walk home, Lidia wrote down the recipe on a piece of brown parcel paper. She tucked it into her clothing on the march that lasted for months. She never lost it. When, weeks and weeks later, she reached the house in Mondovi by the green River Ellero, in the shadow of the mountains that overlook the turquoise Ligurian Sea, she pinned the piece of paper with the recipe up on the living room wall. Seventy-six years later, it is still there.

THE GERMAN AFTERMATH

On 13 November 1972, Kurt Christmann stepped out of the swimming pool at his home in Munich. To his surprise, the police were waiting for him with an arrest warrant. While the former Gestapo officer was towelling himself dry, the Bavarian officers read the warrant: he was wanted on suspicion of the murder of civilians in the Soviet Union.

Christmann was 72 years old that day in 1972, and the Public Prosecutor's Office alleged that he had ordered 105 people to be gassed or shot while he was leading an SS *Einsatzkommando* in Krasnodar in the Crimea. The victims were mostly Jews. Christmann had already been charged before two years previously, but the SS officer – by then an estate agent – had managed to avoid prosecution, claiming ill health.

The Americans had first arrested the former Klagenfurt Gestapo chief in 1945 and interned him in one of the sub-camps of Dachau. He escaped and worked under a false name in the British Zone of Occupation, until an Austrian woman recognised him in a shop. So, travelling on a false Red Cross passport, he bought fake identity papers and reached Rome. He sailed to Argentina, where he took an active part in the SS comrades association, the *Kameradenwerk*. In 1956, he returned to Europe, and in 1987 he died in Munich, never having faced trial.

Theodor Dannecker fled Italy in March 1945 and headed to Austria, where he hid for the summer and autumn in the mountains on the Italian border. American troops arrested him in December 1945, and on 10 December, while in a military prison in the town of Bad Tolz, he committed suicide.

Police Chief Kurt Daluege, the man whom Reinhard Heydrich called 'Dummi-Dummi', or 'idiot', suffered a massive heart attack in May 1943. Hitler relieved him of all of his duties and he spent the rest of the war on an estate in Pomerania, recovering. British troops in Lübeck arrested him in May 1945, interned him in Luxembourg and then put him on trial at Nuremberg. It was his war crimes committed in Moravia and Bohemia, the massacre carried out at Lidice, in reprisal for Heydrich's assassination, that took him to the hangman's noose. All through his trial, he claimed he was only following Hitler's orders, had a clear conscience, and was loved by 3 million normal German policemen. Sentenced to death on 23 October 1946, the Czechs hanged him in Pankrac Prison in Prague a week later.

The capture of Adolf Eichmann in Argentina in 1960, his subsequent covert transfer to Israel and his court proceedings that lasted until 1962, all coalesced into the most high-profile Nazi war crimes trial since Nuremberg. Mossad agents seized him in Argentina and flew him back to face justice. He was eventually convicted on fifteen charges, including war crimes, crimes against humanity, crimes against the Jewish people, and membership of three organisations which had been branded criminal at Nuremberg – the SS, the SD and the Gestapo. He was sentenced to death. Although the judge ruled that the SS colonel had not actually killed anybody personally, he did stress that he had been focally implicated in the execution of the Final Solution. An appeal by his defence team failed and a request for clemency from the Israeli President, Yitzhak Ben-Zvi, was denied after the country's cabinet advised him to reject it. The Israelis hanged Eichmann at a prison in Ramla, central Israel, on 1 June 1962. His last words were:

Long live Germany, Long live Argentina, Long live Austria. These are the three countries with which I have been most connected and which

I will not forget. I greet my wife, my family and my friends. I am ready. We'll meet again soon, as is the fate of all men. I die believing in God.[1]

His body was cremated, and a patrol boat from the Israeli Navy scattered his ashes in the Mediterranean.

Suicide, hanging, imprisonment, death by natural causes, escape, flight, arrest, co-operation with captors – the post-war years saw the end of the story for all of the SS, SD and Gestapo officers who had served in Italy between 1943 and 1945 implementing the Final Solution. Often, it was only after the war that it became evident which men had been working as American or British intelligence assets, which ones only did so after the war's end, and why.

The network of SS double agents inside and across Italy was, as has been explained, just one of the reasons why the implementation of the Final Solution was so ham-fisted, slow and corrupt, often making it not impossible for Italian Jews to sidestep it. The full range of duplicity ranged from officers like Guido Zimmer, who was a triple agent working for the Italians as well; to Karl Wolff, working with the Americans; to Theodor Saevecke, working for the Americans because he hated communism; to Wilhelm Hoettl, who just wanted money.

There were men like Albert Kesselring, released from prison early and pardoned because the Allies had seen and sniffed the wind of approaching communism, felt the frosts of the Cold War, and wanted Germans rearmed and on their side. And others, like Walter Rauff, who had always been out-and-out unprincipled, mercenary gangsters, who then went to work for dictators in Syria and Chile.

By looking at some of the cases of the individual SS men *after* the war, the extent to which they collaborated with the Allies *during* the war sometimes becomes clearer and throws their operations in Italy between 1943 and 1945 into a more comprehensible perspective. It helps to explain why the results of these operations so often turned out the way they did.

Another background factor that helps to explain some of the more problematic realms of the post-war thinking of the Allied political leadership can be gauged from the draft plan of an operation that Winston Churchill proposed in July 1945.

Operation Unthinkable

By May 1945, the Cold War had become a reality. When Trieste was occupied by the Yugoslavs and liberated by the Maori soldiers of the 2nd New Zealand Infantry Division, a dividing line was established across the centre of the Adriatic port. The SS leaders, Rainer and Globocnik, had long since fled, and on one side were the Italians, Americans, British and their Commonwealth Allies, and on the other, the Yugoslavs and just behind them, the Red Army.

Churchill was, by summer 1945, enormously concerned about the coming threat posed by the Soviet Union, and so just before he lost the General Election and his position as prime minister in July 1945, he ordered his senior chiefs of staff to begin planning an extraordinary contingency plan. Like many in Europe, he simply didn't trust the Soviets, nor the Red Army, in their speeches, promises, actions or intentions.

Within weeks, the world inside Europe had spun around on its head. Suddenly, concentration camps had been discovered, then emptied, and the world could see what the Third Reich – particularly the SS – had been about. But within days of soldiers from the British 6th Airborne Division discovering the emaciated corpses of the victims of Belsen, Churchill saw the threat as coming from the other end of Europe. He was perspicacious, and he saw how the threat could develop. So, in this state of mind, he came up with a plan, called it Operation Unthinkable, and set his chiefs of staff to work.[2] 'Oh, dear,' Chief of the General Staff Sir Alan Brooke was reported to have said, when he saw the plan. 'Winston wants another war.'[3]

Apart from the requirements for the invasion of Japan, Churchill was preoccupied that the economic pressure in the US to 'get the GIs home' could suddenly see tens of thousands of American soldiers and airmen withdraw from the territories they had occupied and liberated, such as France, Italy and Germany, and return home. Or naturally, see their forces diverted to the Pacific for the attack on Japan.

Secondly, he was very worried that Washington might also withdraw its remaining troops, airmen and sailors from the European continent because of the enormous human pressure, the domestic unpopularity of keeping a massive army in Europe after four long years of war, expensive in both human and material terms. Britain would, once again, come out of both decisions vulnerable and tactically and strategically exposed.

Meanwhile, the promises and undertakings all three sides had made to each other at the Yalta Conference, the Moscow Conference, Casablanca and Potsdam now seemed, like Stalin's words, as inconsequential as boiling water poured into sand.

The concept was, in essence, a third world war. In May, then June and July 1945, Churchill asked his planners and chiefs of staff to come up with a plan in secret. The basis of it would be an attack against the Red Army, in the centre of its line around Dresden, by the British Army, Navy and Air Force, accompanied by her allies. One of Operation Unthinkable's aims, as the report said, was to impose upon Russia the will of the United States and the British Empire. The will of these two countries could be defined (and this was Churchill's key phrase) in 'a square deal for Poland'. It was to be a protracted war after a pre-emptive strike, and yet it would almost certainly see the beginning of a third world war.

The plan was completely confidential, written by a small group of very senior British officers in the Cabinet War Office who, along with Churchill, numbered about twenty. The plan was to attack and cripple Russia and its forces before the Red Army could do the same to the Western Allies. And in their new war against the Soviet Union, the Allies were going to need reinforcements. The Red Army, despite the failings in the quality of its personnel and its outdated and often cumbersomely inefficient equipment, had a massive numerical superiority in men and material against the Americans and British.

So, one of the requirements of the strategy that Churchill dreamt up was the co-opting of up to 100,000 former German servicemen – including the Waffen-SS – to fight alongside the British, Americans and other forces. The assistance and support of the Americans would obviously be vital, said the report. As the Germans would now be earmarked to attack the Red Army on their own national territory, in their own country, it would open up the possibility of German troops taking revenge on the Russians for crimes inflicted during their invasion of Germany in 1944 and 1945. These crimes were themselves revenge for crimes committed by the Germans in Ukraine, Byelorussia, Russia and the Baltic States in 1941 and 1942. History was in danger of repeating itself very fast.

The Russians outnumbered the Western Allies, realistically, three to one: yet the superior quality of Allied men, training and equipment offset some of these advantages in manpower and quantity of equipment the Russians held. Forty-seven Allied divisions would go head to head with 170 Russian ones. The plan foresaw the possibility that Britain could lose access to Iraqi and Persian Gulf oilfields and Russia could even ally with Japan. Yugoslavia would be involved, undoubtedly, Austria could be invaded by Russia, and there would be a long-lasting and total war in central Europe again, within weeks of the conflict having just ended.

By June, Churchill was ready to review the plan and the options, after the document had been signed by some of the men who had prepared it: the British First Sea Lord, Admiral Sir Andrew Cunningham, General Sir Alan Brooke, Chief of the Imperial Staff, and Air Chief Marshal Sir Douglas Evill, Chief of the Air Defence Staff. Churchill saw it, at that point, as a hypothetical contingency.

The extent to which it would affect Germany was to the tune of 100,000 men, or ten divisions. And so, if it came to it, the co-operation of their generals, the men who still held their loyalty, was vital for Churchill. The operation never made it off the page, but it explains some of the British thinking about former members of the Wehrmacht and SS directly after the war.

Wilhelm Hoettl and Holocaust Gold

Wilhelm Hoettl, who had arranged the transport and receipt of Herbert Kappler's 50kg of gold from Rome to Berlin in October 1943, kept his position at the RSHA until the final moment as the Red Army was approaching Berlin. He had access to German passports and visas for Switzerland, and he sold these. One of the men he sold them to was

Árpád Toldi, a Hungarian SS officer. He was one of the people in charge of the so-called 'Hungarian Gold Train'.

In the summer of 1944, more than 430,000 Hungarian Jews were rounded up and deported to Auschwitz. Their gold, jewellery, paintings, silverware, gems and foreign currency, mainly Swiss francs and American dollars, were confiscated by the SS. As the Red Army approached Budapest, Árpád Toldi and his colleagues loaded the treasure onto a forty-six-car freight train that headed west towards Austria and then Germany. Jewish and Hungarian organisations later estimated the value of what was in the train at approximately US$350 million in 1945 (around US$4 billion in 2007).

As the train crossed into Austria on 30 March 1945, Toldi and his family left the convoy and tried to enter Switzerland, but they were turned back at the border. The Red Army was then only 10 miles behind. So, he offered Wilhelm Hoettl 10 per cent of his personal treasure, which amounted to four boxes of small gold ingots. Hoettl, in return, gave Toldi and his family Swiss visas and German passports. They entered Switzerland and, apart from a brief interrogation by the Allies in Austria a year later, he was never seen again. Much of the treasure from the train fell into the hands of French, Austrian and American officers and subsequently disappeared.

After this, Hoettl had enough gold bullion to be able to escape to South America and begin a new life if he wished, or stay in Europe and adopt a false identity, and certainly not have to work. However, he chose to turn himself in to the American OSS.

In April 1945, Ernst Kaltenbrunner had decided to relocate the headquarters of the RSHA from Berlin to Altaussee, a town sitting at the heart of the Salzburg mountains, where Hitler and the SS had long considered forming an Alpine Redoubt. Hoettl was in Bad Aussee with Kaltenbrunner in April and May 1945, and a number of other high-ranking Nazis had passed through or stayed in the town in the days before the Americans arrived. They included Eichmann, Franz Stangl, who had commanded Sobibor and Treblinka camps, and Anton Burger, who had been in charge of Theresienstadt.

Kaltenbrunner was staying in a villa, and after he left, an Austrian farmer called Johann Pucher made a report to both the Altaussee municipal authorities and the American military authorities. He said that while ploughing his land, he had discovered currency and gold to a weight estimated at 75kg. He said he handed it all to an Austrian partisan leader, Albrecht Gaiswinkler.

Another US Army report from the 319th Infantry Regiment in Altaussee claims that Gaiswinkler presented them with 2,036 British gold sovereigns, other gold coins, some bars of gold bullion and foreign currency in lire, dollars and French and Belgian francs. The two sums may have been part of the same haul. The Americans, in turn, reported that they had handed it over to the Currency Section of the Upper Austrian National Bank in January 1946.[4] Was this part of the 50kg of gold, believed to be the Jewish treasure taken from Rome in 1943, which Kaltenbrunner and Hoettl – the two guardians of the gold – had brought with them to Austria?

After leaving Kaltenbrunner in Altaussee, Hoettl surrendered to a reconnaissance troop of the US Army's 7th Infantry Division, who transferred him to Germany. He appeared as a witness for the prosecution, against his former colleagues, during the Nuremberg Trials.

He said in a sworn affidavit from 25 November 1945 that he and Adolf Eichmann had a conversation in Budapest in August 1944. The deportation of the Hungarian Jews was then at its height. Eichmann had allegedly told him that 6 million Jews had been killed, 4 million in camps, the other 2 million mostly shot by the Security Police in Russia.

After testifying, Hoettl was taken back to Austria, and the Americans released him in December 1947. The Austrian People's Courts wanted to arrest him and put him on trial for his responsibility, as part of the RSHA, for deportations of Austrian Jews. The Americans blocked this. Instead, by autumn 1948, he was intricately involved working as a control chief for a US Counter-Intelligence Corps (CIC) operation in Austria, code-named Mount Vernon. This involved a network of Austrian informers working inside the Russian Zone of Occupation in Austria:

Network MOUNT VERNON was activated on 1 October 1948 by the CIC Gmunden Field Office. This net is generally described as a network of Austrian informants operating in the Russian occupied zone of Austria who are charged with reporting all information that would be of value to the U.S. Armed Forces … penetration of the Cominform … and all Communist organisations, espionage of all Soviet Activities to include industrial scientific and military information.[5]

Hoettl's alias was 'Goldberg' or 'Willi', and the report described him as living in Altaussee and being the control chief both for Mount Vernon and an additional project known as Montgomery. The CIC said that he was:

… an excellent source for ideas, both concrete and theoretical, on the expansion of American Intelligence in Austria. His background as a former Deputy Chief of Amt VI RSHA for southeast Europe enables him to evaluate incoming reports on the Soviets with fairly complete accuracy.[6]

The report then proceeded to list thirty Austrian and German agents, both men and women, who were involved in Operation Mount Vernon. These include former SD officer Werner Moser, an SD captain code-named 'Edi', an SS lieutenant code-named 'Walther', who had formerly operated with the SS commando leader Otto Skorzeny, an SD lieutenant called Erwin, and five former officers and NCOs from the Wehrmacht.

Some of the former officers from the RSHA, like Hoettl, were now protected from arrest by the Austrians and Italians and were, effectively, getting away with murder.[7] As the former Jewish Brigade Group soldiers were helping Holocaust survivors make the journey to Palestine, some of the men who had been instrumental in implementing the Final Solution were now less than 200 miles away, working for the Allies.

The report detailed a hint of intelligence operations at the beginning of the Cold War, carried out at that time by these former SS and SD men, for whom their old enemies, the Americans, had just become their new counterparts:

All reports are handled either by courier or letter-drop. The break-down of these methods by sources is as follows:

10/6343 – Makes a trip once weekly from Vienna over the Enna bridge to Attnang-Puchheim where a package containing reports is picked up, from the courier by a representative of the Gmunden [Counter-Intelligence Corps] Center. When traveling through the Russian zone the courier wraps his reports in an old newspaper and places them on the baggage rack above the person opposite him in the train compartment, upon which bags, coats and other items are placed. Source also makes one monthly trip to the Gmunden Centre. At which time he hides his package of reports inside the water tank of the men's toilets when passing through the Russian Zone.[8]

Hoettl would go on to open a school in Altaussee and worked as its director until 1980. Despite the protests of some surviving victims of the Holocaust, he received a medal. He died in the same Austrian mountain town in 1999, aged 84. He had never served an hour of prison time, nor appeared in court. And largely, the survivors of the Italian Holocaust, in Turin, Milan, Rome, Florence and other cities, never had the slightest idea about what had happened to him.

His former colleague in the SD, Wilhelm Harster, was, however, arrested by the British Army and deported to the Netherlands to face trial. In 1949, he was given a sentence of twelve years for his role in the deportation of 104,000 Dutch Jews, including Anne Frank. Yet, he was to serve only four years of this sentence, before being released early and going on to work as a civil servant in Bavaria, subsequent to which he drew a full pension.

He was tried again in 1967 and received another prison sentence, this time of fifteen years – but he served only one. He died in 1991, a free man.

The man who had overseen the operations carried out in Italy by these SS and SD men was, of course, Ernst Kaltenbrunner. Shortly after he left Eichmann and Hoettl in Altaussee in spring 1945, the US Army found him hiding in a mountain chalet above the Austrian town on 12 May 1945.

The Mayor of Altaussee was told by a mountain ranger that in a cabin on a mountainside, six hours' walk from the town, there was a party of SS men hiding with fake documents. He, in turn, informed soldiers from the US Army's 80th Infantry Division. A CIC agent assembled a search party made up of American soldiers, the town mayor and four ex-Wehrmacht men.

It took them six hours to climb over glacial moraine and mountain slopes to reach the chalet. The search party stormed into the wooden building and the German and Austrian SS men surrendered instantly. The scar-faced Kaltenbrunner, who, at 6ft 4in, was easy to recognise, at first insisted he was a doctor. But arriving back in Altaussee, his mistress was standing in the street. Gisela von Westarp called out to him by name – it was all the American soldiers needed.

At his trial in Nuremberg, Kaltenbrunner said that he hadn't even known about the Final Solution until 1943 and had protested vociferously to both Hitler and Himmler about the treatment of the Jews. He said that Himmler was responsible for everything and – even though one visit he made to Mauthausen was carefully documented – he had never actually been there. He claimed that the head of the Gestapo, Heinrich Müller, had often illegally signed documents in his place. He finally claimed that it had been partly because of his efforts that the Final Solution had been brought to an end.

Not surprisingly, his arguments did not sway the court. He was sentenced to death by hanging and was executed on 16 October 1946. He left behind him a range of subordinates and colleagues, whose judicial fate after the war demonstrated much about post-war justice for war crimes – or the lack of it – and how so many SD and SS officers escaped without facing trial for the crimes committed in Italy.

Herbert Kappler was arrested by the British in 1945 in Rimini and handed over to the Italians in 1947. Tried by a military tribunal, he received a life sentence, which he began to serve at the prison at Gaeta, north of Naples. One of his visitors while he was incarcerated was Monsignor Hugh O'Flaherty, with whom he kept up correspondence. Kappler converted to Catholicism under his spiritual aegis. He also married a nurse called Anneliese in a prison ceremony in 1972.

By 1975, having been diagnosed with terminal cancer, he had moved to a military hospital outside Rome. On a visit in 1977, Anneliese Kappler was reportedly able to carry him out in a suitcase, as the former Gestapo chief's weight had dropped to 47kg. The couple arrived in West Germany, where authorities refused to extradite Kappler. He died six months later in 1978. The Italian Defence Minister resigned as a result of his escape.

Although Himmler, Kaltenbrunner and Karl Wolff had been in charge of the SS hierarchy that oversaw the Final Solution in Italy, Field Marshal Albert Kesselring had been the Supreme German Commander and was indicted for his role in the killings of partisans and civilians in reprisal operations, and for the deaths of the 335 prisoners at the Ardeatine Caves. He was captured by the American 101st Airborne in May 1945 and was put on trial at a British military tribunal in Venice in May 1947. He was given the death sentence, but this was then commuted to life imprisonment after a series of protests by significant politicians and soldiers in Britain, including Winston Churchill and Field Marshal Harold Alexander.

To the fury of the Italians, in October 1957 he was released from prison because of ill health. He died in 1960, and among the mourners at his military funeral were senior SS officers like Sepp Dietrich and Joachim Pieper, the latter at the time wanted for war crimes committed in Italy, around Cuneo in autumn 1943.

A German who fought on the side of good and survived the war was Josef Müller, who had liaised with the Pope over resistance plots against Hitler. Although he was arrested in 1943 and sent to Flossenburg concentration camp, he was spared execution after the July 1944 attempt on Hitler's life. Released in April 1945, he was part of a group of high-value German prisoners who were marched to the South Tyrol and handed over to the Americans. He subsequently became a liberal politician and was deputy prime minister in 1951. He died in 1979.

Conversely, the head of the SS operations in Milan, Walter Rauff, evaded justice for ever. His post-war career saw him recruited by Syrian intelligence in 1948, advising their government on how to operate against the newly formed State of Israel. He then moved to Lebanon, then to Italy, where he avoided arrest with the help of former SS colleagues working for the so-called 'Rat Line' escape network. He sailed to Ecuador and moved to live in Chile. A 1950 CIA report claimed that Rauff was working for Mossad in Syria, and that it helped arrange the immigration papers for him to enter South America.

In a startling intelligence volte-face, Rauff was then employed from 1958 to 1963 by the *Bundesnachrichtendienst* (BND), the Federal Intelligence Service of West Germany. His handler at the BND was reportedly an officer called Wilhelm Beissner, who had worked with Rauff at the RSHA. The worm was not so much turning, as doing somersaults. By 1960, Rauff had even managed to visit Germany to claim his pension from his time in the navy before and at the beginning of the war.

The Chilean authorities repeatedly rejected German and Israeli calls for his extradition, and Rauff disappeared. He died in Santiago in May 1984.

Justice, however, came much faster for Joaquim von Ribbentrop, the Reich's Foreign Minister. He was arrested by a French sergeant working with the Special Air Service (SAS) in Hamburg in May 1945. In his pocket, he had a letter to Winston Churchill in which he criticised Britain's anti-German foreign policy, claiming it was responsible for the spread of Soviet communism, and subsequently the Soviet Army, into Europe. Von Ribbentrop was the first defendant to be sentenced to death at Nuremberg.

One of his subordinates in Italy, Ernst von Weizsäcker, stayed in the Vatican as a guest of the Pope until 1946, before being arrested in 1947 and put on trial at Nuremberg. His son, the future German President Richard von Weizsäcker, appeared as one of his defence lawyers. Their stance was that he had been strongly opposed to Hitler and part of the resistance plots.

The prosecution claimed he had been responsible for deporting French Jews. The latter won, and he received a seven-year sentence, later reduced to five, and then three. He died of a stroke in 1951, and at his funeral he was buried in full Nazi diplomatic uniform, along with the swastika armband.

Five other SS and SD officers who had been central to Holocaust operations in Italy also faced completely different fates after the war. Friedrich Rainer, who governed Trieste and the Adriatic administrative zone, was arrested by the British in Austria in 1945 and appeared at Nuremberg as a defence witness. The Yugoslavs demanded his extradition and he was tried by a military court in Ljubljana in 1947, found guilty, and sentenced to death by hanging. His wife was given a death certificate at the time. Only years later did Slovenian government documents claim that he had worked as an informant for the Yugoslav government and was not executed until 1950.

His SS henchman, Odilo Globocnik, fled Trieste at the end of April 1945 with a group of Ukrainian SS camp guards and his three SS deputies. He took his Holocaust treasure with him. Arrested by British troops from the 4th Hussars in a small mountain hut in the Austrian mountains, he committed suicide in front of his captors in the town of Paternion in June 1945. His gold and valuables were buried on a mountainside in southern Austria by his deputies, somewhere near the Weissensee, the White Lake. They were never recovered.

Willy Tensfeld, from the SS office in Verona, and Theodor Saevecke, from Milan, were arrested by the Allies. The British put Tensfeld on trial in 1947, but he was acquitted, while Saevecke escaped, was sentenced to life imprisonment *in absentia* by a court in Turin but was never extradited from Germany. Both men died in freedom.

Their commanding officer, Karl Wolff, also appeared as a witness at the Nuremberg Trials, having allegedly made a deal with American Intelligence during Operation Sunrise that he would be granted immunity from prosecution. But the West Germans arrested him in 1962 and he received a sentence of fifteen years for his role in deporting Italian Jews. He served seven years. On his release, he became involved in a piece of duplicitous intrigue that, even by the standards of his former colleagues' double dealing, stands out.

In the 1970s, he was asked by a journalist from *Stern* magazine, Gerd Heidemann, to work on a story about the discovery of Hitler's alleged diaries. He and Heidemann travelled to South America, where Wolff helped find war criminals Klaus Barbie and Walter Rauff. It is not known what the reaction of these two former SS officers was to having their hiding places revealed to the media by one of their former colleagues. Wolff died in 1984.

There was to be a cruel irony in the legal proceedings that took place concerning the SS killings on Lake Maggiore. During the autumn and winter of 1943, the *Liebstandarte* Division had itself carried out an internal investigation, after the body of the murdered Jewish man had washed up in Switzerland. The inquiry may have been inconsequential, but it had a crucial outcome and effect on a court case in 1968. Five former soldiers from the SS unit went on trial in the north-western German town of Osnabrück, charged with twenty-two counts of murder; the court found three of them guilty and handed down life sentences. Another pair were charged as accessories and received three years' jail each. On appeal, the case went all the way up to the Bundesgerichtshof, the country's supreme court. The court did not overturn the guilty verdict, but it did do something very unexpected.

Germany had a Statute of Limitations in place for various types of crime committed in the Second World War, and the legal start date for this statute was the end of the war, May 1945. However, because the SS themselves had investigated the incident in autumn 1943, legally this provided a different 'start date' for the statute: 1943. So this meant that, by 1968, the Statute of Limitations had expired and the defendants were freed. Additionally, when it came to the case of the murders of the Ovazza family, an Austrian SS officer called Gottfried Meir was tried in 1954 in Klagenfurt, but the court found him not guilty. In 1955, however, a military court in Turin sentenced him to life in prison *in absentia*, but the Austrians did not extradite him.

And what of the arch-intriguer himself, Guido Zimmer? During the negotiations for Operation Sunrise, and up until their collapse, he travelled to Switzerland. He kept an Allied radio operator in his house in Milan, liaising between the British and Americans from their head-quarters at Caserta, near Naples, and OSS HQ in Berne. When Operation Sunrise imploded, after Moscow accused Washington and London of negotiating behind its back, Zimmer stayed in Italy. He remained in contact with the OSS, introducing them to his Italian contacts. After the war he took a job as private secretary to the Italian businessman Luigi Parilli and moved back to live in Erlangen in Bavaria. German economist Gero von Schulze-Gaevernitz, who assisted the OSS in the Operation Sunrise negotiations, sent a letter to Major-General William Donovan, the head of the OSS, on 20 November 1945. In it, Zimmer was described as 'having played an outstanding part in the secret operations, which resulted in the unconditional surrender of the German armies in northern Italy'. The letter continues, saying that 'Zimmer had proved to be of extreme usefulness. During several weeks he sheltered a clandestine Allied radio operator in his house in Milan.'[9] In 1948, he made approaches to the fledgling West German Intelligence Service, overseen by the Americans, called the Gehlen Organisation. By 1949, hearing rumours that the Dortmund prosecutor's office was looking for him, he sailed to Argentina, arriving in October 1949. He spent nearly thirty years as an agricultural products salesman and never returned to Europe. He died in 1977.

And the German diplomat in Florence, who did more to help the Jews in that city than any other of his fellow countrymen? In 1955, Gerhard Wolf was made an honorary citizen of Florence. The Acting Mayor of Dresden unveiled a marble plaque in his honour on the Ponte Vecchio.

WHAT BECAME OF THE OTHER CHARACTERS IN THE BOOK?

Wanda Abenaim

The last the world heard of Wanda Abenaim was the message written in fountain pen on the postcard, which was either thrown out of a lorry, dropped while walking or pushed through the slats of the cattle car at Verona Station. On arrival in Auschwitz on 12 December 1943, she was gassed immediately. Whether her husband Riccardo saw her and was reunited with her on that same deportation train, whether they didn't know the other was there, or whether they had a last-moment reunification on arrival in Auschwitz remains unclear.

Dante Almansi

The head of the Jewish community in Rome, who met with Herbert Kappler to discuss the 50kg of gold that the Gestapo was demanding, died in Rome in 1949, aged 71.

Gino Bartali

Bartali's cycling feat of winning three consecutive mountain stages – numbers 13, 14 and 15 – in the 1948 Tour de France was unequalled for decades. It is remembered as one of the most astonishing accomplishments in the history of road cycling, and it would take another fifty years before anybody did it again (Mauro Cipollini did it in the 1999 Tour de France, winning four stages). It was also during the 1948 Tour that Gino Bartali came into his own as a national hero.

The country's political scene was incendiary in those post-war years, with the country drifting to and from the brink of civil war. While Bartali was winning one of his racing stages in the Tour de France, the Communist Party leader Palmiro Togliatti was shot in the neck by a sniper as he was leaving the parliament building in Rome. Furious Communist supporters occupied radio and TV stations and factories and MPs had screaming arguments in the chamber.

Then, the country was united by the news of Bartali's win. One later obituary said:

> Just as it seemed the communists would stage a full-scale revolt, a deputy ran into the chamber shouting 'Bartali's won the Tour de France!' All differences were at once forgotten as the feuding politicians applauded and congratulated each other on a cause for such national pride. That day, with immaculate timing, Togliatti awoke from his coma on his hospital bed, inquired how the Tour was going and recommended calm. All over the country political animosities were for the time being swept aside by the celebrations and a looming crisis was averted.[1]

The former prime minister Giulio Andreotti said:

> To say that civil war was averted by a Tour de France victory is surely excessive. But it is undeniable that on that 14th of July of 1948, day of the attack on Togliatti, Bartali contributed to easing the tensions.[2]

In addition to his 1948 French win, Bartali won the Giro d'Italia in 1946. He stopped racing when he was 40 and died of a heart attack in May 2000. Thirteen years after his death, Bartali was recognised as Righteous Among the Nations by Yad Vashem for his efforts to aid Jews during the Second World War.

Rachel 'Becky' Behar

She was just 13 when the SS *Liebstandarte* turned up at her father's hotel in Meina and, as one of the few survivors of the massacre there, she returned to Milan after the war with her father. She found it wrecked and desperate, exhausted by occupation and by Allied bombing. But she would thrive there. She married Pier Paolo Ottolenghi, a Jewish engineer from Ferrara, a partisan who had escaped the German arrest operations, took over her father's antiques business, and ran for the Italian Senate in 1992. But, as she and others wrote, the main focus of her life after the war was to visit and lecture in schools about all forms of discrimination.

Then one day in January 2016, she was out walking in the streets of Milan on the way to meet her daughter, Rosanna, when she had a cerebral haemorrhage. It was to be Primo Levi who testified, after her death, that her main aim in life was to make sure that other people did not suffer the same forms of prejudice that she had.

Giovanni Borromeo

After the war, the doctor from the Fatebenefratelli Hospital became friends with the prime minister, Alcide De Gasperi, who led the Christian Democrats in a coalition between 1945 and 1953. Borromeo joined Gasperi's party and became Counsellor for Public Health of the Municipality of Rome. He died at his own hospital, the Fatebenefratelli, in August 1961. He was awarded a Silver Medal of Civil Valour for his actions whilst he was alive and, forty-three years after his death, he was recognised as Righteous Among the Nations by Yad Vashem.

Gian Galeazzo Ciano

Mussolini's Foreign Minister's time in the sun was short. When his father-in-law was deposed by the Fascist Council of Ministers, Ciano was dismissed from his post by the new, puppet Fascist government in the Salò Republic. Ciano, Edda and their three children fled to Germany on 28 August 1943, thinking they'd be safe. The Germans arrested them and returned them to Italy.

A court run by Mussolini's administration in Verona found Ciano guilty of treason, and on 11 January 1944 he faced a firing squad. To humiliate the condemned men, they were tied to chairs that were turned against the firing squad, so they would be shot in the back. Some accounts claim that Ciano managed to twist his chair to face the firing squad before he was shot. Allegedly, his final words were 'Long live Italy!'

Before he was shot, his wife had tried to barter his personal diaries in which he had recorded details of meetings with Hitler, Ribbentrop, Mussolini and foreign diplomats. The future fashion designer Emilio Pucci, then a lieutenant in the Italian Air Force, hid the diaries at Medesano, near Parma. When Hitler refused to negotiate Ciano's life for the diaries, Pucci helped Edda Ciano and her children escape to Switzerland with five of the diaries, the ones covering the years of the war. The diary from 1939 to 1943, edited by Malcolm Muggeridge, was published in the United Kingdom.

Eugenia Cohen

In 2018, Eugenia Cohen's son with her British Jewish soldier husband, Reuven Donath, met two of the children of the Italian couple who had saved her during the war. Ernestina Madonnini's children, Caterina and Antonella, welcomed Nir Donath in the vast fourteenth-century Castello Visconteo, which serves as the council's headquarters in the town of Pandino. This was where Eugenia hid in the war. Mr Donath read a text message from one of his sisters, Navia, who now lives in Israel. She sent her love 'to the Madonnini family, thanks to whom we are in this world'. Eugenia Cohen, or Noga Donath, died in Israel in 2017.

Lieutenant Colonel Sam Derry DSO MC

Sam Derry's book, *The Rome Escape Line*, was published in 1960 and it inspired a film, *The Scarlet and the Black*, starring Gregory Peck as Monsignor Hugh O'Flaherty. After the war, Derry became a magistrate in Newark, and a municipal councillor. He died in 1996. In his book, he described O'Flaherty as 'one of the finest men it has been my privilege to meet. Had it not been for this gallant gentleman, there would have been no Rome Escape Organisation.'

Ugo Foa

Now in his nineties, Foa lives in Rome. The former community leader who met with Herbert Kappler now runs the Memory Project of the Jewish Cultural Centre in Rome. A sprightly man, he is devoted to the idea that by talking about what happened in the past, it may well prove possible to prevent it happening again in the future.

Sister Mary Hambrough

She never left Rome, nor stopped working at the nunnery in the Piazza Farnese, where she died in June 1966. In 2012, the Vatican took up her case for canonisation.

Pascalina Lehnert

She managed the papal charity office for Pius XII from 1944 until the pontiff's death in 1958. As a sister of the Holy Cross Menzingen Order, she wrote her autobiography in 1959. The Church authorities permitted its publication only in 1982. In around 200 pages, the nun tries to give an idea of some of the qualities of Eugenio Pacelli, with whom she effectively worked for almost forty-one years. There's everything that one would expect – the meetings, the drama of the war, the coronations, the Vatican ceremony, the personal character of the Pope and their daily routine, Castel Gandolfo in the summer, the Vatican at Christmas, diplomats, delegates and dramas. But not surprisingly, no Jews or Nazis or resistance plots. She died in Vienna in 1983, aged 89.

Primo Levi

In terms of his scientific and literary legacy, Levi is probably the most well-known Holocaust survivor. The nervous, gentle, intensely intelligent chemist from Turin's Corso Re Umberto was endlessly immortalised for his words and thoughts about Auschwitz, and the nature of life and death – and chemistry. His most well-known book is *If this is a Man*, published in 1947, which is the story of the year he spent in Auschwitz. Next comes *The Periodic Table*, which is a socio-psychological dissection of the world and life according to chemistry, as defined by the different elements of the Periodic Table. It was described as the best science book ever written.

Nowadays, there's little to remind the passing visitor of his presence, or his life, around his house in Turin. Number 75 Corso Re Umberto is a large, nineteenth-century apartment building, set on one of the elegant, wide boulevards of central Turin, itself perhaps one of Italy's most graceful cities. Rows of chestnut trees line the centre of the avenue, and triangular road signs, edged in red, carry the idiosyncratic warning, 'Beware: Falling chestnuts in the autumn season'. It seems a fitting place for a man of such brains as Levi. After the war it was where he came back to, and where, eventually, he wrote.

In April 1987, Levi died from the injuries he suffered after he fell down the stairwell to the ground floor from the landing outside his third-floor apartment. His death was ruled by an inquest to be a case of suicide, but many people have suggested that this was highly unlikely because he didn't leave a suicide note, there were no witnesses, and he was taking medicine that could have affected his balance. And for somebody like him, a careful, considered man, the idea of throwing oneself down the gap between the ascending flights of stairs strikes one as too chaotic, messy, thoughtless – everything Levi was not.

After the war, Levi spent a great deal of time visiting schools to talk about his experiences in Auschwitz. He rejected the view that the German camps and Stalin's Gulag system were in any way comparable – one was a system of work camps where up to 30 per cent of the inmates died, the other was a system simply designed to kill people, which it achieved at a rate of 90–95 per cent. His view of the Holocaust was that it was an attempt at the triumphalism of presumed superiority of one race over another. That it worked for as long as it did, as effectively as it did, says Levi, was a tribute to the Germans' capacity for organisation and a ruthless, mechanical approach to human destruction. When he died, the Holocaust survivor Elie Wiesel said, 'Primo Levi died at Auschwitz but forty years later.'

Roberto Lordi

Lordi was one of the 335 prisoners executed at the Ardeatine Caves. Nowadays, the site is preserved as a commemorative memorial, set along the shiny paving stones of the Via Appia, under the umbrella pine trees of southern Rome. The city, and its memorial sites like the Ardeatine Caves, have lasted as a tribute to the passing ebb and flow of dramatic human history. In these days of complex, chaotic warfare crackling across countries like Syria, it's hard not to stand at sites like that of the

Ardeatine Caves and question whether mankind has developed, evolved and found ways not to want to destroy itself.

Cardinal Luigi Maglione

He died in August 1944, two months after the Allies had liberated Rome. The relationship between the Pope and Maglione was reputedly so close that one joke went like this: 'Do you know that when the Pope goes out without his *maglione*, he gets a cold?' (It is a pun on the word '*maglione*', which in Italian means 'sweater' or 'jumper'.)

Much of Maglione's work is documented in the twelve volumes of material released from the Historical Section of the Vatican Archives in 1965. As referenced previously, these run to 2,114 pages and are only excerpts of what happened in the war. *Actes et Documents du Saint Siège relatifs à la Seconde Guerre Mondiale* bear reading carefully. They are like a system of mirrors in *Alice in Wonderland*: the reader ploughs through, hoping for more revelatory details about what happened with the Jews in Rome in 1943 or what Hitler did or didn't say to Pius XII.

These details, of course, are exactly what *aren't* in the documents. Their release in 1965, after much deliberation, was designed to sidestep this issue, and present a very large amount of other material that shows the Vatican in a reflective, human, achieving and benevolent light. They go a long way to explaining the Pope's actions through the communications he had with other parties, notably the Germans, Americans, British, Italians and Swiss. They're a picture of a church at war, and a church fighting for its material, human and spiritual survival, and if there are episodes excised or not included in the archive material? Well, not for nothing has the Vatican lasted so long.

Virginia Montalcini

Virginia was arrested near Sondrio on 23 January 1944, deported to Auschwitz on the 30th, and killed as soon as she arrived. Nowadays, there are bronze commemorative plaques set in the pavement out-side her former high school, Massimo D'Azeglio, on Turin's Corso Matteotti.

A group of the teenage students recently got together and launched a project to remember Virginia. With the help of two of their professors, they persuaded the local municipality that it might be possible to have the bronze plaques set outside the school, rather than outside Virginia's former home or the house where she was originally born. So, there are two plaques outside her school, and each time one passes them, they're bright and shining, burnished by the caretakers, as though reminding everybody that the smile for which Virginia was so well known was never really extinguished.

Hugh O'Flaherty

Decorated for his service to the Vatican, Italian Jews and Allied POWs, the Irish monsignor continued to serve Pope Pius XII as Notary of the Holy Office. He was made a Commander of the Order of the British Empire (CBE) and was given awards by the United States, Canada and Australia. He regularly visited Herbert Kappler in the prison at Gaeta, being his only visitor, month after month. He baptised Kappler in 1959. He suffered a stroke in 1960 and died in Ireland in 1963, aged 65.

Sir D'Arcy Osborne

When the end of the war came, the British Ambassador to the Holy See, D'Arcy Osborne, retired and remained in Rome. He lived at the Palazzo Sacchetti on Via Giulia. Fittingly, for somebody who enjoyed such a close relationship with the Vatican, the palace had been built in 1542 by an architect called Antonio da Sangallo the Younger on land given to him by the Pope. The papal coat of arms still stands out, on the outside of the building, along with the chiselled inscription, '*Tu mihi quod cumque hoc rerum est*' ('Everything I have, I got from you').

Osborne worked after the war with the future Pope Paul VI and set up a trade training school for the children of impoverished parents. On a number of occasions, during royal visits to Italy, the Queen and the Queen Mother, old friends of Osborne's, came to visit. He defended Pius XII's wartime record, and when he fell ill at the beginning of the 1960s, Pope Paul VI sent his personal chamberlain to visit Osborne. His dukedom and titles lapsed when he died aged 79, in 1964.

Adriano Ossicini

The student doctor at the Fatebenefratelli Hospital only graduated in medicine at the end of 1944, and once he had done so, he continued to work there. He decided to specialise in psychiatry and neurological diseases, and by 1947 he had become a Professor of Psychology at the Sapienza University of Rome. There he stayed until 1968, when he decided to enter politics. Voted in as a candidate for the Independent Left Party, he held on to his seat in parliament until 1992. He died in 2019, and today the hospital where he worked still stands, still works, still serves, sitting on its little island in the Tiber.

Riccardo Pacifici

Riccardo was gassed on arrival in Auschwitz on 12 December 1944. Even though he was travelling on the same deportation train as his wife, Wanda, it is not known if the two of them were able to meet for one last time on arrival in the concentration camp. At the entrance to the Galleria Mazzini in Genoa, his bronze memorial plaque remembers him. There is also, in Genoa, a square that was named after him in 1966 – Largo Riccardo Pacifici.

Witold Pilecki

In many ways, the story of Captain Pilecki was the story of Poland itself in the second half of the Second World War. After his experiences in Auschwitz and his documenting of the workings of the camp, he returned to Britain and then back to Warsaw, where he re-joined a partisan unit. He fought in the Warsaw Uprising, and in July 1945 was posted back to the Polish Army itself.

By this time, the Second Polish Corps was based in Ancona, on the eastern Adriatic seaboard in Italy. General Władysław Anders was their commander, and the Poles had spearheaded not just the capture of Ancona but the attack on the crucial city of Bologna in April that year. This had allowed the Allied armies to break through the German defensive positions of the Gothic Line and move into the flatlands of the Po Valley.

Anders sent him back to Warsaw in December 1945 to gather intelligence, form a network of former partisans and send information back to London to the Polish government-in-exile. However, the Soviet authorities in the occupied zone where he was operating broke his cover.

Anders ordered him to leave the country. Pilecki refused. The communist authorities arrested him in May 1947 and he was tortured. Messages sent to the acting prime minister, Josef Cyrankiewicz, fell on deaf ears, even though the political leader was himself a survivor of Auschwitz.

Pilecki was shot and his burial place was never found.

Clotilde Piperno

She returned with her family to live near the Via Portico D'Ottavia and the extended family began trading again in textiles on the Largo Argentina, near the old ghetto. Clotilde died in 1964.

Pope Pius XII

The Pope died in October 1958 of heart failure. His funeral procession was estimated to be the largest gathering of human beings ever seen in the history of Rome. It wasn't just the fact that the Pope himself came from Rome, it was also the fact that, like the Italians around him who mourned, he had been through the war. On 11 October 1958, Cardinal Angelo Giuseppe Roncalli, who was later to become Pope John XXIII, wrote in his diary that it was probable that no Roman emperor had had such a tribute and this was a reflection of the spiritual dignity and majesty of Pius XII.

Lidia Rolfi

When she finally arrived back in her hometown of Mondovi, in Piemonte, in 1945, Lidia started teaching again. She discovered, of course, that she was not the only woman in the area among the network of former partisans who had survived Ravensbrück. She also tried to work out who, in that mad summer and autumn of 1944, had betrayed her to the Germans. One of the main priorities she gave to her work was with the Historical Institute for the Resistance of Cuneo and with the National Association of ex-Deportees.

She saw her friend Monique frequently after the war, some fifteen or twenty times, and the recipe for orange marmalade, brought back from Ravensbrück, is still in her son's house in Mondovi.[3] There's a drawing, too, of Lidia, done in the camps. It's faded with the years, but it's still possible to see the pencilled outlines and the fragile yet determined beauty of the woman whose son says had 'a pair of balls bigger than a man's'.[4]

She returned to Ravensbrück for the first time in 1949, and although she didn't talk about her feelings very much, in 1959 she met a group of other women who had been in the same camp. She worked tirelessly for almost thirty years to raise awareness about what had happened in the camps for deported women. In 1978 she wrote, along with another survivor, *The Women of Ravensbrück*, which was the first book about the deportation of women to concentration camps in Nazi Germany, and 1996 saw the publication of the second, *The Exile's String of Memory*, about returning to the camps and reintegration into civilian life. Primo Levi – whom she knew – was a great supporter of her writing and he wrote the introduction to her last book, about growing up under a dictatorship, which was published posthumously in 1997. She died in 1996.

Today, her memory is that of a local hero in the town of Mondovi and in the circles of former partisans, modern writers, women's rights activists and campaigners across Italy. Her diaries were taken back to Ravensbrück in 2018 and presented to the museum.

The street in which her son Aldo lives is named after her. It's a narrow, twisting lane that runs parallel to the River Ellero. In the early autumn sun, large chub bask in the bottle-green, transparent waters. The house is full of papers, diaries, books and pictures. It is something of a shrine to Lidia Beccari Rolfi and to her two brothers who fought on the Russian Front.

Aldo, a calm and individual man, keeps the flame of memory burning bright. A martial arts instructor and owner of a leather goods shop, he clearly remembers one evening in January 2020, just before the Covid-19 pandemic swept across Italy. He'd been asleep at home when he heard scuffling and scurrying in the street, followed by banging and knocking. He looked out of the window, but saw nothing. The next morning, he discovered, to his surprise and horror, that there was a message left on the front door in black paint. A dribbling daub of a paintbrush had left the image of a Star of David and the words '*Juden hier*'.

The irony of the incident, said Rolfi, and the hundreds and hundreds of neighbours and citizens of Mondovi who gathered in a candlelit vigil the night afterwards, was that Lidia was not Jewish. So stupid was the person who left the message that they couldn't even be bothered to find out, said Aldo. The family were Catholics, like almost everybody else in Mondovi.

As you talk to Lidia's son, the feeling you get from his recollection of the incident is that it heightens the sense of triumph of people like his mother, who survived the Holocaust, knowing that stupidity can be beaten and overcome. The message, and feeling, that good, love, common sense, knowledge and intelligence will triumph in the face of brutal exterminationism is a common thread with Lidia Rolfi, Eugenia Cohen, Primo Levi, Ya'akov Hollander and the others.

Augusto Segre

The jovial and positive rabbi from the Piedmontese town of Casale Monferrato spent the war fighting as a partisan with the Langhe Division. He then became a lawyer, the secretary of the Italian Jewish Federation and head of the cultural department of the Italo-Israeli Community. He moved to Israel in 1979 and died there in 1986.

Enzo Sereni

Sereni, who helped organise the Jewish parachute unit of the British SOE which sent agents into occupied Europe, was himself arrested in Italy and shot by the Germans in Dachau in November 1944. (Another famous agent who parachuted into Europe was Hannah Szenes, whose SOE mission was to jump into Yugoslav territory, which she did, and then move into Hungary to try and help some of the Hungarian Jews who were then being deported. Arrested at the border with Hungary in November 1944, she was put in front of a firing squad.)

A *kibbutz* is named after Enzo Sereni in Israel, as are several streets.

Myron C. Taylor

Myron died aged 85 in New York City in 1959. President Harry C. Truman paid tribute, noting:

The Honorable Myron C. Taylor performed great services for both me and my predecessor in the White House to the Vatican, at a time when it was essential that the United States be represented in that quarter. Undoubtedly, no one could have performed the job as well as he did. All of us should be deeply grateful for the unselfish works of this fine man and able public servant.

FURTHER READING

These are just a few of the many works of historical non-fiction written about Italy in the Second World War and the implementation of the Final Solution in that country and its aftermath. The following stand out as exceptional examples of good writing, excellent research, engaging storytelling and analytical interpretation of history.

Alvarez, David & Robert Graham, *Nothing Sacred: Nazi Espionage against the Vatican 1939–1945* (UK & USA: Frank Cass, 1997).

An extremely well-researched book, drawing on numerous declassified intelligence files, which argues masterfully that the Germans considered the Vatican as nothing short of an enemy state, allied to and assisting the British, Americans, Russians and other Allied and neutral countries.

Atkinson, Rick, *The Day of Battle: The War in Sicily and Italy, 1943–1944* (USA: Henry Holt, 2008).

The second volume in Atkinson's *Liberation* trilogy, this book begins with the American and British armies as they depart from north Africa to invade Sicily and then the Italian mainland. It progresses northwards from Salerno and Monte Cassino to the liberation of Rome.

Bettina, Elizabeth, *It Happened in Italy: Untold Stories of How the People of Italy Defied the Horrors of the Holocaust* (USA: Thomas Nelson Inc., 2013).

Bettina tells the story of the triumphant, unseen populace and how her grandmother's village in Italy had hidden hundreds of Jews during the Second World War. This leads her on a trail of discovery across the country that reveals quite how many Italians, of all backgrounds and professions, helped conceal so many Jews.

D'Este, Carlo, *Fatal Decision: Anzio and the Battle for Rome* (HarperCollins, 1991).

The Allied amphibious landing at Anzio, their failure to push towards Rome and the subsequent five-month battle was one of the great missed opportunities of the war. D'Este's exhaustively researched book tells what happened and why.

Gallagher, J.P., *The Scarlet and the Black: The True Story of Monsignor Hugh O'Flaherty, Hero of the Vatican Underground* (UK & USA: Ignatius Press, 2009).

A reprint of Gallagher's book *The Scarlet Pimpernel of the Vatican*, published in 1967. The story of how one Irish Catholic priest based in the Vatican helped hide thousands of Jews using a network of convents, seminaries and escaped Allied POWs.

Holland, James, *Italy's Sorrow: A Year of War 1944–1945* (UK & USA: HarperCollins, 2009).

The first-hand accounts of Italy's civilian population caught up in the fighting make a powerful counterpoint to Rick Atkinson's military perspective. Together, these two books explain most clearly the Allied strategic and tactical decision to invade Italy, the complete uncertainty of the campaign's outcome, and what it was actually like for the soldiers and civilians of all sides who fought and lived there.

Houston, Ivan J., *Black Warriors: The Buffalo Soldiers of World War II* (USA: iUniverse, 2011).

The fighting in Tuscany in summer and autumn 1944 described from the point of view of a junior NCO serving with the African American soldiers of the US 92nd Infantry Division. A unique and rare look at the unit and what it was like to fight with them, as well as what Tuscany was like in that year of war.

McConnon, Aili and Andre, *Road to Valour: A True Story of WWII Italy, the Nazis, and the Cyclist Who Inspired a Nation* (UK & USA: Broadway Books, 2013).

The story of how a national hero, the Italian cycling champion Gino Bartali, who won the Tour de France and Giro d'Italia, also risked his life to help Jewish families during the war.

Moorehead, Caroline, *A House in the Mountains: The Women Who Liberated Italy From Fascism* (UK: Chatto & Windus, 2019).

Probably the best book written in English about the Italian girls and women who fought with and operated for partisan groups. In Moorehead's account, the lives of four women in wartime revolve around their roles as couriers with resistance groups in and around Turin.

Riebling, Mark, *Church of Spies: The Pope's Secret War against Hitler* (UK & USA: Basic Books, 2016).

Riebling's book is the one that best presents the Pope-as-unsung-hero argument. The author alleges that Pius XII and the Vatican's intelligence networks were secretly supporting multiple assassination attempts against Hitler, explaining why the Pope's public stance on the Holocaust was more understated than it otherwise could have been.

Stafford, David, *Mission Accomplished: SOE and Italy 1943–1945* (UK: Vintage, 2012).

A fascinating and beautifully in-depth look at what the Special Operations Executive actually did on its many missions inside Italy. It is so good because Stafford has had complete access to SOE's records and describes the idiosyncratic deployments of the even more idiosyncratic agents and exactly what they achieved.

Sullam, Simon Levis, *The Italian Executioners: The Genocide of the Jews of Italy* (USA: Princeton University Press, 2018).

A Professor of History at the University of Venice, the author's authoritative revisionist account tells how many ordinary Italians participated in operations to deport Italy's Jews.

Walters, Guy, *Hunting Evil: How the Nazi War Criminals Escaped and the Hunt to Bring them to Justice* (UK: Bantam Press, 2009).

A comprehensive 700-page account of the hunt for the major German war criminals after the war. It concentrates on the high-profile individuals such as Eichmann and Josef Mengele, while also providing one of the best accounts of the 'Rat Line' escape routes that enabled wanted criminals to escape to South America and Spain.

Weale, Adrian, *The SS: A New History* (USA: Little, Brown, 2010).

To understand the military operations, policing and internal security duties of the SS a thoroughly researched and clearly explained account of its history, background, motivations and *raison d'être* is needed. Adrian Weale provides just that.

Zuccotti, Susan, *The Italians and the Holocaust: Persecution, Rescue and Survival* (USA: University of Nebraska Press, 1996).
Zuccotti, Susan, *Under His Very Windows: The Vatican and the Holocaust in Italy* (USA: Yale University Press, 2001).

Both are studiously researched, academic and balanced accounts of the actions and policy of the Vatican during the Holocaust and the widely varying experiences of Italy's Jews in the Second World War.

NOTES

Prologue

1   Wanda Abenaim's postcard from that day at Verona Station is in the archives of the *Fondazione Centro Di Documentazione Ebraica Contemporanea CDEC Onlus (CDEC)* (The Foundation for Contemporary Jewish Documentation) in Milan, and is preserved online in the section of CDEC's website called The Shoah Museum, in Section 20, 'Deportations.' shoahmuseum.cdec.it/albums/le-deportazioni/.

2   The details of the story of the Pacifici and Abenaim families, before, during and after the war, are, among other places, online on the CDEC website, in the section called 'Archivio' of the Shoah. Wanda's elder son Emanuele Pacifici became a historian after the war, when he grew up, and in 1993 published an autobiography entitled *Non ti Voltare: Autobiografia di un Ebreo* (*Don't Turn Around: Autobiography of a Jew*), Casa di Editrice Giuntina, Florence, 1993.

3   The original list of personal effects for Jewish deportees was given to those of Rome's Jews who'd been arrested in October 1943, and the contents of the list remained subsequently identical for SS, SD and Gestapo deportation operations until April 1945. It's held in the archives of CDEC's Shoah Museum, in Section 17, 'The anti-Jewish politics of the German occupiers, September to December 1943': shoahmuseum.cdec.it/albums/la-politica-antiebraica-delloccupante-tedesco-settembre-dicembre-1943/.

4   'Here on the 3.11.1943 Reuven Riccardo Pacifici, Chief Rabbi of Genoa, was arrested. Born in 1904, he was murdered on 11.12.1943 in Auschwitz.'

All *Stolpersteine* in Europe are written in exactly the same way, with the dates, names, ages, place of birth and place of death laid out.

5   7,680 is the figure used by Yad Vashem, The World Holocaust Memorial Centre.

6   Record Groups HW 237–240 are in the National Archives in London. Record Group HW 16 contains messages about logistics and Holocaust transports on the German and Reich Railway Network.

Chapter 1

1   Mussolini's truculent early character and his paternally inherited stance as a politicised intellectual are described in the Australian historian Richard Bosworth's two biographies of both man and country: *Mussolini* (London: Hodder & Stoughton, 2002) and *Mussolini's Italy: Life Under the Dictatorship 1915–1945* (London: Allen Lane, 2006).

2   The comments were made after the speech and after a meeting with Hitler.

3   Ovazza described the meeting with Mussolini in the Introduction to his book *Politica Fascista*, published in 1933, according to *Quest: Issues in Contemporary Jewish History*, Issue 11, October 2017. The magazine is the journal of the CDEC, the Jewish Contemporary Documentation Centre in Milan.

4   Quoted in a letter sent by Ettore Ovazza to Mussolini on 15 July 1938, Archivio Centrale dello Stato, Rome, Spd / Co / File no: 211.398.

Chapter 2

1   The Museum of Turin has kept a record of every single RAF and USAAF raid during the Second World War: www.museotorino.it/view/s/44cae5aed5 3148d79f25343763106fe0.

Chapter 3

1   Pope Pius XI's private secretary was Monsignor Carlo Confalonieri, quoted in his autobiography *Pius XI – A Close Up* (Altadena, California: The Benzinger Sisters Press, 1975) p.373.

2   *Non Abbiamo Bisogno*, encyclical of Pope Pius XI on Catholic Action in Italy, 29 June 1931, paras 36 and 44: www.vatican.va/content/pius-xi/en/ encyclicals/documents/hf_p-xi_enc_29061931_non-abbiamo-bisogno.html.

3   Quoted by Martin Gilbert in 'Hitler's Pope?', *The American Spectator*, 16 July 2006.

4   *Ibid.*

5   Sam Derry, *The Rome Escape Line* (New York: W.W. Norton, 1960) p.43.

6 The Brazilian visa petition, which continued for three years, is one incident documented at great length in selected Vatican correspondence from the Pope and cardinals, which was released in 1965 from the Vatican's Historical Archives. Absent from this archive release were allegedly some of the detailed communications the Pope and Cardinal Maglione had with their nuncios abroad, as well as with the Germans, concerning the Jews of Rome in 1943 and 1944. See *Acts and Documents of the Holy See Relative to the Second World War*, translated from the French, *Actes et Documents du Saint Siège relatifs à la Seconde Guerre Mondiale*, 12 volumes (Editrice Vaticana, 1970) www.vatican. va/archive/actes/index_en.htm. In subsequent notes, any references are just prefaced *Actes et Documentes*, along with the volume and page number, date and the nature of the letter or note.

7 Pope Pius XII, *Summi Pontificatus: On the Unity of Human Society*, 20 October 1939, paras 6 & 7.

8 London: Hutchinson and Co., 1942.

9 'The Polish White Book', 'The Black Book of Poland' / G.P. Putnam's, New York and Hutchinson and Co., London, 1942.

10 Jewish Telegraphic Agency, 8 September 1942.

11 The report, translated from the Polish, can be found at witoldsreport. blogspot.com/2008/05/volunteer-for-auschwitz-report-by.html.

12 api.parliament.uk/historic-hansard/commons/1942/dec/17/united-nations-declaration.

13 The *New York Times*, 11 December 1942.

14 Quoted in Michael Phayer, *The Catholic Church and the Holocaust 1930–65* (Bloomington, Indiana: Indiana University Press, 2000) p.54.

15 Letter from Myron C. Taylor to Cardinal Maglione, 26 September 1942, copy held in the Franklin D. Roosevelt Presidential Library and Museum: docs.fdrlibrary.marist.edu/PSF/BOX52/a467aq01.html.

16 Pope Pius XII, Christmas Address, Vatican Radio, 25 December 1942.

17 A report from the Prague detachment of the Reich Security Main Office, on 27 December 1942, quoted in Pinchas Lapide, *Three Popes and the Jews* (London: Souvenir Press, 1967), p.137.

18 Both extracts and quotes are included in Galeazzo Ciano, *Diarios 1937–1943* (Milan: Rizzoli, 2004) pp.504–08.

19 David G. Dalin, *The Myth of Hitler's Pope: Pope Pius XII and his Secret War Against Nazi Germany* (New York: Regnery, 2005) p.76.

20 *The Villa, the Lake, the Meeting: Wannsee and the Final Solution*, Mark Roseman, Allen Lane, London, New York, 2002, pp.110–11.

21 *The Origins of the Final Solution: The Evolution of Nazi Jewish Policy, September 1939–March 1942*, by Christopher R. Browning, University of Nebraska Press, 2007, p.413.

22 *Eichmann: His Life and Crimes*, by David Cesarani, Vintage Publishers, London, 2005, p.114. Minutes of the meeting were given to each participant,

but after the war all copies but one were destroyed or disappeared. The surviving copy was found by US Prosecutor Robert Kempner (who was German) in the files of the Reich's foreign ministry in 1947. Kempner, who prosecuted at the Nuremburg Trials, used it in evidence.

Chapter 4

1   Michael Phayer, *Pius XII, the Holocaust and the Cold War* (Bloomington, Indiana: Indiana University Press, 2008) pp.253–4.
2   Ralph McInerny, *The Defamation of Pius XII* (South Bend, Indiana: St Augustine's Press, 2001).
3   See Chapter 5 – Codes of the Holocaust – as to how the Vatican, British and Germans achieved this.
4   John S. Conway, University of British Columbia, 'The Meeting Between Pope Pius XII and Ribbentrop, pp.103–04. A paper published in the CCHA Study Sessions of 1968, in which Conway investigates and analyses the multiple recent books, opinions and points of view about this meeting: www.cchahistory.ca/journal/CCHA1968/Conway.pdf.
5   The *New York Times*, 14 March 1940.

Chapter 5

1   The intercept copy and the decrypt of the Mogilev Police message are held in the US National Archives, and copies of both of them – as well as the cryptanalytical background to their interception – can be found in Robert J. Hanyok, *Eavesdropping on Hell: Historical Guide to Western Communications & Intelligence and the Holocaust 1939–1945* (Centre for Cryptologic History, National Security Agency, 2005) pp.51–52: www.nsa.gov/Portals/70/ documents/about/cryptologic-heritage/historical-figures-publications/ publications/wwii/eavesdropping.pdf.
2   Anson Rabinbach and Sander L. Gilman, *The Third Reich Sourcebook* (Berkeley, California: University of California Press, 2013) p.335.
3   Callum MacDonald, *The Killing of SS-Obergruppenführer Reinhard Heydrich* (New York: Macmillan Publishing, 1990) p.175.
4   ATS Corporal Joan Bradshaw quoted on the website of the museum of the village of Quorn in Leicestershire, next to Beaumanor. 'Quorn in WWII: the Girls Who Listened', Sue Templeman: www.quornmuseum.com
5   Based on a series of interviews with the Head of Historical Research at Bletchley Park, David Kenyon, carried out January–July 2021.
6   *Ibid.*
7   Author's note.
8   *Ibid.* Interview with David Kenyon.

9   Documents of Hut 6 of GC & CS, held at Bletchley Park and in the
    National Archives in Record Group HW43/72, pp.1–3, numbered
    Sec. 1.8132 / 1942 'The Orange Age', paras 1 & 4. Author's documents
    courtesy of Bletchley Park.

Chapter 6

1   www.nsa.gov/Portals/70/documents/news-features/declassified-documents/
    european-axis-sigint/volume_1_synopsis.pdf, pp.9 & 37. The main summary
    of Pers Z S successes is on p.9 and Italian successes on pp.34–6. Further
    analysis of Pers Z S is in Vol. VI, pp.1–75, www.nsa.gov/Portals/70/
    documents/news-features/declassified-documents/european-axis-sigint/
    Volume_6_foreign_office_cryptanalytic_section.pdf.
2   Group XIII/52/ROME TO BERLIN/RSS32/7/10/1943.
3   Now held by the British National Archives.
4   Record Groups HW 237–240 are in the National Archives in London.
    Record Group HW 16 contains messages about logistics and Holocaust
    transports on the German and Reich Railway Network.
5   These code-books are now in the archives of the German Ministry of
    Foreign Affairs. They took a lengthy fifty-five-year-long trip to get there,
    being stolen by the Gestapo in 1941 from the Vatican, captured by the
    Americans at the end of the war, then handed to the British, who returned
    the files to Germany in the year 2000 as part of the declassified resources of
    the US Target Intelligence Committee.
6   'European Axis Signal Intelligence in WW2 as Revealed by TICOM
    Investigations' – Volume 6, the Foreign Office Cryptanalytic Section /
    US Army Security Agency / National Security Agency Library, file S47-61.
7   Arlington Hall memo about the decipherment of KIF-Purple.

Chapter 7

1   *Libera Stampa* newspaper, Lugano, 23 October 1943.
2   Alexander Stille, *Uno su Mille: Cinque Famiglie Ebraiche durante il Fascismo*
    (Milan: Garzanti, 2018) p.89. (Translated: *One in a Thousand: Five Jewish Families
    during Fascism*.)
3   Atlas of Nazi and Italian Fascist Massacres in Italy – Intra,
    Verbania, 5–17.10.1943, www.straginazifasciste.it/?page_id=38&id_
    strage=2424&lang=en.
4   Becky Behar's testimony of the events of her life, and the killings in
    Meina in 1943, are documented in the book *La Strage Dimenticata: Meina
    Settembre 1943, il Primo Ecidio di Ebrai in Italia* (Novara: Interlinea, 2003).
    (Translation: *The Forgotten Massacre: The First Killings of Jews in Italy*.)

Documents on her life are also in the Istituto Storico Resistenza 'Piero Fornara' in Novara. Author's visit to Meina, October 2020.

5   This from Behar's testimony of her life in *La Strage Dimenticata*, but it's also quoted on the website of the Istituto Storico Resistenza in Novara, at anpi. it/media/uploads/patria/2009/1/E_INSERTO_p_6.pdf.

6   A monument now stands in Meina at the site from which the boat pushed off, bearing a Star of David and a memorial tribute to the victims. (Author interview, visit to Meina, October 2020.)

Chapter 8

1   Ronan Manley, 'From Gold Trains to Gold Reserves: Banca d'Italia's Mammoth Gold Reserve', Bullion Star, 23 September 2016.

2   *Actes and Documents*, Vol. 9, p.491 – 27 September 1943, letter from Cardinal Maglione's notes.

3   A copy of her original receipt is in the archives of the Jewish Documentation Centre, the CDEC, in Milan, and online in their Shoah Museum exhibition: shoahmuseum.cdec.it/albums/la-politica-antiebraica-delloccupante-tedesco-settembre-dicembre-1943/.

4   Marco Misano, romanjews.com, 8 December 2019, 'The Gold of Rome: An Incredible Story of the Nazi Occupation'.

5   *Actes et Documentes*, Vol. 9, p.526 – 29 September 1943, letter to Cardinal Maglione from the Special Administration of the Holy See. A note adds that it was not clear which Catholic communities had given this gold.

6   *Activity Report of the Commission for the Recovery of the Bibliographic Heritage of the Jewish Community in Rome, looted in 1943*, paras 2, 7 & 8: lootedart. com – The Central Registry of Information on Looted Cultural Property 1933–45.

7   Signal from Wilhelm Hoettl, RSHA, Berlin, Amt VI, to Herbert Kappler in Rome, Signal XIII/52 Berlin to Rome, RSS 107, 7 October 1943, held in NARA RG 226 of the messages of the OSS, contained in the declassification in 2000 by the Nazi War Criminal Records Interagency Working Group.

8   'Background of Dr Wilhelm Hoettl, 5 August 1949', p.2: www.cia. gov/readingroom/docs/HOETTL%2C%20WILHELM%20%20%20 VOL.%203_0061.pdf.

9   *Ibid.*, to note (5) – Signal RSS 118, 187 – 7 October 1943.

10 OSS message held in National Archives, RG 226, Entry 212, Box 40, Folder J: 6 October 1943. Declassified 28 June 2000, Office of Strategic Services, Washington DC, Boston Series No. 9, Copy No. 8.

11 Quoted in Margherita Marchione, *Consensus and Controversy: Defending Pope Pius XII* (New York: Paulist Press, 2002) p.71.

12 *Actes et Documentes*, Vol. 9, p.629 – 17 September 1943, letter to Cardinal Maglione from Ambassador Hildebrando Accioly of Brazil.

13 Message from Herbert Kappler in Rome to Ernst Kaltenbrunner in Berlin, 6 October 1943, 2022hrs GMT. Message No. Group XIII/52 Rome to Berlin RSS 32 /7/10/43.

Chapter 9

1   Encoded SS and Pers Z S cable from Berlin to Rome from SS Obergruppenführer Ernst Kaltenbrunner to Herbert Kappler, 11 October 1943, signal number RSS 256/7458.
2   Owen Chadwick, *Britain and the Vatican During the Second World War* (Cambridge: Cambridge University Press, 1988) pp.275–6.
3   *Ibid.*
4   The account of Sonnino Speranza's escape is detailed in the Jewish newspaper *Forward* by Giancarlo Buonomo, 17 October 2018. The experiences of another Sonnino Speranza, who was 39 at the time of the round-up, was deported to Auschwitz and did not survive, are in the CDEC Digital Library of the Shoah Museum in Milan.
5   José M. Sanchez, *Pius XII and the Holocaust: Understanding the Controversy* (Washington DC: Catholic University of America Press, 2002) p.26.
6   Signal from Herbert Kappler, Rome to Berlin, 19 October 1943: Group XIII/52 ROME to BERLIN / RSS253 19/10/1943.
7   *Actes et Documentes*, Vol. 9, p.512 – 18 October 1943, notes from Monsignor Montini concerning a letter to Cardinal Maglione.
8   *Actes et Documentes*, Vol. 9, p.511 – 17 October 1943, letter from Don Igino Quadraroli to the Secretary of State.
9   *Actes et Documentes*, Vol. 9, p.518 – 23 October 1943, notes from the Secretary of State.
10 *Actes et Documentes*, Vol. 9, pp.508 & 674 – 16 and 18 October 1943, letters from the Vatican to Italian military authorities, letter from Monsignor Marchioni to Cardinal Maglione.
11 Tarciso Bertone, Cardinal Secretary of State, is quoted as saying this in 2007 in defence of the Holy See's record in the Second World War. Phillip Pullela, 'Vatican says tried to enlist Jews as guards in WW2', Reuters, Rome, 5 June 2007.
12 Group XIII/52 ROME TO BERLIN RSS 160/19/10/1943.
13 *Actes et Documentes*, Vol. 9, p.560 – 25 October 1943, letter from Bishop Agostini in Padua to Cardinal Maglione.
14 *Actes et Documentes*, Vol. 9, p.530 – 28 October 1943, notes by the Vatican Secretary of State.

Chapter 10

1   MI5 / Security Service, file no. KV 2/1970/, SS-Standartenführer Walter Rauff. File released to the National Archives on 5 September 2005. It includes a record of a British interrogation of Rauff.

2   *Ibid.*

3   Author's research visit to the former Gestapo headquarters in Klagenfurt, the Lendorf concentration camp outside the city and the town, railway station and marshalling yards at Tarvisio, July and August 2018.

4   Nuremberg Trial Document NO-059/60 details reports from Globocnik to Himmler on 'Valuables turned in from Operation Reinhardt'.

5   *Actes et Documentes*, Vol. 9, p.594 – 15 November 1943, notes from the Cardinal Secretary of State.

6   *Actes et Documentes*, Vol. 9, p.578 – 26 November 1943, letter from Cardinal Maglione to the German Ambassador to the Holy See, Ernst von Weizsäcker.

Chapter 12

1   See Chapter 16, The Diary of an SS Double Agent, and the inclusion of the material from SS Lieutenant Guido Zimmer's diary.

2   Caitlin Hu, 'An Italian doctor explains "Syndrome K," the fake disease he invented to save Jews from the Nazis', Quartz Magazine, 8 July 2016. qz.com/724169/an-italian-doctor-explains-syndrome-k-the-fake-disease-he-invented-to-save-jews-from-the-nazis/. This is a translation from the original video interview with *La Stampa* newspaper: video.lastampa.it/importati/adriano-ossicini-cos-ho-salvato-gli-ebrei-durante-le-perse-cuzioni/56065/56064.

3   Martin Gilbert, *The Righteous: The Unsung Heroes of the Holocaust* (New York: Doubleday, 2002) p.311.

4   Martin Gilbert, *The Holocaust: The Jewish Tragedy* (London: Collins, 1986) pp.622–3.

5   *Actes et Documentes*, Vol. 7, p.124 – 2 December 1942, letter from D'Arcy Osborne to Cardinal Montini.

6   The Goldenberg family confirmed the story after the war, as Bartali's fame increased. The Jewish newspaper *Pagine Ebraiche* and *La Gazzetta della Sport* printed the story – these details from it are found in the archives of the National Association of Partisans (ANPI) and the Museum of the Deportation in Florence. Retold by Simon MacMichael on road.cc on 28 December 2010, in 'Gino Bartali hid Jewish family in Florence home to protect them from the Holocaust'.

7   In September 2013, Piero Piperno, then 84, gave an interview and wrote an article for *Pagine Ebraiche (Jewish Pages)*, which is the monthly newspaper of the Union of the Italian Jewish Community in Italy. Piero describes the time

hiding around Siena and in the convent in Rome, as well as some of his family's background. It was reprinted in the pages of *Avvenire*, an Italian daily affiliated with the Catholic Church, on 3 September 2013: www.avvenire.it/agora/pagine/qunado-le-brigidine-salvarona-i-piperno.

8   The details of the time that the Piperno family spent in hiding at the Brigidine convent in Piazza Farnese in Rome were confirmed and clarified by written emailed interviews with the Mother Superior and other nuns of the order in August 2021, as well as by a research trip to the convent itself.

Chapter 13

1   The blast holes can still be seen today on the pavements and walls of the Via Rasella.

Chapter 14

1   Oly Givon's interview for the Olin/Cooper 2012 production about the Jewish Brigade Group, called *In Our Own Hands*. This section comes from outtakes of the interviews for the documentary, which are archived at the State Library of Illinois, at guides.library.illinois.edu/ld.php?content_id=26908202.

2   Interviews with David Kenyon, Head of Historical Research at Bletchley Park, January–July 2021.

Chapter 15

1   Author's research visits to the museum at Via Tasso in Rome, between 2014 and 2019. It is now called the Historical Museum of the Liberation of Rome, and as well as preserving the original cells, with the original messages scratched on the walls by the prisoners, it holds one of the largest archives in Rome on the arrests and deportations of Rome's Jews and partisans.

2   *Actes et Documentes*, Vol. 11, p.362 – 5 June 1944, address of Pope Pius XII to the Romans.

3   28 December 2010, road.cc.

Chapter 16

1   Zimmer's personal case file from the CIA, derived from that compiled by OSS agents in Berne in 1945, was part of the Interagency Working Group on Nazi War Crimes documents declassification in 2000–04: www.archives.gov/iwg/declassified-records/rg-263-cia-records/rg-263-zimmer.html.

2   The Zimmer Notebooks consist of 167 separate memos from May 1944 to March 1945, built into four main volumes. They are heavily annotated and written in a German shorthand, with multiple references to a wide variety

of soldiers, civilians and intelligence agents of Italian, German, British, American, Spanish and other nationalities. The annotated and translated OSS / CIA typed and translated version is filed under Memo JRI-3748, United States SCI/Z Milan, 28 June 1946, held in the CIA Reading Room online at: www.cia.gov/readingroom/docs/ZIMMER%2C%20GUIDO_0059.pdf. (Subsequent notes from here are simply mentioned as Zimmer Notebooks with a page number.)

3   *Ibid.*, the Zimmer Notebooks, pp.8–9.
4   At 2021 comparative rates, this means that $2,200 would be worth fifteen times that amount, or $33,000.
5   The Zimmer Notebooks, pp.21–2.
6   *Ibid.*, p.34.
7   *Ibid.*, p.64.
8   *Ibid.*, pp.96–7.
9.   *Ibid.*, p.97.

Chapter 17

1   Prime Minister's personal telegram, number T.1652/4, 23 August 1944. From Churchill to Roosevelt it was also numbered 765. The telegrams between the two leaders about the establishment of the Jewish Brigade Group can be found at: www.yadvashem.org/docs/churchill-and-roosevelt-on-establishment-of-jewish-brigade.html. Yad Vashem cites these as being excerpted from Tamar Lubshinski-Katko, *Halochem Hayehudi Bemilchemet Haolam Hesheniya* (translation: *The Jewish Fighter in World War II*) (Shiryon Press, 2005) p.112. An image of the original of Churchill's telegram, drawn from the Churchill Archives Centre in Cambridge, can be found at: www. loc.gov/exhibits/churchill/interactive/_html/wc0213_1.html.
2   Quoted by Jewish Telegraphic Agency, 26 March 1945: www.jta. org/1945/03/26/archive/gen-mark-clark-welcomes-jewish-brigade-to-italian-front.
3   'Jewish Brigade in action in Italy', *Jewish Telegraphic Agency Daily News Bulletin*, New York, Vol. XII, no. 69, 26 March 1945.
4   *Ibid.*, Jewish Telegraphic Agency, 26 March 1945.
5   Morris Beckman, *The Jewish Brigade: An Army with Two Masters* (Stroud: Spellmount Publishers, 1998) p.97 (published in a separate edition by The History Press in 2008).
6   Quoted from an interview with Yohanan Peltz, included in the Olin/ Cooper 1998 film & TV documentary production, *In Our Own Hands: The Hidden Story of the Jewish Brigade Group in WWII*: www.youtube.com/ watch?v=uhWBCHYg_NA andmediaburn.org/video/in-our-own-hands-the-hidden-story-of-the-jewish-brigade-in-world-war-ii/.

7   Quoted in Julian Kossoff, 'Jewish Brigade shot Nazi prisoners in revenge',
    The Independent, London, 23 October 2011.
8   The War Diaries of the 1st, 2nd & 3rd Battalions of the Palestine Regiment,
    Imperial War Museum, London, and quoted in Beckman, *The Jewish Brigade:
    An Army with Two Masters*, p.85.
9   *Ibid.*, p.81.
10 Ernest M. Young, who flew with 432 Squadron of the 17th Bomber Group,
    quoted on its site: sites.google.com/site/bombgroup17/brenner-pass.
11 Interview with William C. Wildman, *The State* newspaper, Chapin,
    20 October 2008: www.thestate.com/news/local/military/
    article14334551.html.
12 Beckman, p.82.
13 Part One Daily Orders, 1st, 2nd & 3rd Battalions, The Jewish Brigade
    Group, 6 March 1945. Quoted in War Diaries of the Jewish Brigade Group,
    Imperial War Museum, London; Beckman, p.83.
14 Beckman, p.83.
15 Chuck Olin, *In Our Own Hands*, an Olin/Cooper Production, 2012:
    www.youtube.com/watch?v=uhWBCHYg_NA and mediaburn.org/
    video/in-our-own-hands-the-hidden-story-of-the-jewish-brigade-in-
    world-war-ii/. (Excerpts from the outtakes of the interviews featured in
    the documentary are also collected, along with contributors' biographies, at
    the website of the State of Illinois Library: guides.library.illinois.edu/olin/
    jewish-brigade).
16 These sections of Peltz's answer come from the above website of the Illinois
    Library.
17 From the broadcast version of *In Our Own Hands*.
18 *Ibid*.
19 *Ibid*.
20 This is a claim by Morris Beckman himself, in Julian Kossoff, 'Jewish
    Brigade shot Nazi prisoners in revenge', *The Independent*, London,
    23 October 2011.
21 *Ibid*. Israel Carmi, as quoted by Beckman in *The Jewish Brigade: An Army with
    Two Masters*.
22 *Ibid*.
23 Yohanan Peltz, *In Our Own Hands* documentary interview outtakes at
    Illinois State Library.

Chapter 18

1   Press dispatch written by Major Cameron Coffmann, Public Relations
    Officer, 71st Infantry Division, AP 360, US Army: 5 May 1945,
    Gunskirchen, Austria. Original held in the United States Holocaust
    Memorial Museum, Washington DC. The four pages can be found

on this sequential link: www.ushmm.org/information/exhibitions/
online-exhibitions/special-focus/liberation/documents-from-liberators-
gunskirchen/cameron-coffman-page-1.

2   Captain Pletcher's report is on the Jewish Virtual Library, 'Allied Liberators:
Liberation of Gunskirchen Lager': www.jewishvirtuallibrary.org/liberation-
of-gunskirchen-lager.

3   Ya'akov Hollander's account of his experiences during the Holocaust are
among those collected in text and video link on the 'Torchlighters' section
of the Yad Vashem website. Each year, six Holocaust survivors are invited to
light the six memorial torches at Yad Vashem on the annual State Opening of
Holocaust Remembrance Day. Each torch is designed to represent 1 million
of the 6 million Jews who are estimated to have died in the Holocaust.
Hollander lit the torch in the 2007 ceremony: www.yadvashem.org/
remembrance/archive/torchlighters/hollander.html.

4   *Ibid.*

5   Throughout the war, the SS used the acronym 'KL' as shorthand for their
concentration camp system, while inmates and others often preferred to use
'KZ', especially as it sounded phonetically harsher.

6   Ya'akov Hollander's description of his trip from Austria to Italy is collected
on a video link on the Yad Vashem website, in the section called 'DP Camps
and Hachsarot in Italy after the war', Section 1: 'The Encounter between
survivors & soldiers from Eretz Israel serving in the British Army': www.
yadvashem.org/yv/en/exhibitions/dp_camps_italy/index.asp.

7   Quoted in *In Our Own Hands* documentary.

8   *Ibid.*

9   'DP Camps and Hachsarot in Italy after the war', Section 1: 'The Encounter
between survivors & soldiers from Eretz Israel serving in the British Army':
www.yadvashem.org/yv/en/exhibitions/dp_camps_italy/index.asp. And
from the subsequent sections, including 'Selvino: A colony of Eretz Israel in
the Italian Alps': www.yadvashem.org/yv/en/exhibitions/dp_camps_italy/
index.asp#selvino'.

10   *Ibid.*

11   *Ibid.*

12   *Ibid.*

13   *Ibid.*

14   *Ibid.*

15   Interview with Eugenia Cohen's son, Nir Donath, in *The Jewish Chronicle*,
published on 3 June 2018 and later, on moked.it, by Rosie Whitehouse.

16   Interview with Eugenia Cohen, who changed her name to Noga Donath,
included in the Yad Vashem exhibition, 'DP Camps and Hachsarot in Italy
after the war' in Section 3, 'Selvino – A colony of Eretz Israel in the Italian
Alps': www.yadvashem.org/yv/en/exhibitions/dp_camps_italy/index.asp,
and in video link: www.youtube.com/watch?v=uMP9l3a5Uno.

17 *Ibid.* Interview carried on the Yad Vashem site.
18 Interview with Eugenia Cohen's son, Nir Donath, and the Madonnini family, Pandino, Lombardy, *Jewish Chronicle*, 15 May 2018, by Rosie Whitehouse.
19 Interview with Aldo Rolfi, the son of Lidia Rolfi, and visit to Lidia Rolfi's house in Mondovi, 22 October 2020.

Chapter 19

1 David Cesarani, *Eichmann: His Life & Crimes* (London: Vintage, 2004) p.321.
2 'Operation Unthinkable: Russia – Threat to Western Civilisation', British War Cabinet Joint Planning Staff, 22 May, 8 June and 11 July 1945. Public Record Office, CAB 120/691/109040/002. All thirty-seven pages of the document can be viewed and downloaded here: web.archive.org/web/20101116152301/http://www.history.neu.edu/PRO2/.
3 Quoted by Sir Max Hastings in the *Daily Mail*, 25 August 2009, 'How Churchill wanted to recruit defeated Nazi troops and drive Russia out of Eastern Europe'.
4 Reports between Colonel Hanna, Major O'Rourke and Major Simonini of the US Army, Altaussee, January 1946: web.archive.org/web/20120916042600/ and www.clintonlibrary.gov/assets/storage/Research%20-%20Digital%20Library/holocaust/Holocaust-%20Gold%20Series/Box%2053/902534-master-set-folder-58-230724-230814A-4.pdf.
5 US Counter-Intelligence Corps Field Report on Operation Mount Vernon, October 1948, pp.2–4, signed by Thomas A. Lucid, CIC Chief, Upper Austria. The report was declassified in 2000 by the CIA as part of the Nazi War Crimes Disclosure Act: www.cia.gov/readingroom/docs/ARMY%20CIC%20NETS%20IN%20EASTERN%20EUROPE_0002.pdf.
6 *Ibid.*, p.5.
7 *Ibid.*, pp.6–11.
8 *Ibid.*, p.12.
9 The letter is held in the Donovan Nuremberg Trials Collection at Cornell University Law Library: hydraprod.library.cornell.edu/fedora/objects/nur:00674/datastreams/pdf/content.

Epilogue

1 Obituary of Gino Bartali, *Daily Telegraph*, London, 9 May 2000.
2 Obituary of Gino Bartali, *New York Times*, 6 May 2000.
3 Interview with Aldo Rolfi by the author, 22 October 2020, Mondovi, Piemonte.
4 *Ibid.*

INDEX